Bridgw

Nortoık

Sidestrand Church

Bridgwater's
Norfolk

Hickling Pleasure Staithe

Beth Bridgwater

Encompass Press   Norwich

For Richard

First Published 1995

© Beth Bridgwater (Text) 1995

© Beth Bridgwater (Photography) 1995, except that on p.115

© Richard Green (Maps) 1995

Encompass Press, 45 The Street, Aylmerton, Norwich NR11 8AA.

A CIP catalogue record for this publication is available from
The British Library.

ISBN 1 897924 04 6

Printed in Great Britain by
Broadgate Printers, Aylsham, Norfolk.

Preface

Tired of the hustle and bustle of city life, I first visited Norfolk during the Easter of 1987. Travelling alone, and with only friends' comments about its flatness, remoteness and backwardness for company, I must admit to a certain amount of trepidation about what that trip might produce. I had booked myself into an inn on the north coast - the only stipulation I had made; a room overlooking the sea. In that respect, I was not disappointed, for my lasting memories of Norfolk will always be of an icy North Sea, at once both inviting and intimidating. Nor did it take me long to realise that far from being flat, Norfolk enjoys an especially varied and gently rolling countryside which not only soothes the soul but also allows an open-spirited response. Remote! yes I suppose it is: at the northern and eastern most tips of a bump bulging its way into the waters, and an awkward distance from central England, making northern and southern access rather tiresome. Perhaps this helps explain though why Norfolk has, thus far at least, escaped the ravages of too much so-called development. Backward, though, it certainly is not. Its people somewhat reserved but always helpful and charming, and its cultural traditions - both past and present - very much alive. In fact, I loved it so much that by the end of the 1980's, I had upped and left London for a peaceful Norfolk retreat, a stone's throw from the sea, and a local man, later to become the most interesting and adoring of husbands. We still live in Norfolk and we still find much to learn and enjoy here. In what follows, I hope the visitor too will be able to share in some of that fun and excitement.

Beth Bridgwater
August 1995

Acknowledgements

A great many people have helped in the making of this title and to all those I offer my sincere thanks and appreciation. Particular thanks must however, be extended to Simon, Barbara, Richard, Caroline, Kirk and Luke without whose efforts I may not have got beyond the first page. Love and thanks to you all.

Using This Guide

In an attempt to help visitors get the best out of any stay in Norfolk, the bulk of this guide has been broken down into area Chapters. Wherever possible these Chapters follow a particular feature of the landscape - for example, Broadland, Breckland, King's Lynn and the Marshland Fens all have Chapters in their own right. The coast has been split into three Chapters - Western, Central and Eastern - and these also provide coverage of those inland areas falling within their ambit. The Waveney Valley, although not as such a specific physical area, is covered in a brief Chapter of its own for this part of the county is quite dissimilar from the rest of Norfolk, being more akin to the bordering lands of north Suffolk. A separate Chapter is also devoted to Norwich.

By arranging the Chapters thus, you can quickly decide where you want to go within a radius of only a few miles i.e. by using the maps accompanying each Chapter, a tour of that particular locality can easily be put together, and places to spend time identified. Additionally, as the countryside is best enjoyed and understood on foot, 34 walks have been included, spread across the various Chapters. These walks vary in length from two to ten miles and can be enjoyed by anyone who is reasonably fit. Good footwear is always advisable (especially as many of the paths can be a little muddy) as are local maps: the Ordnance Survey Landranger series being more than adequate. Walks around Norwich, King's Lynn and Great Yarmouth have also been included.

In addition to identifying local attractions - anything from stately homes to museums, gardens and unusual leisure activities - we have included as many pubs, restaurants, hotels and the like, as we have been able to sample, and consider good in terms of value for money, service and quality. *At no time has hospitality or payment been accepted in return for these establishments' inclusion in this Guide. They have been sampled independently and anonymously by our own team and are included on a merit only basis*. In this way, the visitor should have a greater degree of confidence in what is reported.

Finally, your comments on what you find are welcome, just as are suggestions for what might be included in later editions. Please use the following Freepost address for these purposes only: The Editor, Encompass Press Guides, Encompass Press, Freepost, 45 the Street, Aylmerton, Norwich NR11 8BR.

Norfolk

Contents

List of Illustrations

All photographs by Beth Bridgwater, except page 115

Colour Plates

Front Cover: Oby Mill
Back Cover: West Runton Beach

Illustrations in the Text

List of Walks

All maps by Richard Green

Introduction

Only a short stay in Norfolk and the visitor will appreciate the way in which Norfolk's landscape offers an unassertive beauty, a gentle and peaceful charm, all of it understated. It was not until the 19th Century, however, that peoples' eyes were opened up to the boundless landscapes, lofty skies and broad horizons that the Norfolk countryside affords. These glimpses of Norfolk's beauty were first brought to the public's attention courtesy of two local painters - John Crome and John Sell Cotman.

Geologically speaking, Norfolk is still relatively young, resting as it does on Jurassic chalk. The general line and character of the Chilterns and Cambridgeshire Gog Magog Hills stretch north through west-Norfolk from Thetford to Castle Acre, Great Massingham, the Ringstead Downs and so to the sea at Holme. The elevation achieved, however, is little more than 200 feet and in Breckland this has been covered over with sand gravel, silt and clay, making the chalk over most of the county east of the Peddars Way almost unrecognisable. This chalk surface slopes gently underground to the east, and can still be found in Norwich and on the coast at Sheringham and further east at Trimingham. To the west of a line through Hunstanton and Stoke Ferry there is, however, no substratum of chalk to be found. Instead, here we find the beginnings of much older rock formations from red chalk to carstone and gault clay.

Over the centuries, the coastline has changed considerably, the last great flood occurring in 1953. Inevitably, over time rivers have changed their course, ports have come and gone, for example at Wiveton, and whole towns and villages have been lost to the sea; Shipden once being further north than Cromer. Today, the prospects for this coastline are not brilliant - cliff erosion, certainly during the last few summers, especially hazardous and rising sea levels making the area vulnerable for those following us into the 21st Century. Water is though a characteristic feature of the Norfolk landscape whether it be the sea, the tidal estuaries, the marshlands on the coast , the relatively swampy lands towards the Fens, or the man-made peaty Broads.

The coastline curves its way round north and east from the Wash (near King's Lynn) to Great Yarmouth. At the western end, the Wash is subject to a huge overflow from the Fenland rivers and to some phenomenally high tides. The sand banks and mussel beds are ideal for seals - not so good for the fishermen - and large flocks of migratory waders are another feature. At Hunstanton one cannot help but be impressed by the huge chalk and sandstone cliffs, huge that is, for Norfolk. Further to the east one arrives at the marshland coast, one of the finest examples of salt marsh in Britain, with its large colonies of terns and waders. The dune reserves of Scolt Head Island and Blakeney Point further concealing extensive salt flats and tidal creeks. 'Twitchers' abound along this stretch of coast, humping their increasingly elaborate equipment from one hide to another or setting up wherever they will. At Cromer, the coastline begins to bend south-easterly and then runs very straight down to Winterton-on-Sea and Great Yarmouth. In places, the cliffs - composed of glacial drift - are very low, but at others, for example at Trimingham, they are over 200 feet high. Beyond Happisburgh, they disappear altogether replaced by a long ribbon of dunes carrying the shoreline down to the Broads and Great Yarmouth.

Norfolk's Marshland Fens, not to be confused with the coastal salt marshes between Holme and Cley nor with the peaty Cambridgeshire/Lincolnshire Fens, occupy an area south and west of King's Lynn, stretching to Burnham Market in the south and Wisbech to the west. This marshland is a result of periodic sea and fresh water flooding, and was once rich pasture land ideal for sheep rearing. At the time of the Norman Conquest (1066), this was one of the poorest areas in England but by the mid 1300's it had become one of the most prosperous, and in some cases the populations of these Marshland villages had increased tenfold. This Medieval prosperity is today best gauged by the ecclesiastical architecture which has survived and most evidently at the two Terringtons' churches, the three at the Wiggenhalls and not forgetting that sumptuous offering at Walpole; all of them funded by the profits derived from sheep farming. Today, the sheep farming is no longer, the land so fertile it is now well under the plough.

King's Lynn itself owed its prominence as a seaport during the Middle Ages and indeed its survival later on to the fact that it is at the mouth of a very extensive navigable waterway system. Four Fenland rivers - the Wissey, Welland, Nene and Great Ouse - all find their exits into the Wash. Much of the prosperous livings of Cambridge, Ely, Bury St. Edmunds and Thetford would also have seen their surpluses traded through the port at Kings' Lynn. Today, this is an area little explored by the traveller, who is perhaps unaware of the simple beauty to be found here, so all the more reason for doing so.

The Broads occupy an area of approximately 220 square miles and are fed by three main rivers ; the Waveney in the south (along the Norfolk and Suffolk borders), the Yare in the middle forming the sea route between Norwich and the coast, and the Bure in the north which is probably the most characteristic of the three as it winds its way around to connect with most of the Broads and has the most tributaries. The Broads are, however, an industrial landscape, man-made to the end. During the early Medieval period, the digging of peat and turf for fuel was a major source of income for many of our ancestors. Norwich, at this time, the second largest city in England, provided a flourishing market for the same. As the sea levels during the Middle Ages rose so did these old peat workings become flooded forming a series of lakes which now make up the Broads. Many of these lakes are connected to rivers which eventually flow together and enter the sea at Great Yarmouth. Some contraction in the extent of the Broads is apparent from the heavy colonisation of reed beds and alder woods but it is these which continue to form a valuable habitat for wetland wildlife.

To the east of what is strictly the Broads is an area of flat, well-grazed grassland crisscrossed by long drainage dykes, as at Halvergate. This is another largely man-made landscape formed by reclaiming land around a huge estuary. The accumulation of the gravel pits on which Great Yarmouth now stands eventually caused these estuary waters to silt up and so form a marsh. Over the centuries, this marsh was gradually drained to produce the rich pasture land we now see today. Monuments to this drainage process are the hundreds of windpumps which are dotted along the horizon, most of them now derelict, but others such as the Berney Arms, the Stracey Arms and that at Horsey Mere offer a superb reminder of what once was.

The Broads offer over 200 miles of navigable waterways and these once provided an essential lifeline for isolated communities, facilitating a commercial route for the transportation of all manner of goods:-coal,timber, foodstuffs, and reeds etc, by wherry to the ports of Norwich (yes, Norwich was once a major port) and Great Yarmouth and vice versa. Today, it is one of England's favourite holiday resorts with hundreds of pleasure cruisers plying their way along the narrow stretches of waterway. Inevitably there is some conflict of interest between the farmers, the conservationists, and the tourists; but for the most part a median balance is struck for the benefit of all concerned. It should be recalled though that the Broads have suffered in recent years from overstimulate algae which has resulted in the demise of thousands of fish and waterfowl. The otter is now extinct and there has also been a rapid disappearance of Norfolk reed. The Broads Authority, which only received the status of National Park in 1989, is doing its utmost to regenerate the area and some parts have now been dammed off and the polluted mud and water pumped out. By the mid 21st Century, it is hoped that all of the Broads will have been revitalised in this way.

Breckland, the central Norfolk area around Thetford, was once very sandy and a mass of wild heaths. Today, it is impressively afforested with some of the largest coniferous plantations in England; inevitably, therefore, it is the most geometric landscape in the county. During pre-historic times, the area was densely populated resulting in the lands conversion from deciduous woodland to open heath. At Grimes Graves, a network of over 300 pits, dug by our neolithic ancestors in search of flint, have been revealed. Much of this flint probably finding its way into axe heads to fell the trees and so clear the land for growing crops. The importance of the area during the Bronze Age is attested by the numerous round barrows that are still visible.

By the Middle Ages though the poor quality of the land here ensured sparsely populated villages, all concentrated around the fringes of the heath and in the river valleys. Central Breckland being given over to sheep pasture. After the Medieval period, the population declined further and, hence, the frequency of ruined Medieval churches in this area. The 18th and 19th Centuries saw much of this heathland enclosed with long lines of Scots pines planted to shelter these enclosures and stabilise the light, sandy soils. During our own 20th Century, more and more of this heathland was given over to forestry production and, hence, the environment we can now see. Breckland is, however, sprinkled with small meres or lakes, supplied erratically by water rising from the underlying chalk - one of the largest and best known being The Devils Punchbowl, just north of Thetford. These meres were especially important during the Saxon and Medieval periods - for example, six parishes are known to have converged on Ringmere. The raised chalky rims of these meres support a rich and varied plant life whilst the heathland around is patterned by heather, bracken, larger shrubbery and trees. The Nature Reserve at East Wrenthem (just north east of Thetford) is probably the easiest place to enjoy this environment.

That Norfolk was once so densely populated and flourishing economically is evidenced by the amount of superb architecture which has survived intact. Much of this was the result of trade with Continental Europe and with ports along Britain's eastern shoreline. Such trade inevitably gave rise to a prosperous middle class of farmers, cloth-makers and merchants all keen to consolidate their new found wealth in the buildings they chose to inhabit. However, given there is so little in the way of indigenous building stone, much of Norfolk's best architecture employs flint as its core material.

There are many variations in the method of flint structuring from the use of whole flints to its blending with freestone in flushwork. Indeed, this flushwork is Norfolk's chief speciality, made up from a patterning of freestone and knapped flint i.e. where the flint is split in half (knapped) and the flat smooth surface exposed. One of the best examples of this work being Trinity Guildhall at King's Lynn. In north and east Norfolk, you will notice many houses built with randomly laid flints where the rough unbroken stones have been gathered from the fields. Along the coast, however, flint pebbles from the beach are also used - being rather more uniform in shape than the field cobbles - and often laid in neat courses as they are usually relatively small. Brick or stone corners and surrounds being pre-requisite for the rest of the buildings main structure.

Due to its close contact with Continental Europe, Norfolk was one of the first county's to import bricks, later establishing a great many brickyards for local manufacture. It was not until the 17th Century, however, that bricks were used in any quantity for smaller houses. Of the early brick built houses, Oxburgh Hall (1482) has to be the most sumptuous, and later buildings on an equally grand scale include Blickling and Felbrigg Halls. Further evidence of Norfolk's close contact with the Low Countries can be found in both the frequency of crow-stepped or Dutch gables - both of Flemish origin - and in the use of roof pantiles. Replacing local thatch, the latter vary in colour from red to brown, and until local manufacture began in the 17th Century, these too were imported.

Norfolk reed, the Prince of Thatch, is considered the best available reed for thatching, lasting well over 70 years; demand, however, far exceeds supply so it is more often wheat straw that is employed today. The reeds are harvested in standing water from December to March and left to dry along many a roadside. Norfolk reeds enable a more steeply pitched roof thatch to be achieved with sharper angles and heavier ridges. Ironically, though thatched roofs in Norfolk are now only an occasional feature of the county's architecture, being much more common in Suffolk and Cambridgeshire.

You will also notice the occasional use of chalk in church interiors and in this sense it is usually referred to as 'clunch'. Yet another material to be found is carstone - especially in the King's Lynn, Sandringham and Hunstanton area - and noticeable by virtue of its reddish-brown appearance. Often used with yellow or red brick dressings, carstone was a favourite amongst many Victorians who employed it as the main wall surface for their buildings. Here the mortar is set well back such that the carstone appears as if it has been laid dry.

Norfolk woodwork is especially good within church interiors - witness the number of splendid hammerbeam roofs in the county - but externally, as timber-framed housing, there is now very little. Those buildings which have survived include the Greenland Fisheries (King's Lynn) and Lovell's Hall (Terrington St. Clement), both in the west of the county.

Nor should we forget that Norfolk is a county of windmills - postmills, towermills and wind pumps - further reminding us of its similarity to the Continental Lowlands. Indeed, to help in digging channels and dykes, and in land reclamation the services of Dutch drainage experts were essential. Early attempts to drain the marshes concentrated on the digging of dykes to take the water off the land and into the rivers. Drainage mills and windpumps not following until the 1750's. At the outset these would have been small wooden smock type mills, later to be replaced by brick tower mills. It is believed that at one time there were over 200 such mills working throughout the Broads. Steam and oil driven engines replaced their forbears and the death-knell of these later versions sounded with the introduction of electricity; now it was possible to just press a switch instead of relying on the vagaries of the weather.

Norfolk's relative remoteness from the rest of Britain cannot be denied. It is that bump on the country's eastern flank which pushes out to the North Sea. Its isolation though is also its charm. There are no motorways, only a handful of major roads, and inland a motley collection of narrow country lanes, meandering here and there and often poorly signed (maps are advisable if you want to explore this hinterland to full advantage). There is only one small airport and this more geared up for flights to Amsterdam than anywhere else.

Although it is the fourth largest county in England, Norfolk is an incredible 23rd in terms of population density. This works to the visitors advantage, for even in high season, Norfolk is never bursting at the seams. The Angles (Danes) originally established the Kingdom of East Anglia in the 6th Century, i.e. once the Romans had left. Until King Egbert united England into a single Kingdom in 829 AD, East Anglia consisted of just Norfolk (Northfolk) and Suffolk (Southfolk). During the Middle Ages, Norfolk was the most densely populated county in England and as late as 1723 Daniel Defoe, in his *Tour Through the Eastern Counties* (1724), was still able to record that no other county could boast three towns, namely King's Lynn, Great Yarmouth and Norwich, "*... so populous, so rich and so famous for trade and navigation.*"

Today, there are no large cities, Norwich remains pretty compact, and no heavy industry. It is a land of farms (although fewer and fewer labourers work the land) halls, churches, windmills, villages and small market towns. Farming and food production, whether it be of the sea or the land, are the main avenues of employment. Industry is very much short on the ground and it is this which is needed if the local economy is to be revitalised and sustained.

Village life, however, is not what it was. Many churches are now redundant or enjoy irregular services and attendances, most priests serving as many as five parishes. Additionally, the majority of village shops and schools are now closed and many old rectory's are now either restaurants, or small hotels. Perhaps one of the last stalwarts to survive this process of depletion though is the village pub - the greater proportion of them still extant and doing a good job serving both incomers and locals alike. But this pattern is probably no different from anywhere else in rural Britain and we can only hope that new avenues for rural community living are found and enjoyed in the future.

Norfolk has at times been called 'Tory' country, or alternatively a 'mecca' for Royalists. This cannot truthfully be denied but thankfully it is a Toryism with a rural, feudal heritage, and not that imbibed upon us by the likes of Lady Thatcher's monetarism. But it is also true to say that Norfolk is traditionally non-conformist, and this perhaps is a reflection of its physical isolation which has in turn left its mark upon the character of the people here. Not for nothing was this the centre of trade with Continental Europe, not for nothing did Cromwell recruit many of his fierce parliamentary Ironsides from here during the Civil War. Other political radicals who have also made their lasting non-conformist marks include Robert Kett, leader of the Peasants' Revolt, and Thomas Paine, a prime mover behind the American Independence movement but who spent his early life in Thetford.

Norfolk has also been home to some of the most advanced revolutions in farming techniques, and it is to the likes of Thomas Coke (Holkham Hall) and Lord 'Turnip' Townshend (Raynham Hall) that we must look for significant advances in early crop cultivation and cattle breeding. With over production a feature of today's farming though, it is good to see in Norfolk a return to some of the more traditional farming methods which seek to preserve the landscape and its animal and plant life, and so enable resident and visitor alike to enjoy the countryside for what it should be.

King's Lynn and the Marshland Fens

Our tour of the Marshland Fens must of necessity begin at King's Lynn. From here we move in an easterly direction first to Castle Rising, and then south-east to Great Massingham. The last part of this Chapter will then see us travelling west and south-west to the Wiggenhalls, Walpole St. Peter, and to the great sluice gates at Denver. The Marshland Fens are an area little explored by visitors; most people are unaware of what beauty and charm there is to be found here. The same goes for King's Lynn which is well worth a couple of days exploration as shall be seen from what follows.

King's Lynn

Perhaps surprisingly, as seen from its relatively ugly outskirts, King's Lynn remains one of the best preserved towns in England, and holds a collection of Medieval merchants' houses and warehouses probably not surpassed anywhere in the country. As ample testimony to this, King's Lynn was recently used as the prime location for the filming of *Revolution*, an examination of the American War of Independence, and for which period housing was a pre-requisite.

Prior to 1537, King's Lynn was known as Bishop's Lynn; Herbert de Losinga had paid William II a sum of money in 1094 in return for the Office and Title of

Bishop of Norwich. As penance for his simony, the Pope demanded the building of a number of priories and churches in de Losinga's diocese, in addition to the Cathedral at Norwich; hence his efforts in King's Lynn. Not to be outdone, his successor Bishop Thurbe of Norwich (1146-74) built his own town a mile or so to the north of de Losinga's, and endowed it with St. Nicholas' Church.

Two towns, therefore, evolved separately until 1204 when a Charter from King John saw them united. They were brought even closer together by a bridged link over Millfleet constructed in 1250. The Medieval markets, however, could not survive without Royal approval, but King John allowed both - Tuesday and Saturday - to continue at Bishop's Lynn. The Tuesday Market Place retains its grand urban space; its prosaic Corn Hall built in 1854 for the sale of grain but now used for concerts, sports and exhibitions; and the imposing Duke's Head Hotel. Here also once stood a fine market cross and the town pillory where convicted witches were burned.

> In 1590, at Tuesday Market Place, **Margaret Read** was burned at the stake. Legend has it that her heart burst from her body and flew across the Market Place landing high on the north-east wall of the corner of the Market. The Place is marked to this day by a diamond shaped brick with a heart carved on it.

Other than the weekly market, the main festivity is now the King's Lynn Mart Fun Fair, granted by a very early Charter and one of an incredible 15 Charters variously awarded the town. The Fair is held for one week, beginning on St. Valentines Day (February 14) and marks the opening of the season for Britain's travelling fairs. By contrast, the Saturday Market Place is now characterised by a relatively recent shopping precinct at one end and the stunning Trinity Guildhall at the other, but in actual fact its history predates that of the Tuesday Market Place.

Tuesday Market Place

In 1294, Lynn (as it is popularly known today) was granted the right by Edward I to levy murage - a tax on goods brought into the town - the proceeds of which were used to finance the building of the town's defenses. These defenses were essentially little more than earthworks, although those around Bishop Thurbe's side of town were constructed from stone. Only two of the four gates have survived; the much restored North Guanock Gate and that at South Gate. Gatekeepers had the job of charging tolls on goods entering the town, it was also their responsibility to close the gates at dusk and to keep out those with insufficient reason for entering; 1723 saw the end of this system.

> In 1558, King's Lynn was amongst 100 or so English boroughs granted the right to its own MP, though in fact it had two MP's, thus putting it in the category of a **'rotten borough'**. At one time both seats were even held by the same man - Thomas Howard, 4th Duke of Norfolk.

Lynn has been a prosperous trading port for centuries and continues to thrive on trade both with Continental European and other British ports. Its 11th Century merchants are known to have exported wool, fish and salt, and to have imported furs and cloth. A century later and with East Anglia now the wealthiest part of the country (made prosperous from its sheep-rearing and trade in wool and cloth), buyers from Brughes and Ghent were a familiar sight. King's Lynn merchants as well as those in Boston, Lincolnshire, also served the richest hinterland of England; they were, after all, at the mouth of the only navigable outlets to the sea for the corn growers of Marshland and Fenland, the leadminers of Derbyshire, the Lincolnshire and Norfolk salternes, and the wool growers of East Anglia and the East Midlands. Particularly with the Abbeys of Ely and Peterborough shipping out vast consignments of wool through Lynn, more and more exotic commodities were brought in to satisfy theirs and others demands for luxury items: furs, hawks and falcons from Norway, wine from Gascony, beeswax from Russia, timber from Finland, wood and madder from Picardy, rafters, masts, furniture, tar and potash from the Baltic countries, and even fish from Iceland.

Although the Suffolk coastal ports concentrated their efforts on fishing, Lynn, as we have seen, grew wealthy from its emphasis on commerce. Indeed, Daniel Defoe tells us that in the early 18th Century, Lynn imported more coal than anywhere between Newcastle and London, and more wine than any other port excepting Bristol and London. Its merchant fleet was additionally and repeatedly requisitioned as 'men of war' when hostilities with other nations dictated their need as such. At the Siege of Calais, for example, Lynn was represented by 16 ships and no less than 382 mariners. Nor did this prevent Lynn from sending a number of whalers to Greenland each summer and conducting a very profitable business on the basis of the same. Today, Lynn port continues to handle large volumes of grain and other commodities and acts as a clearing house for goods particularly from Rotterdam in the Netherlands but destined for the British Midlands.

At Fisherfleet (*fleet* meaning shallow), a narrow creek on the Lynn side of the

Great Ouse, fishing still goes on albeit on a very small scale. There are very few fish in the Wash as it is a breeding nursery for seals and they take what stocks there are. Nonetheless, the area around Fisherfleet is crowded with small boats specifically designed for shell fishing - the shrimps being boiled on board as soon as they are caught.

> **Shrimps** are widely available on the Norfolk coast. There are two varieties - pink or the small brown. The brown are the most readily available, have the sweeter flavour but are a nuisance to peel.

Otherwise, mussels and cockles are raked up by the fishermen from the sand and mud as the tide goes out. Fisherfleet was once twice its current length, but in the late 1800's it was reduced to make way for the then new Bentinck Dock.

Places to Visit

Museums:

The Lynn Museum (01553 775001), *Market Street.* Go here for natural and local history exhibits especially those illustrating King's Lynn's history. The displays are housed in a former, 1859, Non-Conformist Chapel built in high-Gothic style. Look for the Museum's collection of pilgrims' badges, the largest outside London. Also of particular interest are the engineering achievements of local man Frederick Savage. *Open Mon-Sat, 10-5, closed Public Hols. Admission charge. Wheelchair Access.*

> **Frederick Savage** began his engineering career by inventing a winnowing machine and tackle for ploughing. He is best remembered though for his steam engine which transformed the formerly handcranked rides of the travelling Showmen. His name cannot be separated from the development of Britain's fairground rides into the extravaganzas they are today. Savage's works continued to operate in King's Lynn until the 1970's and a monument to the man was set up on the corner of Guanock Terrace.

Town House Museum of Lynn Life (01553 773450), *46 Queen Street.* Particular emphasis is placed on the social and domestic history of west Norfolk. *Open Tue 10-5 & Sun 2-5, May to September. Also open Tue-Sat, 10-4 in October.*

Trinity Guildhall, *Saturday Market Place.* Built in 1421,shortly after St. George's Guildhall, Trinity Guildhall is one of King's Lynn's most striking buildings, its beautiful chequerboard facade making use of alternate blocks of knapped flint and limestone. In Medieval times, these guilds fulfiled a variety of roles from town's council to tradesmen's federation, benevolent society, bank and early trades union; all with religious overtones. A powerful combination whatever the political climate, and one clearly too influential for Edward VI who, in 1547, took the unprecedented step of disbanding all such guilds and seizing their assets for the Crown. Thereafter, from 1571-1937, the cellars of Trinity Guildhall were used as the local prison. Not until the 1950's was Trinity restored, its undercroft now a Museum with many important treasures on display.

Foremost amongst these are the enamelled and embossed King John Cup with its silver gilt cover, the oldest secular loving cup in England and made around 1340 in the reign, not of King John, but of Edward III. Also on display is the King John Sword, with its Latin inscription which we can render as: '... this sword was given by King John from his own side and long Live King Henry VIII in the 20th year of his reign'. All rather confusing, but it is thought that the sword is Tudor in origin and so mention of Henry VIII would at least appear to be accurate. Another item to look out for is the original parchment Charter granted by King John in 1204, as are later Charters, as well as the Red Register used throughout the 1300's to record wills and deeds. Behind the main Hall are two further buildings dating from 1767; these are the Assembly and Card Rooms. An audio-visual tour called *Tales of the Old Gaolhouse*, housed behind the Tourist Information Office *(01553 763044)* is *open Fri-Tue, 10-5, November to Easter, & daily, 10-5, Easter to November. Admission charge. Wheelchair access. Note: 1996 opening times may be subject to some variation, so it is advisable to phone first.*

True's Yard *(01553 770479), North Street.* A Museum concentrating on Lynn's fishing industry and housed in a former fisherman's cottage. *Open daily, 9.30-4.30. Admission charge. Wheelchair access.*

Ecclesiastical & Public Buildings:

St. Margaret's Church, *St. Margaret's Place.* Originally founded in 1100 by Bishop de Losinga as part of a Benedictine Priory, and built from Northamptonshire limestone transported by lighter along the River Great Ouse, St. Margaret's is now adorned with two towers. Look for the clock installed in 1603 on the outside of the south tower. Unusually it does not remind us of the time but instead of the next high tide; if the 'L' represents midday and the 'G' midnight, then the letters equate to LYNNHIGHTIDE.

The early English chancel and brasses here, especially that to Adam de Walsokne (d. 1349), are considered of national importance. This brass commemorating Walsokne and his wife, depicts allegorical scenes of everyday rural life: workers in the vineyard and a man carrying corn to the mill. Another, the Peacock Brass, depicts Robert Braunche (d. 1364), his first and second wives, angels above their heads and a lavish feast at their feet of roast peacock, musicians and 12 guests. The scene recalls Braunche's banquet for Edward III in 1349 - a feast to which the host himself was unsure if he would be permitted to attend! Once in the nave look for the 18th Century rack which holds the town mace when the Mayor visits St. Margaret's on official business, and the richly decorated pulpit thought to be the work of Matthew Brettingham who was also responsible for the elaborate staircase at Holkam Hall. The reredos behind the altar celebrates Felix - a shipwrecked preacher who was washed ashore near Sandringham and when his fellow men failed to come to his aid, he was befriended by the badger population. Felix went on to become Bishop of Dunwich (Suffolk), and Felixstowe (also in Suffolk) is named after him.

The organ at St.Margaret's was installed at the instigation of Charles Burney, then struggling for a living as an organist and music tutor of the local gentry. His *History of Music* became famous, though probably less so than the work of his daughter Fanny d'Arblay. Her novel *Evelina*, recounting a young lady's entrance into the larger world, was much praised by the then intelligentsia.

Although she could neither read nor write, **Margery Kempe**, thought to have been born during the mid 1360's, left behind the first English autobiography (c. 1435). Daughter of one of Lynn's mayors, she married a local merchant and is thought to have had 14 children. At some point during her life, she claimed to have received strange visions. Some consider her a mystic, others a charlatan, but she nevertheless held onto the belief that she had been called to 'sainthood'. As a result, she was arrested on many occasions for heresy. During her lifetime, she undertook many pilgrimages ranging from visits to Canterbury to longer explorations to the Holy Land, and many places in between. She was undoubtedly an intrepid lady traveller, but one who always returned to her family in Lynn. *The Book of Margery Kempe*, recounting her persecution at the hands of the devil and by men, was published in an abridged version in 1501 but then disappeared. It was not rediscovered until 1934 and the manuscript is now housed in the British Museum, London. Kempe died around 1440.

St. Nicholas' Chapel, *St. Nicholas Street,* was founded in 1145 as a chapel-of-ease but was not completed, at least in its current form, until 1420. Unusually, the nave and chancel are one unit, thus giving great height and elegance to the interior. This is further enhanced by the tie-beam roof carved as it is with angels. If you do manage to go inside, look for a carved bench-end depicting a 15th Century ship with its furled square mainsail and furled lateen mizzen. This is a typical representation of the type of vessels built in King's Lynn during the 1400's. Sadly, the Chapel suffers from severe subsidence and is not normally open except for concerts during the town's annual Festival; the two-storied south porch has also at times been used as a schoolroom and as a library.

Red Mount Chapel, *The Walks,* built circa 1485 beside the ancient pilgrims' way to Walsingham, was specifically intended for pilgrims' use. This octagonal, tiny, red-brick Chapel is noted for its fine fan-vaulted roof and its especially strange shape, both aspects making it an extremely rare building. The two staircases provide glimpses, through peepholes, of the altar. Today, the Chapel stands in a public park called The Walks.

Greyfriars Tower, *Tower Gardens, St. James Street* is all that is left of the former Greyfriars monastic settlement, a victim of Henry VIII's Dissolution of the Monasteries. The Tower still retains its fine lantern top and other remains of the Priory walls are evident in the public gardens.

All Saints Church, *off All Saints Street,* was formerly known to its more superstitious Saxon originators as All Hallows, and was substantially rebuilt during the 14th Century. The thing to look for here is the anchorhold - a cell for voluntary hermits locked in almost as prisoners would be for the rest of their lives, but this time as an act of faith rather than as penance for any misdemeanour. The daily needs of the anchorite or anchoress would be looked after by a servant living in the next room but with access to the hold. On the outsides of the south wall, you can still see fragments of the former servants' quarters.

Thoresby College, Queen Street, was built around 1500 to house priests belonging to the Trinity Guild but after the Dissolution it became a merchant's house with adjoining warehouses. Although it is now a Youth Hostel and also provides flats for the elderly, do open the central door and go into the courtyard. On the ground on the north side is a slate marking the site of the 13th Century Quayside; a clear indication that the present Quay makes use of reclaimed land.

The Hanseatic Warehouse, St. Margaret's Lane, was built in 1475 by and for the Hansa, a substantial north European league of merchants, and used by them as a goods depot until 1751 when they sold it. Restored in 1971, the building is now used by the Norfolk County Council as its King's Lynn offices.

> **The Hanseatic League** was little more than a Medieval protection society for merchants trading overseas. Its members were mainly drawn from the cities/ports of Bremen, Cologne, Hamburg and Lubeck. Its powers were much depleted during the Thirty Years War (1618-1648) and disintegration followed quickly thereafter.

Marriott's Barn, South Quay. Standing parallel to the Hanseatic Warehouse on the riverside is this barn, its stone walls specifically designed to withstand any high tide. Its timber upper structure is thought to be 16th Century and crafted by German labourers, probably in the employ of the Hansa merchants.

St. James Street

Clifton House, *Queen Street.* Although the main house here was remodelled in the early 18th Century, it retains its splendid Elizabethan watch tower in the courtyard. Additionally, the warehouses which still stretch back to the river are thought to precede the tower and the undercroft is undoubtedly 15th Century. More recently, a 14th Century pavement of Clare tiles has been uncovered and is considered the most substantial secular pavement of its age to be preserved *in situ* in England.

Hampton Court, *Nelson Street.* Although begun before 1200 and remodelled during the 14th Century as a merchant's house- with the west, east and north wings added variously during the 15th and 16th Centuries - Hampton Court has been well restored by both private individuals and the King's Lynn Preservation Trust. The block once contained the merchants' and apprentices' residential quarters, counting house and the warehouses fronting on to what was then the riverbank. It is not open to the public but you can nevertheless enjoy easy viewing from the outside.

The Greenland Fishery, *Bridge Street.* A rope merchant and former mayor of Lynn, John Atkin, was responsible for this building which dates from 1605. Subsequently, during the 18th Century, it was used as an inn by whalers and hence its name. It is now a private home (again, easy external viewing is afforded) but during restoration, elaborate 17th Century allegorical wall paintings and texts are known to have been uncovered.

> **George Vancouver** was born in a house in New Conduit Street in 1757. Aged 14, he joined Captain James Cook as a junior officer aboard *Resolution* for a four year voyage around the world. A year after his return he signed on as midshipman on Cook's last voyage aboard *Discovery*; they failed to find the North West Passage but they discovered Hawaii instead. Vancouver was among those sailors to recover Cook's murdered body from the islanders. In 1791, he was to lead his own expedition taking western Australia for the Crown, and persuading Hawaii to become part of the British Empire. From there he sailed to Canada, persuading Spain to cede what later became known as British Columbia to the Crown; today the Province's largest city is named Vancouver in his memory. He also explored the tiny inlets around the Gulf of Georgia, which also bears his name.

The Bank House, *King's Staithe Square.* One of the town's finest houses with its 1685 statue of Charles I and where Samuel Cresswell Gurney of North West Passage' fame was born. The building's frontage was probably altered during the mid 18th Century. Again, it is not open to the public.

The Customs House, *Purfleet Quay,* was originally built in 1683 as a Merchant's Exchange, only becoming the Customs House in 1718. Its building was financed by Sir John Turner of Warham but its designer and builder twice held the office of mayor; his name Henry Bell. A statue of Charles II can be found over its entrance, and on one of the walls sculpted heads adorned with ears of corn and grapes (symbols of trade both 'out of' and 'into' port) can also be seen.

The Customs House

The South Gate, *London Road*, once formed part of the town's comprehensive defence works and was built in 1437 with 16th Century embellishments. The outer wall is of grey stone whilst its inner face uses a more mellow and subdued red brick. ***Open occasionally*.** Phone the Tourist Information Centre *(01553 763044)* for precise details.

Live Entertainment:

St. George's Guildhall *(01553 774725)*, *King Street*. Although St. George's was originally founded in 1376 and received a Charter from Henry IV in 1406, the current Hall was not built until 1420. Nevertheless, it remains the oldest Guildhall in England. It is an unassuming place with its brick-faced front but the roof inside is heavily beamed. A wide tunnel runs under the range of buildings here which themselves stretch right down to the Quay. The Hall is now owned by the National Trust and is home to a theatre - Shakespeare and his troupe are thought to have performed here - art galleries, a restaurant and coffee bar. In summer, the building is also the Headquarters of the King's Lynn Festival; the Festival operates a varied programme of events and is well worth enquiring about should you be visiting the town during the summer months. ***Open all year, Mon-Fri (except Good Friday), 10-5 & Sat 10-12.30. General admission is free of charge.***

27

Factory Visits:

Caithness Glass (01553 765111), *Old Meadow Road, Hardwick Industrial Estate.* At the former and once much larger Caithness Crystal works, ex-company employees have set up their own small-scale glass-making works. Known as *Creative Glass of King's Lynn* demonstrations of their skills can be watched. Caithness Glass also have their own shop on site.

Sports Venues:

Hang Gliding: Lejair Ltd (01362 687000), 8 The Watlings, Scarning, Dereham. Courses and tuition for beginners and for experienced pilots wanting to begin Tow Launching for themselves.

Horse Riding: Runcton Hall Stud (01553 840676), Church Farm, Runcton, nr. King's Lynn. BHS approved.

Motor Sports: King's Lynn Speedway, (01553 771111). Motor cycle racing.

Swimming: St. James Swimming Pool (01553 764888), Blackfrairs Street.

Tenpin Bowling: Strikes (01553 760333), 1-5 Lynn Road, Gaywood.

> **The Peter Scott Walk**, also known as the Wash Coast Path, is a remote walk along the estuary between the Rivers Nene (Lincolnshire) and Great Ouse (Norfolk). It is ten miles long if you start at West Lynn and continues to the lighthouses flanking the mouth of the Nene. To shorten the distance, as you would normally return by exactly the same route, try starting at Ongar Hill, following the path initially to the outer sea bank. This would give a total walk distance of approximately 12 miles. Allow five hours for completion. The walk itself is dedicated to Sir Peter Scott who lived in one of the lighthouses during the 1930's and who spent much of his life conserving the areas wildlife and their natural habitats.

Food & Accommodation

Hotels:

The Duke's Head (01553 774996), *Tuesday Market Place.* Owned by Forte Heritage, furnished in typical Forte style, and offering accommodation and service to their accustomed standards. This is a particularly handsome hotel with its distinctive 17th Century Georgian facade, and painted a striking shade of pink. It is ideally situated in the centre of King's Lynn and overlooks the attractive and colourful Tuesday Market. *Wheelchair access.*

Restaurants:

Riverside (01553 773134), *King Street.* The menus here are flexible enough for all pockets - from light lunches to one course meals and full dinners. Set in the Arts Centre, the building itself is of Medieval origin and exposed brickwork and beams abound.

Rococo (01553 771483), *Saturday Market Place.* The menu here is characterised by light sophistication through to full blown formality, and much care is taken in its preparation. Lunches are especially good value and you can even get away with a simple bowl of soup and bread. *Wheelchair access.*

Swinton House (01366 383151), *Stow Bridge, nr. King's Lynn.* A warm welcome can be expected at this restaurant and a strong local following has been gained. The emphasis is on local produce and the menu leans towards modern English. *Wheelchair access.*

Pubs:

The Lattice House (01553 777292), *Chapel Street.* Originally built in the 15th Century and undergoing significant but careful restoration by the Borough Council in the early 1980's, the building's fine structure is nonetheless clearly evident. *Wheelchair access to public bar only.*

Tudor Rose (01553 762824), *St. Nicholas Street.* Also dating back to the 15th Century, Tudor Rose still retains its half-timbered front complete with a Medieval oak-studded door. Both bars are well used by locals as is the raftered upstairs restaurant. Bedroom accommodation is simple but comfortable. *Wheelchair access.*

Walk 1: King's Lynn

Directions:

1. From the Car Park on St. James Street, take a look at Trinity Guildhall, and then go left into Queen Street passing the former Thoresby College. 2. Turn left into Purfleet Quay to see the Custom House and retrace your steps to turn left into King Street. 3. Go along King Street passing St. George's Guildhall on your left and continue along the edge of Tuesday Market Place to go right into St. Nicholas Street. 4. Turn right into Chapel Street and right again into Market Lane (note the Lattice House 15th Century pub at this junction). 5. Go left into the High Street passing the Duke's Head Hotel on your left. Continue along the full length of the High Street. 6. Turn left into St. James Street, noting Tower Place on your right. Continue a little further up St. James Street to visit Greyfriar's Tower and gardens. Retrace your steps and go into Tower Place. 7. Turn left into Millfleet for a short distance to see the small brick enclosure that was once the Jewish Cemetery during the first half of the 19th Century. Retrace your steps to the junction and turn left. After a short distance follow the path on your left leading through Hillington Square, a council estate, to All Saints Church. 8. Leave the Church via the gate leading to All Saints Street and turn tight along here and then right into Bridge Street . 9. Go straight across at the junction with Stonegate Street and Boal Street and then left into Nelson Street passing The Valiant Sailor on your right just before the left turn into St. Margaret's Lane. 10. Go down St. Margaret's Lane to join South Quay where you turn right. 11. Turn into College Lane to return to the junction with Queen Street and with the Guildhall in front of you.

Approx. Distance: 2.75 Miles
Approx. Time: 2 Hours.

Castle Rising

A few miles north-east of King's Lynn is Castle Rising, a delightful village with much to offer the unsuspecting visitor. First to the Castle with its fine mid 12th Century domestic keep, set in the centre of massive defensive earthworks. The Castle was begun circa 1138 by William d'Albini who was also Lord of the Manors of Buckenham, Happisburgh and Snettisham. Needing major repairs in 1327, it was sold to the newly crowned Edward III who incarcerated his mother, Queen Isabella, here for her suspected part in the murder of his father; the screams of her ghost are said to haunt the Castle. Eventually it passed to the Black Prince (Prince of Wales and Duke of Cornwall) although he died in 1376, only a year before he would have become king. He did, however, decree that the Castle be passed in perpetuity to the Duchy of Cornwall. His bequest was granted until 1544 when Henry VIII granted the Castle and Manor to Thomas Howard, 3rd Duke of Norfolk, in exchange for lands around Felixstowe. It remained in Howard hands until 1958 when it passed to the State. The site is managed by English Heritage and is *open daily, 10-6, April to October, and Wed-Sun, 10-4, November to March. Admission charge. Wheelchair access to exterior only.*

Although much of the Church of St. Lawrence is Victorian - the saddle roof was added in 1880 and replaced the original battlemented tower - its west end

Castle Rising

retains one of the finest pieces of Norman blind- arcading in the country. At the east of the nave, the Norman arch and triforium arches provide access to a passage which runs round each side of the tower and to a belfry staircase. Across the road from the Church is the Hospital of the Holy & Undivided Trinity (also known as the Howard Bede House) which was built by the Earl of Northampton in 1614 for a " ... *governess and 11 poor spinsters*" in memory of his grandfather, the 3rd Duke of Norfolk. Candidates for this almshouse must be "*.. .no common beggar-haunter of inns and alehouses*" but "*religious and grave...*"and "*...able to read...and at least 50 years of age.*" The Hospital still functions in this way, and its lady residents can occasionally be seen walking to Church in their red cloaks with Howard badges and black steeple hats.

Castle Risings former importance - it was a well established settlement even before the building of the Castle - is attested to by the following piece of verse:

Rising was a seaport town
When Lynn was but a marsh
Now Lynn is a seaport
And Rising fares the worst.

It was also once a rotten borough, regularly returning two MPs to Parliament during the period 1558-1832. Sir Robert Walpole of Houghton Hall being amongst these. As for employment, at least until the end of the 17th Century, Castle Rising's inhabitants were able to take advantage of the local saltpans and of fishing facilitated by the then tidal waters of the River Babingley.

Close to Castle Rising is **Roydon Common**, a large and important Nature Reserve managed by the Norfolk Naturalists Trust and mainly comprised of dry, acid heath with its colourful array of heather and bracken. Sphagnum mosses are also widespread. As for its birdlife; nightingales, nightjar, curlew and tree pipit can regularly be seen, as can merlins and hen harriers in winter. Also of note is **Reffley Wood**, half a mile north-east of King's Lynn, where a tem

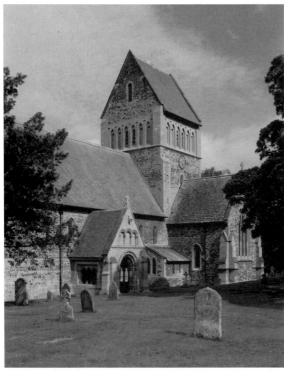

St. Lawrence's Church

ple is said to have been built in 1789 by members of a Royalist Society. Little is known of the Society except that it was founded in 1651 during the Commonwealth and membership was restricted to 30 men, the largest number that could legally meet together at that time. The Society still exists - its membership remains 30, and they still meet in the woods!

Walk 2: Castle Rising & Ling Common

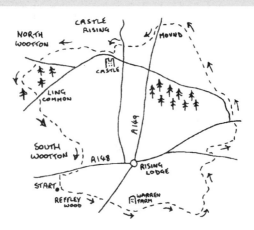

Directions:

1. From the park at the bottom of Sandy Lane near the entrance to Reffley Wood continue along Sandy Lane (i.e. ignore the stile) which soon becomes a footpath. 2. Cross over the busy A 149 and continue along Sandy Lane, now a farm track, to Warren Farm. 3. Keeping the house on your left, continue along the track as it skirts the north western fringe of Grimston Warren. 4. About half way along the edge of the wood, look for a path on your left which winds its way across the heath. Ignore the secondary paths which intersect with this and follow to the lane. 5. Turn left at the lane and after approximately 150 yards follow the path on your right which leads to a group of trees. 6. Instead of following this straight on, turn right just before the trees to follow the right hand edge of a field. Continue along here skirting a small wood until you reach a track. 7. Turn left into this track and follow it until you reach the A 148. Cross over the road, taking the minor road opposite you. Where the road begins to descend, look for a wooden farm gate on your right which leads to a well used woodland path which forks left (ignore the right hand path). Continue along here ignoring all secondary paths to your left and right until you reach a group of houses. 8. Just before these houses look for a path which leads up to the A 149. Cross this with care looking for a path on the other side of the road which leads to Castle Rising. 9. At the road, turn right and follow the road round to your left (taking in the quaint old almshouses and St. Lawrence's Church). From the Church follow the road round to your left to the crossroads. To visit the Castle, go straight on, otherwise go right along the lane until you come to another lane on your right just before a series of bends. 10. Go along this lane and where it bends right ignore this instead going on a little way before turning left along a track. At a barn, take the left hand fork which leads you through Wooton Carr. 11. Just before a cottage, go left but rejoining your path going straight on into North Wooton and so ignoring a private road on your left. 12. Upon reaching the road, go left for a few yards and cross the road to a path leading through Ling Common. After a short distance, the path forks and here you go to your right. After a while the path runs parallel with a road and then goes left again through the wood to the road running between the Wootons and Castle Rising. 13. Cross the road, go to your right and look for a narrow path running beside the wood. Continue along this path - in places it can be quite overgrown - until it bends sharply right, leading down to the A 148. 14. At the main road, go right for a few hundred yards until you see Sandy Lane on your left which will take you back to your starting point.

Start: Sandy Lane, near Reffley Wood off the A 148.
Approx. Distance: 9 Miles
Approx. Time: 4 Hours
Map: Landranger 132

Great Massingham

Food & Accommodation

Congham Hall Hotel(*01485 600250), Grimston.* An 18th Century Georgian manor house set in substantial and secluded, private parkland. Richly and warmly furnished throughout, Congham Hall also offers a highly proficient kitchen and cellar. Evening meals usually call for smart dress though a more informal atmosphere pervades the lunchtime scene. The proprietors have created a traditional 17th Century potager and herb garden which supplies the hotel kitchen on a daily basis. This is well worth a visit its own right - over 200 labelled herbs are grown here and approximately 150 of these are on sale. *The gardens are open daily, excluding Sat, 2-4, April to October. Wheelchair access to restaurant and gardens only.*

Also north-east of King's Lynn is Great Massingham. A charming village unusually endowed with two village greens and ponds. At one time, the village had its own fair but this is now non-existent, as is the Priory, originally founded by Nicholas de Syre in 1260 as a cell of that Castle Acre. The scanty remains of the Priory can be found in the house and outbuildings of Abbey Farm, though these are now naturally private. The 15th Century Church of St. Mary's has a large pinnacled tower and lofty porch suggesting a larger community than that which is current; the church is usually locked but details of the key holder are posted at the entrance. Massingham Heath - known for its flint mines - and Weasenham Lings with its series of burial mounds provide good walking.

Walk 3: Great Massingham and the Peddars Way

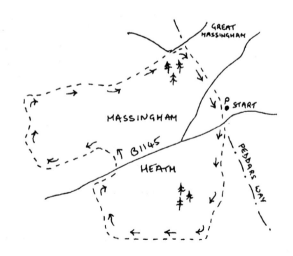

Directions:

1. From the B 1145 Gayton to Litcham road, park on the right hand side of the Peddars Way (marked), a few hundred yards before the turn to Great Massingham. Head south along the way for a short distance until you come to a fork where you bear right off the Peddars Way. 2. Continue along this track over Massingham Heath until it joins another single track route. Again, bear right for just over a mile and take the second path on your right as it skirts a copse. 3. Upon meeting the B 1145 turn right until you come to a footpath heading off to your left. Follow this up the Heath and round to the left again for approximately one mile. 4. Then bear right over the northern elevation of the Heath. At the end of this, where it joins another track, bear right for about one and a half miles until it joins the road to Massingham. Walk along the road (it is not that busy) for about a quarter of a mile until you join the Peddars Way crossing. 5. Turn right and walk the Peddars Way until you return to the start.

Start: on the B 1145, near Great Massingham
Approx. Distance: 6.5 miles
Approx. Time: 3 Hours
Map: Landranger 132

Middleton

Although substantially rebuilt in the late 1800's and early 1900's, **Middleton Towers**, a few miles south-east of King's Lynn, were originally begun in the 1400's and the elegant 15th Century gatehouse with its four turrets still stands, all surrounded by a moat. The older parts of the building were begun by Lord Scales, who met a violent end at the hands of the Yorkists during the Wars of the Roses and following his escape from the Tower of London; Scales was a Lancastrian. Nor did his successors fair much better - his son-in-law, Lord Rivers, was executed by Richard III in 1483.

Not far from the Towers is **Middleton Mount**, thought to be the remains of a motte but signs of a bailey are noticeably absent. Furthermore, just over a mile south-east of the village are the scanty remains of Blackborough Priory, founded in the mid 1100's for the Benedictines. Clearly then, this was once a wealthy part of the country and defensive structures would have been an inevitable aspect of this environment.

Close by, still only five miles south-east of King's Lynn, is **East Winch Common.** This is is a fine example of acid heathland, surrounded by oak and birch woodland. The site is exceptionally rich in its bird life - nightingales, garden warblers, blackcaps, yellow hammers, linnets and finches - and in its population of butterflies and dragonflies. Adders and common lizards can also be found during the summer. Please keep to the pathways if you visit the Common as it is a fragile environment.

Heading further south, we arrive at **Wormegay.** Standing isolated from the village is St. Michael's Church, substantially rebuilt in late Victorian times but originating from the 13th Century. But the village itself is also somewhat unusual occupying as it does something of an island. In earlier times it must have been of strategic importance as the unusually large motte and bailey site of Wormegay's former Castle can still be explored; it was clearly designed to fortify against attack standing as it does across a narrow stretch of marsh. The base and shaft of a Saxon village cross can be found at the east end of the village.

Walk 4: Wormegay and the River Nar

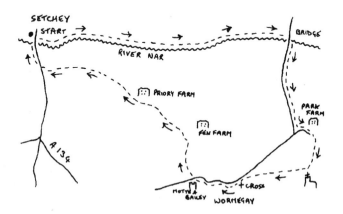

Directions:

1. From your park in the lay-by just north of the bridge at Setchey on the A 10, go down to the riverbank and walk along the northern banks of the River Nar as far as High Bridge (approximately two miles). 2. Once you have climbed the banks, cross High Bridge and go south along a lane towards Park Farm. 3. Turn left into Park Farm and within a few yards go right along a track which takes you to the isolated Church of St. Michael's. 4. From the Church, go left towards Wormegay and just on the village outskirts you will pass the base of a Saxon cross. 5. Go through the village but remembering on its western fringe to look round the Norman motte and bailey of the Castle. 6. Just after the Castle, look for a path on your right which leads alongside a group of houses, and which works its way around to a raised bank. 7. Follow the path along this bank until it brings you once again to the River Nar. 8. Go left along the banks of the Nar until you reach the southern element of the bridge at Setchey where you climb the bank, and return to your start over the bridge.

Start: Off the A 10 just north of Setchey Bridge.
Approx. Distance: 7 Miles
Approx. Time: 3.5 Hours
Map: Landranger 132 (essential)
Note: Parts of this walk may be overgrown due to lack of use.
Shorts are, therefore, not advisable.

Downham Market

Now to Downham Market and the Marshland Fens proper for the town was once a thriving port on the banks of the Great Ouse. It is now, sadly, a quiet and not especially attractive market town. Its demise can be attributed first to the coming of the railway and second to a drainage cut, both of which separated the town from its former prosperous river base. There has been a settlement here since Roman times and if you walk along the riverbank, four old settlements collectively called The Wiggenhalls, can be found. In the Market Place, once famous for its butter trade, a fine cast-iron Gothic Clocktower, can now be found. Built in 1878 and painted in green and white livery, it is a particularly handsome feature.

Nearby at **Welle Manor Hall,** *Upwell,* Norfolk Punch is produced. Made from an ancient recipe in the traditional way, **Norfolk Punch** is a herbal health drink reputed to have 'pick-me-up' qualities; over 30 different herbs and spices go into its preparation. It is widely available throughout Norfolk, as it is in the rest of the country. The Hall, not open to the public, is a Medieval fortified, ecclesiastical, manor house once belonging to Benedictine monks (974-1539); two of the early fortified towers still stand. Also here is the only selenium mineral spa in England.

For those of an horticulturalist bent, try **Whispering Trees Nurseries** *(01366 388752), Wimbotsham, nr. Downham Market,* specialist growers of fruiting plants, ornamental trees and shrubs. *Open daily 10-5.*

Denver

A couple of miles west of Downham Market, the original old sluice at Denver was built by the Dutch engineer Vermuyden for Charles I to limit the run of the tidal sea waters up the Great Ouse, and to provide the foundations for an ambitious but ill-fated market town to be called Charlemont. The Sluice was subsequently destroyed by a group of men calling themselves the Fen Tigers; as these men made their livings by eeling and wildfowling, they were vehemently opposed to drainage of the Fens. In any case, the Sluice, was further damaged by a high spring tide combining with local flood waters in 1713. A larger and stronger structure was built by Sir John Rennie, also responsible for the old Waterloo Bridge, London, and has subsequently been remodelled and steel gates fitted. The double locks operating here enable vessels passing through at low tide to do so on the downhill from south to north, and uphill at high tide. Prior to the cut-off Channel, water draining from 800, 000 acres of land would pass through the Sluice. Now with the Channel open this load is somewhat lighter and is further supported by the New Denver Sluice which opened at the end of the 1950's.

An interesting six-storey Towermill, built in 1865, and with adjoining steam mill and granary stands midway between the Sluice and the village; plans to renovate and open it up to the public are currently underway. Although the village

Denver Mill

of Denver has no particularly unusual features to commend itself, it should, nevertheless be recorded as the birthplace of George Manby. At school he was a contemporary of Lord Nelson and he would also spend his life in pursuance of maritime interests. Manby had watched a ship go down with all hands off Great Yarmouth, and this spurred him to invent first a mortar and then a rocket as life saving equipment; these are still in use today albeit with sophisticated and up-to-date modifications. By 1823, his equipment had saved the lives of over 200 seafarers. Manby is buried in the churchyard at the nearby village of Hilgay.

Food & Accommodation

Hare Arms *(01366 382229), Stow Bardolph.* Opposite Stow Hall, this is a popular ivy-clad country pub-cum-restaurant. Inside, it has been sympathetically decorated, and has a regularly changing menu offering straightforward classics as well as some original dishes. Fresh local produce is the key, shell fish and game being regularly featured. ***Wheelchair access.***

Methwold

Methwold is an unspectacular county border town but nevertheless interesting for exactly that reason. It is almost large enough to be a town and especially given the array of substantial farmsteads within it. The buildings use a mix of chalk, carstone, flint and brick and make for a motley collection. Built in Perpendicular style, the Church here, and unusually for Norfolk, has a steeple.

Methwold Hythe, once a port, is now two miles from the River Wissey, cut off from its navigation head as a result of Fenland reclamation. An interesting group of buildings can be found between the chalk uplands and Fens and there are fine views across the expanse of Fenland into Cambridgeshire.

The Wiggenhalls

The Wiggenhalls are a collection of four villages, just south-west of King's Lynn, and form the centre of Norfolk's Marshlands clustered as they are along the River Great Ouse. Do not confuse these Marshlands, which are closer to the sea and on higher land, with the Cambridgeshire Fens.

Wiggenhall St. Germans is amongst the most picturesque, and was once a principal mooring for the Fen lightermen; hence its pubs. In the Church of St. Germaine (note the different spelling) are a good set of 15th Century carved bench ends from traditional poppy-heads and grotesques to the more elaborate priest blessing a kneeling person and a couple of lovers. An unusual iron hourglass stand is attached to the pulpit. Nearby, the late 17th Century St. Germaine's Hall faces the river (this is not, however, open to the public).

In St. Mary's Church, at Wiggenhall St. Mary, is another especially attractive set of early 16th Century benches with carved ends and motifs on their backs. At Wiggenhall St. Mary Magdalene, the last remaining professional eel catcher lived until recently by the Great Ouse. Smelts, once a Royal delicacy, were also a regular catch though very rarely heard of today. The Church here has some interesting Jacobean panelling and 15th Century stained glass. Most attractive though are the early 17th Century cottages just east of the Church with their stepped gables. The best place to walk from is probably Wiggenhall St. Peter where there is a good bank, on the east side of the river, to Wiggenhall St. Mary Magdalene. St. Peter's Church is an impressive ruin, standing below the level of the raised bank, its walls still pretty well complete, only roofless.

Terrington St. Clement

Visitors to Terrington St. Clement, west of King's Lynn, cannot help but feel the change in the landscape, the Fens, bulb and flower fields of Lincolnshire just miles away. Appropriately, here too are specialist garden nurseries and the like.

African Violet Centre *(01553 828374), Terrington St. Clement.* A Chelsea Flower Show gold medallist winner, propagating a large variety of African violets - bi-colours, mini's and trailers. They also offer a large selection of seasonal quality plants. *Open daily, 10-5 or dusk if earlier.*

More than anything else, however, the landscape around here is dominated by St. Clement's Church, often called 'The Cathedral of the Marshes'. Built almost entirely from Barnack stone in the shape of a cross with aisles and transepts, the immediate impression is one of largeness. The interior is equally grand with its fine clerestory and flying buttresses. The large screen of 1788 cost £13 to erect - probably a small fortune at the time - and once supported a musicians loft. In both 1613 and 1670, the tower served as refuge for the local population when the sea broke through the dyke. Story has it that whilst the floods continued, these refugees were fed by boats which travelled up from King's Lynn to their aid. Dorothy L. Sayers was to use the church for the setting of her book *The Nine Tailors*.

Walk 5: The Wiggenhalls

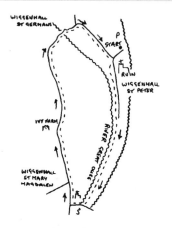

Directions:

1. From your park near the Church ruins of Wiggenhall St. Peter, head towards the River Great Ouse turning left to follow its eastern bank. 2. Cross the bridge into Wiggenhall St. Mary Magdalen and walk through the village past the Church and turn right. 3. Follow this lane for approximately two miles until you reach the outskirts of Wiggenhall St. Germans. The lane bends right and at a T junction turn left and then right to cross the River. 4. Once on the opposite side, turn right to follow the riverbank once again to Wiggenhall St. Peter.

Start: Wiggenhall St. Peter's Church
Approx. Distance: 5.5 Miles
Approx Time: 2.5 Hours
Maps: Landrangers 132 & 131

Walpole St. Peter

At nearby Walpole St. Peter, the Church, also St. Peter's, is one of the most impressive churches of the Norfolk Marshlands - the locals refer to it as 'Queen of the Marshlands' - built between 1350 and 1400. In particular, note the fine bosses on the south porch, the 'sanctus bell' in the bellcote and the passageway under the High Altar called the 'bolt hole'. The latter is said to have been built so as to continue an ancient right of way and even has rings for tethering horses. A number of screens have also been retained, the finest dates from the 17th Century and runs across the nave and aisles. The village itself derives its name from the Walpole family. They first lived here during Norman times and it is from their descendants that Britain was to experience its first Prime Minister.

40

The North-West Coast

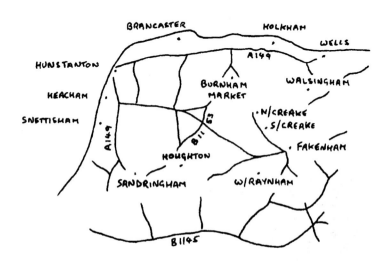

NORTH SEA

BRANCASTER   HOLKHAM
    WELLS
HUNSTANTON   A149
    WALSINGHAM
HEACHAM   BURNHAM MARKET
SNETTISHAM   N/CREAKE
    S/CREAKE
A149   FAKENHAM
HOUGHTON
SANDRINGHAM   W/RAYNHAM
    B1145

A ny visitor to this part of the county invariably finds their way to Sandringham, a favourite residence of the Queen's, and we shall not be the exception. This is an area replete with lavish estates and inevitably, therefore, both Houghton and Holkam Halls are also examined. The coastline itself, offers an interesting balance between the huge cliffs, (huge that is for Norfolk), at Hunstanton and the mud flats of Brancaster Staithe. Inland sees us to the likes of Heacham with its abundant lavender fields, to the Burnhams with their associations with Horatio Nelson, and to Walsingham, a 'mecca' for pilgrims and Britain's holiest shrine.

Sandringham

To Sandringham then, where the Estate was first bought by the Royal Family in 1862 for £220, 000, and which was intended as the then Prince of Wales (Edward) country retreat. One of the visitors first glimpses of the Estate are the huge, decorative cast and wrought iron gates made by Barnards of Norwich the same year. When Prince Edward married Princess Alexandria, the house was considered too small for their needs. Consequently, the main block was demolished and a new house, in Jacobean style, using brick and carstone was put up in its place. This was also the opportunity to replant the grounds, Capability Brown's design being taken as the model, although the gardens to the north of the house were designed for George VI by Sir Geoffrey Jellicoe. The gardens are best visited in spring and autumn. Don't miss the enormous rock garden, built from local carstone, nor the grotto built for Queen Alexandria as a boat and small summer house.

The House and Gardens can be visited (except when a member of the Royal Family is in residence) and of the House interior, the main rooms open are the two-storey saloon with its minstrel's gallery; the main drawing room; dining room and ballroom. Another popular attraction is the Museum housed in the Coach House, the Fire Station and Estate Power House; the line up of Royal cars being the envy of most discerning automaniacs.

The Estate itself, occupies 7, 000 acres and takes in seven parishes though there is no actual village of Sandringham. The Country Park outside the immediate grounds affords free access to nature trails, walks and a picnic area. Otherwise, the Estate is run commercially. Traditional crops grown include cereals and sugar beet but there is also a fruit farm (PYO), two studs and substantial acres of managed forestry. *Opening hours for the House and Garden are complex and you are best advised to phone first (01553 772675). For 1995, however, the following is accurate. The House being open 13 April - 17 July & 4 Aug - 1 Oct, 11-4.45. The Grounds and Museum open 13 April - 22 July & 3 Aug - 1 Oct, 11-5. Admission charge. Wheelchair access.*

Other places to visit are the Church of St. Mary Magdalene in the grounds of the Estate, and the railway station at Wolferton. The former holds many gifts from royalty and other distinguished visitors, and is home to a solid silver altar and reredos. Even the oak pulpit is covered with silver. A spectacularly ornate Church which should not be missed.

Sandringham House

One of the first things you will notice upon entering *Wolferton* is its unusual village sign depicting Fenrir and Tyre. According to legend, Fenrir, an evil wolf, once terrorised the villagers, until Woden, the Norse God, sent assistance in the form of a miraculous slender cord. The villagers persuaded Fenrir to pit his strength against one of their own using the cord; he agreed, but only on condition that villager Tyr put his right arm into Fenrir's mouth. At the end of it all, Fenrir was shackled but Tyr's hand had been bitten off in the process. This is classic Norse mythology and perhaps suggests some past Nordic link with the area.

Built from carstone during the early 13th and late 14th Centuries, St. Peter's Church has a number of unusual features which deserve mention. First the alternating tie-beam and hammerbeam roof, and then the peculiar Gothic mid-19th Century bookcase, thought to be German, but documented as being from Windsor Castle. Additionally, inside the south doorway are a number of stone coffins variously dating from the 12th and 13th Centuries.

Perhaps, however, the main attraction here is the *Station Museum (01485 540674)*, with its collection of Royal memorabilia, a reconstruction of an 1890's Royal carriage, and the Royal retiring room originally built for Edward VII in 1989. Needless to say there is no longer a rail line operating from here; it first began in 1847. The Museum is *open Mon-Sat, 10.30-5.30 & Sun 1-4.30. Admission charge.*

Food & Accommodation

Appleton Water Tower *(01628 825925), managed by The Landmark Trust.* Designed by Robert Rawlinson and built in 1877, here is your chance to stay in a once truly functional building. Although living accommodation was originally built-in for the custodian, this has been improved upon and now also makes use of the second floor. Excellent views of the surrounding countryside can be enjoyed from the top terrace. (Sleeps 4.)

The Feathers *(01485 540207), Dersingham.* A Jacobean inn once frequented by Edward VII before he became King. The atmosphere is relaxed and welcoming - open fires, wall settles and the like. Reasonably priced bar food and a stunning array of real ales. Accommodation is also available.

Park House Hotel *(01485 543000), nr. Sandringham.* Set in its own grounds close to the Sandringham Country Park, this Victorian country house hotel is principally geared towards the needs of the disabled. Carers, friends and relatives of the disabled are equally welcome. The facilities are good and comprehensive, for example, hoists and batri-cars are on hand, and the staff are dedicated professionals.

In Medieval times, *Dersingham* was a port and its fishermen were granted the freedom of the seas by Henry IV. Today it is a good two and a half miles from the sea. Where there were once, in wealthier times, seven manors in

Dersingham, today the Royal Estate owns much of the village. It is an attractive village however, built almost entirely of the local, reddish carstone. The Church of St. Nicholas is mainly 15th Century, its chancel preceding the rest by almost 100 years. Of particular interest is a 14th Century chest carved with birds and with the emblems of the Evangelists. In the northwest corner of the churchyard, is the Great Barn with its stepped gables and built in 1671.

Houghton Hall

A few miles east of Sandringham is *Houghton Hall*. Built in the early 18th Century for Britain's first Prime Minister, Sir Robert Walpole, it is today the home of the Marquess of Cholmondeley (pronounced Chumley). Designed by Colin Campbell in the Palladian style, Walpole originally devoted the ground floor to his and his guests' hunting needs. The first floor aimed at elegance and circumstance, and the second floor held the guests' bedrooms and State Apartment. But perhaps the most lavish part of the Hall is the White Drawing Room with its richly decorated and gilded ceiling and its furniture designed by William Kent. The most astounding features though are the Royal Thrones as used by the Queen, Prince Philip and the Prince & Princess of Wales for the State Opening of Parliament.

The collection of paintings and tapestries is not as rich as it once was, many have been sold to the Czarina of Russia in 1770 and now to be found in The Hermitage in St. Petersburg. The best collection of all though is that which amounts to over 20, 000 model soldiers and is claimed the most important in the world. The Battles of Culloden Moor and Waterloo are amongst those which are permanently set up. *The Hall (01485 528569) is currently undergoing major restoration work and is scheduled to re-open in 1996.*

Sir Robert Walpole, born in 1676, inherited the Houghton Estate after the early deaths of his two elder brothers; another brother, Charles, became 2nd Viscount Townshend, the 'Turnip' Townshend of Raynham Hall. He first entered Parliament as the Whig Member for Castle Rising. Following a move to the other family seat at King's Lynn, he rose to Secretary of War to the Treasurer of the Navy. He is best known, however, for having persuaded Queen Anne in 1713 on her deathbed, to consent to the Whigs taking over the country's administration. This they did in the face of hostile opposition from both the Tory's and the former Queen's Catholic step-brother. With George I now King, Walpole moved to First Lord of the Treasury and Chancellor of the Exchequer. Always a shrewd politician, he created the position of Prime Minister, a post which he himself occupied for 22 consecutive years. He later accepted No. 10 Downing Street as a gift from George II on the basis that it would always be the official residence of the Prime Minister. Walpole resigned in 1742 and was offered a peerage as the 1st Earl of Orford. He died in 1745 leaving the Estate heavily in debt and despite his once having saved the country from bankruptcy following the South Sea Bubble Scandal.

At nearby **Bircham** two places deserve our attention. The first is *Great Bircham Windmill (01485 578393)*, Norfolk's finest tower cornmill, which stands in unspoilt countryside and on a site which has been used for milling since the 1700's. Privately owned, and built in 1846, you can still climb the five floors to the top and at each stage see the machinery in sound working order. The ovens and bakehouse have been restored and now tea rooms, a bakery and gift shop adjoin the Mill. Bicycles can also be hired from here. *Open daily, 10-6, Easter to end September. Bakery closed Sat. Admission charge.* Also look for the *Bircham Art Gallery (01485 578604), Church Lane.* Set in a traditional brick and flint cottage, the gallery hosts an exciting programme of changing exhibitions including Modern British and Contemporary East Anglian Fine Art, Sculpture and Ceramics. *Open Mon-Sat, 11-5.30.*

Walk 6: Great Bircham and the Peddars Way

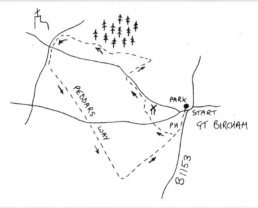

Directions:

1. From your park in the centre of Great Bircham walk down the street, past the pub and turn left down a lane which runs in a south-westerly direction. Look for a track after a short distance on your right. Follow this to the road and go straight across so as to pass the Windmill. 2. Turn left at the lane, and after about half a mile turn right onto a track with trees on the right of it. Continue along here for another half mile until you come to a track heading up hill on your left and just after an old pit. 3. Go along here for just over a mile and a half - the track will soon narrow to a path and then revert to a track. At the road, turn left into the village of Fring. 4. Continue straight on at a junction along Sherborne Road, ignoring a road to your right. Near the top of the hill, turn left to commence your return along the Peddars Way. Stay on the Way for just over two miles, crossing a minor road and ignoring two further tracks on your left. 5. Take the third left hand track, at a crossing of tracks, and continue along here for about a mile and a half bringing you back to your starting point.

Start: On the B 1153 in the centre of Great Bircham
Approx. Distance: 7 Miles Approx. Time: 3 Hours
Map: Landranger 132

Snettisham

Heading further north and just inland from The Wash is Snettisham. Few will not have heard of the hoard of treasure found here in 1985, and comprising a stunning collection of gold torqs dating from around 70 BC. Much of this collection can now be found in the British Museum, London. Previously, in 1948, three hoards of coins were dug up, all of which suggest the area around Snettisham having enjoyed considerable wealth during its early history.

The village is also known for its Coastal Park, an important refuge for wildlife, and run by the local District Council. Open all year, there are two waymarked walks through part of the Park: the yellow trail takes about half an hour, and the blue up to an hour and also provides a bird observation on the shingle sea bank. The hide is great for watching waders, ducks and geese. Other birds to keep an eye out for include curlews, spotted flycatchers, kingfishers and short-eared owls. There are also many different species of butterfly and moth including gatekeeper, burnet and large hawk. The flora has of necessity to be salt tolerant, so sea holly, sea poppy, sea lavender and the like grow in abundance.

Nor is the beach here to be missed. At high tide the sands, with their ancient and evocative names - Thief, Pandora, Seal and The Gat - are still plentiful but do be careful at low tide as much mud is exposed, as it is elsewhere along this stretch of coast. Occasionally, you may even catch a glimpse of the fishermen who use the low tide to rake cockles. The tide here comes in quickly and if you are not careful it is all too easy to get cut off.

Snettisham is also home to the carstone quarry which supplies local building efforts, and to a Watermill. The latter can be found on a path running down to the beach, and was built by public subscription in 1800. It is now restored to working order, grinding flour, which you can buy on the premises. *Snettisham Watermill (01485 542180) is open Wed & Thur, Easter Week, and from late May to early September.*

Another interesting outlet is **Park Farm** *(01485 541244), Snettisham,* known for its venison and free-range eggs, all of which can be had from the farm shop. For those interested in farming, there are three farm trails to follow, supported by an interpretation centre using audio-visual displays to depict life on a typical, working farm.

Heacham

Originally an old settlement on the Wash, Heacham, today, is best known for its lavender farm at Caley Mill. Much of the village's peculiar history, however, is worth summarising here. In 1614, a local man, John Rolfe, married Pocahontas, a Red Indian princess. Rolfe had sailed for Virginia, USA, in 1609 but lost his wife and baby in a shipwreck on the way. Rolfe settled in Jamestown where he fell in love with the 14 year old daughter of Chief Powhaten, and after their marriage he pioneered the cultivation of tobacco. Following a return visit to

England in 1615 with their son, Thomas, and after being received at the Court of James I, the Rolfe family prepared to sail back to Virginia in 1617. Sadly, Pocahontes was to die of consumption in Gravesend before their return journey had even begun. Rolfe, however, did go back only to be killed at the Massacre of Henrico in 1622. In memory of this sad tale, an image of Pocahontes appears on Heacham's village sign.

Heacham is also important for its part in the early history of trades unionism. On the 5th November 1795, over 200 poor farmers and day labourers met in the Church to organise their claim for a reasonable wage. The attempt failed as a result of Anti-Sedition Laws introduced that same month, and after William IV's carriage had been bombarded with mud and stones as he made his way to the State Opening of Parliament. The Heacham attempt at organised labour preceded that of the Tolpuddle Martyrs by an incredible 39 years.

Food & Accommodation

Sedgeford Hall *(01485 570902), Sedgeford, nr. Heacham.* A Queen Anne building set in over 1, 000 acres of woodland and pastureland, and close to both Sandringham and the coast. Much of the bedroom accommodation is in the adjacent cottage. As above, this is a private guest house, offering stylish and upmarket B & B accommodation and where the dinner menu is no-choice, and guests all share one large table.

King William IV *(01485 571765), Sedgeford, nr. Heacham.* A pleasant and lively pub on the edge of the Peddars Way. The straight forward bar food is always well prepared and look for the various ciders on offer during summer, and the range of guest beers. The restaurant gets very busy at weekends, so it is best to book to avoid disappointment.

Norfolk Lavender Ltd (01485 570384), Caley Mill, Heacham, is England's only lavender farm. This is a must to visit during July and early August when the lavender fields around here are harvested; this is when tours of the fields themselves and the distillery at the Mill can best be enjoyed. At other times of year, the National Collection of lavenders can be seen here, set in two acres of grounds around the 19th Century Watermill. The Mill stands on the banks of the River Heacham, the course of which was redirected to serve as the Mill's power source.

The farm was originally founded in 1932 by Linnaeus Chilvers, and now occupies over 100 acres. Five varieties of lavender are grown for distilling and a further two for drying. From an incredible 250 kilogrammes approximately only half a litre of oil is obtained; this is then compounded with other ingredients, using an 18th Century recipe, to produce a quintessentially English fragrance. Also here is a gift shop, tea room and small nursery. *Open daily, 10-5.30, April to October, and weekends, 8.30-4, October to April. Admission charge for guided tours only. Wheelchair access.*

Hunstanton

The main resort along this stretch of coast is Hunstanton, developed during Victorian times in response to the increasing demands for tourist-like facilities. Its main attraction, however, has to be the 60 feet high cliffs with their layers of carstone and red and white chalk giving the appearance of a large, striped stick of rock. From the top of these, on a clear day, you can see right over the Wash to Boston Stump, Lincolnshire, and the tower of St. Botolph's Church, Boston.

The town lost its pier in a heavy storm during 1978 but has since added a number of other attractions including *The Sea Life Centre (01485 533576), South Promenade,* where you can walk the reinforced plastic tunnel out to sea and watch the fish at swim around you. *Open daily, excluding Christmas. Admission Charge.* Alternatively, take a cruise aboard a catamaran to Seal Island, a sand bank in the Wash, or take a trip on an American World War II amphibian troop-carrier. All leave from the Promenade and details can be had from the Tourist Information Centre *(01485 532610)*; bookings are through *Searle's* kiosk on the Promenade. Permits and licenses are not required for boat and beach fishing, and for the latter it is best attempted from the north end of the Promenade. If it is golf you are after then visitors are welcome at the *Hunstanton Golf Course (01485 532811), Old Hunstanton.* You will need your own club membership card as well as your handicap certificate.

Food & Accommodation

Ancient Mariner *(01485 534411), at Le Strange Arms Hotel, Golf Course Road, Old Hunstanton.* The Ancient Mariner stands to the rear of this 17th Century house, the grounds of which run down to the sea. The decor captures the mood of the high seas in its interesting use of old fishing nets and in an old rowing boat mounted over the bar. Decent bar food can be had here, or for something a little more formal try the restaurant in the conservatory extension. **Wheelchair access.**

The Gin Trap Inn *(01485 525264), Ringstead, nr. Hunstanton.* A former 17th Century coaching inn tastefully renovated in the late 1980's. Some of the old traps have been cleverly converted to electric wall lights, and other decoration is in the form of rural implements which cover the ceiling. An original set of stocks can be found in one of two car parks, so good behaviour is called for! Decent bar food and a good range of ales including the pub's own are to be had. Situated close to the Peddars Way, this is a popular haunt with walkers.

Sutton House *(01485 532552), 24 Northgate, Hunstanton.* Some of the rooms in this comfortable Edwardian house enjoy views over the sea and all are furnished to a high standard. Additionally, guests to this B & B establishment have use of the first floor sitting room and balcony area. Evening meals and light snacks are available.

Old Hunstanton, half a mile to the north, is mostly residential and nestles behind the sand dunes. This is one of few places in Britain where the foreshore is privately owned; the le Strange family have been Lords of the Manor for over 800 years, hold the title Lord Admiral of the Wash, and own, according to Charter, everything in the sea as far as a man on horseback can throw a javelin at low tide. Story has it that in the 1930's, this right was exercised when Mercedes Gleitze, the German long-distance swimmer, swam the Wash from Lincolnshire to Norfolk. Once ashore, she was claimed as the legal property of the le Stranges! At least, temporarily so.

East of Hunstanton is *Ringstead Downs*, one of very few chalk grasslands left in Norfolk. It is well known for its rich plant life which includes rock rose and the stemless thistle. The area is also very rich in its birdlife as it is with butter-flies. A public right of way runs though the full length of the Reserve but the woods are privately owned.

Holme-next-the Sea

Holme not only marks the north-western corner of Norfolk, but also the meet-ing point of several long distance paths or ways, as it does the end of the Wash and the beginning of another shore. From here eastwards to Cley, the sea is sep-arated from the land by wide sands and a series of natural harbours protected by dunes, saltings and marshes.

The Holme Dune Nature Reserve occupies an area of about 600 acres and is run by the Norfolk Naturalists Trust. There is a variety of habitats here but the dom-inant ones are the sand dunes and salt marshes. Species of plant to be found include sea lavender, sea rocket, prickly saltwort, hounds tongue, the rare grey hair grass, and a range of orchids. Over 280 species of bird have been recorded including osprey, rough-legged buzzard and harriers. Bird-watching facilities on the *Holme Bird Sanctuary* are however only available to permit holders.

The dunes themselves provide good walking and way marked paths skirt the golf links and the Bird Sanctuary. Otherwise, the sands stretch to the sea, and if you notice black patches visible in the water, these are thought to be the remains of a once ancient forest.

The village itself marks the Norfolk end of the Peddars Way, the Icknield Way and the North Norfolk Coastal Path. It is a small and pleasant enough place and probably best known for its fine 15th Century Church. St. Mary's was built by Henry Notingham (a Judge to Henry IV) but was much demolished in 1788. For those who enjoy horseriding, try *Home Farm Riding Stables* (01485 525233) which is BHS approved.

A little further east is *Thornham*, an attractive village built largely of clunch with some flint. It is part of a transitional area between the main carstone and flint regions of Norfolk. Thornham's natural harbour is small, not as well known as others along this coast, and, therefore, not overly crowded. Mussel, crab and cockle fishing is still a feature of the locals' lifestyle. The beach, with its excellent sands and dunes, is only reached after a mile long walk along the Norfolk Coastal Path, but it is well worth it.

An Iron Age earthwork of circa 40 AD overlooking the Wash, measuring 133 by 175 feet, has been excavated here, and later Roman artefacts found in the area are now held in the Castle Museum, Norwich. Further excavations revealed a Saxon Cemetery holding more than 20 skeletons. Indeed it was the Saxons who first began All Saints Church, though much of the building is mid 14th Century. Extensive repairs particularly during the last century are evident but the huge ilex trees still stand around it.

Just south-east of the village is Thornham Hall (not open to the public) begun by George Hogge in 1788. His descendants married into the Ames Lyde family and endowed the village with considerable fame by beginning, in 1887, a wrought iron foundry. These works were responsible for the kitchen garden-gates at Sandringham, and for those of the Royal Pavilion. The business collapsed in 1914 followed by closure of the smithy six years later.

Food & Accommodation

The Lifeboat Inn *(01485 512236), Thornham.* This former 16th Century smugglers' inn faces out over the open marsh and beyond to the sea. Oak beams, low ceilings and traditional furniture abound ,as do antique lamps, guns, traps and farming tools. It is a popular haunt for families, and certainly at weekends it can get extremely busy. Good food and traditional ales. Most of the bedroom accommodation is housed in an extension to the inn, but some can be found in the original part, and most look out over the marshes.

Titchwell Manor *(01485 210284), Titchwell, nr. Thornham.* A typi-cally, English family-run hotel in a solid Victorian building. Old fash-ioned but comfortable, unpretentious decor is the key. A choice of accommodation is available including self-contained units in the annex.

The White Horse *(01485 525512), Holme.* A rather basic local but the welcome is always warm. Good if limited food. Note; this too gets very busy during the summer.

Brancaster

Formerly called Branodunum, the Romans established their northern most Norfolk fort at Brancaster; its commander given the accolade 'Count of the Saxon Shore'. But it was not until 1960 that the remains of a Romano-British Cemetery, together with Christian burials of the 4th Century, were discovered near the site of the current 14th Century Church. Today, Brancaster's inhabi-tants survive on tourism and shell-fishing.

The Staithe here developed as Scolt Head Island grew and flourished in both the 18th and 19th Centuries. In 1797, the Staithe boasted a malt-house claimed to be the largest in England at that time; it was demolished in 1878. Mussels continue to be farmed in the harbour - transplanted here for three years from spawning grounds in the Wash - and whelks are dredged from the sea bed. We are reminded of the dangers inherent in a life on the sea by a plaque in the Church commemorating the village's lifeboats responsible for the rescue of many seamen who would otherwise have drowned.

The National Trust operates an *Information Centre* at the Staithe, known as Dial House *(01485 210719)* and this is open weekends, March to late July, and daily from late July through August. You can hire bicycles from here. Additionally, there is a Golf course out on the marshes by the sea; *The Royal West Norfolk Golf Club* *(01485 210223)* is a treeless links course dominated by the surrounding marshes and dunes. Visitors are welcome by prior arrangement with the Secretary.

Alternatively, why not take a boat from the Staithe to *Scolt Head Island*, an important site for four species of tern and for oyster catchers and ringed plovers. Just under four miles long, the Island is continuously changing shape, its northern coast a series of sand dunes which protect the salt marsh on its southern shore. The Island was originally bought from Lord Leicester (Holkam Hall) in 1923, and in 1945 the Norfolk Naturalists Trust purchased the eastern tip. Following a 99 year lease granted in 1953, it is now managed by the Nature Conservancy Council. A marked trail ensures minimum disturbance to the varied birdlife on the Island and the ternery is closed to visitors during May and

Brancaster Staithe

June. Access is by boat (by prior arrangement with local boatmen) from the Staithe, and times depend upon both the weather and the tides. Please note, it is strongly advised that you do not try to walk out to the Island at low tide - the salt marshes and salt flats can be very dangerous if you are not wholly familiar with them.

> The Brancaster coastline is the only EEC pollution-free harbour in Britain and is renowned for its **mussels**. The tools for mussel farming are simple: - a small locally built boat called a flat; a long handled net with a metal rake at the end known as a dydle; purse shaped nets with a curved wooden handle; and a grader for sizing the mussels. At low tide, visitors can walk out to the mussel beds; you will need appropriate footwear though. Mussels can also be bought from the Staithe during season (September to April).

The Burnhams

The Burnhams form a pretty group of villages spread along the valley of the River Burn, and which collectively once represented a not inconsiderable port. Their importance in times past is confirmed by a snippet of Medieval verse:

"London, York and Coventry
And the Seven Burnhams by the Sea."

The Burnhams include **Burnham Norton** to the north which lies on the edge of the reclaimed salt marshes. St Margaret's Church here boasts a hexagonal Jacobean pulpit, claimed as England's best, and on the west side of the north porch is a bread oven, presumably used for baking the Communion Wafers. Just west of the village are the remains of a Carmelite Friary founded in 1241. Although the Friary was granted a license to extend its premises in the mid 1300's, it was neither an important nor large monastery. Some of the ruins have survived, including the earthwork banks and a sizeable part of the two-storey, decorative, flint-knapped gatehouse. Other features of the Friary - a 14th Century doorway among them - can be found in the adjoining farmhouse.

Close by are **Burnham Overy** and **Burnham Deepdale**. Burnham Overy has an unusual Church with a square central tower surmounted by a bell turret. The Staithe here also boasts a fine range of granaries and maltings cared for by the National Trust; today only small pleasure boats are sailed from the Staithe. A privately owned watermill strides the river on the B 1155 and the National Trust owns the other Watermill, on the A 149, where the recently renovated complex of buildings date from the late 18th Century and include a malting floor; two of these flats are available as holiday lets, see below. The nearby windmill is also owned by the National Trust, built in 1816 and restored in 1986. None of the mills are open to the public as all have private tenants *in situ*.

During the Middle Ages, the River Burn ran out to sea from Burnham Deepdale but it has since changed its course. Now, Deepdale is detached from the other Burnhams and instead is joined to Brancaster Staithe. The Church is well worth a few minutes if only to see the 11th Century font made from Barnack stone and on which the 12 months of the year are represented in carvings depicting country life.

Burnham Market is made up of the former Burnhams Westgate, Sutton and Ulph. This most attractive town is dominated by the Church of St. Mary Westgate with its fine 14th Century flint tower and its fine, typically English, green is lined with dignified Georgian styled homes and an array of interesting little shops, many of them trading as antique dealers. The battlements to the Church are thought to be early 16th Century and enjoy an unusual gallery of sculpted panels representing, for the most part, scenes and figures of a Biblical nature.

> Born in 1758, **Horatio Nelson** attended the Royal Grammar School, Norwich, and Paston School in North Walsham. Aged 13, he joined the Merchant Navy and for years plied the route between England and the West Indies. In 1793, he was made Captain of the *Agamemnon*; Britain at this time was at war with France, and five years later he was honoured as Baron Nelson of the Nile for his part in sinking Napoleon's fleet at Aboukir Bay. Unfortunately, the Siege of Calvi saw Nelson lose his right eye and during an attack on Santa Cruz he lost his right arm. In 1805, as victor of the Battle of Trafalgar, Nelson lost his life. He is buried in St. Paul's Cathedral, London, and honoured by the 170 feet high granite column in Trafalgar Square which all of us must have some familiarity with.

Lord Horatio Nelson was born at ***Burnham Thorpe*** parsonage in 1758; the house no longer stands but its site is marked with a plaque beside the road. In the 13th Century Church of All Saints, the cross and lectern are both made from timbers taken from *HMS Victory* and flags from the same battleship hang in the nave. Other concessions to Nelson include a pre-1801 Naval ensign which flies from the tower on appropriate days; the hassocks display *Victory* under full sail and a bust of the great man adorns the chancel wall. In all this talk of Nelson though, mention must also be made of the superb brass monument in the central aisle to Sir William Calthorpe (d.1420), once Lord of the Manor. Not that you can miss it though.

Typical flint-built cottages at Burnham Deepdale

The Market Place, Burnham Market

Food & Accommodation

Fishes Restaurant *(01328 738588), Burnham Market.* As its name suggests a restaurant specialising in fish fare, and usually best visited outside the busy summer season. Look out for the local catches, whether crab, lobster or sea bass for example. This is not an elaborate fancy environment but rather one which places emphasis on good value food.

The Hoste Arms *(01328 738257), Burnham Market.* Once a staging inn and now offering a good and varied wholesome menu, friendly service, and well-above-average accommodation throughout; if staying overnight ask for the spacious four-poster rooms. Built in the 17th Century, the local assizes were at one time held here. Additionally, the inn is named after Sir William Hoste, born 1780, who served under Nelson in several campaigns. *Wheelchair access.*

The Lord Nelson *(01328 738321), Burnham Market.* Don't be misled by the pub's appearance; it is far more attractive inside than out. The quality home cooking here has a strong seafood bias and traditional ales are on tap. Look out for the wild mushrooms behind the bar: picked locally, pickled and very edible!

The Lord Nelson *(01328 738241), Burnham Thorpe.* A most unusual and unspoilt pub which does not even boast a bar counter - just a small room with antique settles arranged against the outside wall. Until recently, the landlord Les Winter, adorned the walls with an array of Nelson memorabilia he had collected; these were all sold at auction in 1993.

The National Trust *(01225 791199)* has two self-catering cottages for holiday lets in the beautifully converted Watermill at Burnham Overy. (Sleeps 4-6;4.)

Walk 7: The Burnhams

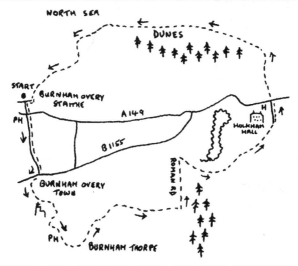

Directions:

1. From your park at the Staithe, head back to the A 149 and cross over to the pub. Continue along the lane (Gong Lane) in front of you, past the Post Office and as it becomes a sandy track leaving the village behind. At a meeting of footpaths continue straight across until you join the B 1155 on the edge of Burnham Overy Town. At the road, turn right passing a handful of houses and take the left hand path over the field to the now dismantled railway track. 2. Go left along the track for about 100 yards, keeping your eyes peeled for a footpath sign and stile on your right. Once over this, cross the meadow using the left hand corner as your goal but avoiding the pond on your right. Climb the stile in front of Burnham Thorpe Church and follow the path round the north and west aspects of All Saints. 3. At the road, turn left which leads you into the village and past the pub. After the pub, go left again passing the edge of the village playing field and then straight over at the crossroads and up a relatively steep hill. 4. At the top, go left and after about 200 yards take the right turn into a sandy track which leads due east to a wall forming part of the Holkam Estate boundary. 5. At the wall, fringing Lucas Hill Wood, go left onto what was once a Roman road. At West Lodge, go right into Holkam Park; although this is a public right of way please ensure dogs are on leads and that you do not deviate from the drive. Once beyond the garden centre, on your left, and the cattle grid into the deer park, the Hall comes into view. Continue along the drive as it skirts the south-easterly edge of the lake and the Hall's courtyard. At the next cattle grid, go left and so to the entrance gates and beyond to the estate cottages. 6. At the end of this lane you once again join the A 149 (the Victoria Hotel on your left). Cross straight over the road into Lady Anne's Road. At the end of this lane go straight across through Holkam Meals and onto the beach. Once on the beach go left, in a westerly direction for about two miles. Thereafter you will notice a

number of wooden posts in the dunes which protect a nesting colony of terns, At the end of these, take the slatted path which leads you to another footpath on the top of the sea defenses. Follow this as it twists along the edge of Overy Creek and so back to your starting point.

Start: Burnham Overy Staithe
Approx. Distance: 9.5 Miles
Approx. Time: 5 Hours
Map: Landranger 132

The Creakes

Further inland, North and South Creake are two attractive villages whose buildings are comprised of a mix of chalk and flint. *Creake Abbey* (North Creake) belonged to an Augustinian community founded by Sir Robert de Narford and his wife in 1206. Sited on the River Burn, it was originally, in the 12th Century, an almshouse and hospice for the poor. In 1206, it was established as an Augustinian Priory and its status further raised to that of an Abbey in 1231. Although it was destroyed by fire in 1378, Richard II, following appeals from the Abbot, contributed to its re-building. To no avail, however, for during one week in 1504 all the monks died from the plague and the Abbey ceased to operate. Story has it that before the monks demise, they hid their valuables on the premises. Today, no record of these having been found exists, although a monk was tried by Sir Thomas More, during Henry VIII's reign, for 'practicing magic' in an effort to discover them. What is left of the Abbey is managed by English Heritage and is *open throughout the year, free of charge.* Abbey Farmhouse, next door, has some of the remains of the cloister and conventional buildings amongst its properties.

At North Creake can be found *Forge Museum (01328 738910).* A living Museum to the blacksmiths art and retaining its old-style charcoal forge fired by bellows. The River Burn runs through the adjoining tea gardens. The Museum is *open during Easter Week and throughout the summer months, 10-5. Admission charge.*

Walk 8: The Creakes

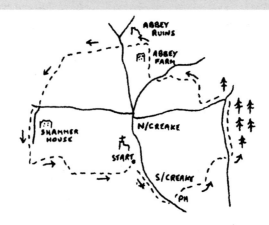

Directions:

1. From South Creake Church, head back to the B 1355 and turn right along there until you see a track on your left just before the pub. 2. Turn left once this reaches an old Roman Road and go straight across at the crossroads, thus entering East Common Wood. 3. At a T junction, go left into Whin Hill, ignore a lane off to your left, and instead take a right-hand track a little further along. Once past some farm buildings, take the left -hand fork to a lane and go left again. 4. Turn right into a bridleway which leads to Abbey Farm and continue to a cottage. 5. Go left here, visit the Abbey ruins, and continue to the B 1355. 6. Cross the road and continue along this track until it forks (ignore an earlier track to your left) and go left again to a junction. 7. Go left here, and at the crossroads straight across past Shammer House. After this, take the third track to your left and after about half a mile, turn right onto the edge of a field. 8. At the end of this, go left along a track for about one mile. Where it bends right, go straight ahead along a footpath to South Creake Church.

Start: South Creak Church
Approx. Distance: 10 Miles
Approx. Time: 4.5 Hours
Map: Landranger 132

Holkam

Continuing to hug this west Norfolk coast will see us to Holkam where the Hall was designed by William Kent for the Coke family (now the Earls of Leicester) between 1734 and 1759, and where the building is faced with sand-coloured brick made on the Estate itself. The many unusual features inside include the Marble Hall - considered one of the finest Palladian rooms in the country - the Great Statue Gallery containing an incredible collection of classical statuary. The Dining Room, in the north aspect, is a perfect cube and its ceiling was designed by Inigo Jones; the floor carpet echoes this design. Additionally, the furniture is contemporary with the house, made by Goodison from Kent's designs, and the library holds one of Britain's largest collections of books. Works by Gainsborough, Reubens, Van Dyck and others grace the many walls. *The Hall (01328 710227) is open Sun-Thur & Bank Hols, 1.30-5, end May to end September. Admission charge.*

The Estate here is perhaps best known for its development of progressive agricultural practices, especially under Thomas Coke (1754-1842) who devised the first four year crop rotation programme - wheat, turnips, barley with clover, and finally clover on its own. This method revolutionised farming and permitted livestock to be fed over winter instead of being slaughtered. Coke had learned from 'Turnip' Townshend (Raynham Hall) and indirectly from Jethro Tull (b. 1741) who had earlier devised the horse-drawn seed drill, thus doing away with hand sowing. In turn, all three had reaped benefits from the Enclosures Act which enabled land to be owned outright; pressure on owners to plan their crops and improve the fertility of the soil were direct outcomes of this development.

The Park at Holkam is also one of the finest in the country and was landscaped by Capability Brown; he created the lake and planted thousands of ilex trees. The six acre walled *kitchen garden* though was designed by Samuel Wyatt and built in the 1780's. It still holds the orangery and vinery, but the glasshouses have been extensively renovated. It is now a *Plant Centre (01328 710374) open throughout the year.*

The old stable block, north of the Hall, houses the *Bygones Collection (01328 710806)*. The Collection contains steam and fire engines, a smithy and laundry, household items and an exhibition on farming. *Open Sun-Thur, 1.30-5, end May to end September. Admission charge. Wheelchair access.*

The dunes still further north of the Hall are known as the Norfolk Meals, and were planted with Corsica pines in the 19th Century to stabilise them, and thus enable the land behind to be reclaimed from the sea. An ancient Iceni fort is thought to be somewhere along these marshes. The sands here are huge, the shells countless and very often horse-drawn buggies are driven hard across them. Bird hides are also available to the public. But best of all take the walk (about three miles) from the car park which goes left through the forest (not straight on to the beach), past an estate cottage, round to the dunes and back along the sands. Alternatively try the Burnhams walk above which includes both Holkham Park and the beach.

Wells-next-the Sea

Wells is our last port of call along this stretch of coast, and it derives its name from the springs of fresh water held by the underlying chalk bed on which the town is built. These were once tapped as the local water supply and many houses even had their own wells situated literally outside their back doors. Earliest mention of the town was made in the 13th Century, though little is really known until a 1675 Act of Parliament created the Wells Harbour Commissioners; a body which could charge a levy on goods handled by the port. A later Act fixed this duty at a shilling per ton of the ship's registered tonnage and this practice still applies, though naturally monetary conversions are now somewhat different.

Nine years later, in 1844, the Commissioners were granted the right to buy property along the waterfront and from that began the present Quay; a stipulation however, accompanying this right, ruled for the provision of a lifeboat. Furthermore, a heavy fine was to be imposed for every day that the lifeboat was not seaworthy. Built in 1869, the first lifeboat house was stationed at the southern end of the Quay. Imagine then having to first row the boat along the mile long channel before reaching sea and those at risk. At low tide, the task was even more complex: horses had to be caught and harnessed and then the lifeboat pulled along the mile-long stretch. Close to this first lifeboat house is a memorial commemorating the 11 man crew of the *Eliza Adams* who lost their lives when the boat capsized and the mast embedded itself in the sand, thus preventing it from righting itself. Today, the lifeboat shed is more sensibly placed at the seaward end of the channel.

As a port, Wells prospered during the period 1850-1914, although the railway (arrived 1857) nevertheless depleted sea trade to some extent. Typical cargoes at this time would have been malt and barley exports and coal imports. After World War I, new exports in the form of potash and sugar beet were thriving, and today imports consist of animal fodder and fertilisers. Having said that, relatively few vessels other than fishing boats and pleasure craft now use Wells but keep a close eye out for a Dutch Schooner, complete with sails, which is a regular trader here; you can even sail to the Netherlands with her for a small fee and providing you are prepared to help on deck.

Two small fishing fleets continue to trade from Wells. The traditional fleet being Whelkers and the other Spratters. The Quay at Wells has still retained its charm, perhaps most evidently assured by continuing use of the overhanging grain hoist, and by Quay moorings for transient yachties and fishing boats. There is also a well stocked Chandlery at the east end of the Quay. Gift shops, fish and chip shops and the like also abound but if you cannot enjoy the latter at Wells then you will never enjoy our great British feast anywhere.

Don't be deceived by the plethora of caravan sites on the road leading down to the beach as Wells beach, with its graceful mix of old, dilapidated, and new and brightly-coloured beach huts, flanked by dunes and conifer plantings, is one of the most attractive around. It has rightly been designated an Area of Outstanding Natural Beauty. But you must heed the tidal warnings, (a loud horn is sounded), as the waters flow fast and furious and it is all too easy to get cut-off from the shore.

Wells Quay

Wells Beach

Food & Accommodation

The Crown Hotel *(01328 710209), The Butlands, Wells.* Despite its Georgian facade, the Crown predates this quite significantly as proven by its bowed beams in the bar. Some interesting maps and prints depicting Wells in both the 18th and 19th Centuries are to be enjoyed. Reasonably priced bar food, good ales on tap and a restaurant should you prefer something quieter. **Wheelchair access.**

Mill House *(01328 710739), Northfield Lane, Wells.* A few minutes walk from the town centre, Mill House was, as its name determines, owned by a local miller and retains its distinctive Flemish gables. Well furnished B & B accommodation throughout. Home-cooked evening meals are available, excepting Saturday and Wednesday.

The Moorings *(01328 710949), Freeman Street, Wells.* Fish accounts for most of the menu and it is especially good, fresh and fashionably presented. Vegetarian, meat and poultry dishes are also available. All round good value is the key here, and this is carried through to the wine list as well.

The Three Horseshoes *(01328 710547), Warham.* An 18th Century cottage pub in a typically flint built village. There are two small bars, simply decorated with cottage antiques, original gas lighting and open fires. Note the American Mills one-arm-bandit machine still in working order, and the Norfolk twister on the ceiling (give it a twist and if it stops in front of you it is your round!). A separate-dining room and a children's room increases the space, as does the garden. Fresh, local seafood is the house speciality.

The town itself has little, architecturally, to truly make its mark but its narrow streets and inter-connecting passages (akin to the Rows of Great Yarmouth) are quaint. There is also The Butlands, an especially pleasant oblong green, lined by trees and for the most part, Georgian houses. It probably derives its name from a 16th Century stipulation requiring regular longbow practice for all adult males.

Wells Museum (*01328 711744*)) can be found at the back of the Harbour Master's office and is especially interesting in its documentation of Wells maritime, fishing and wildfowling history. ***Open Tue-Fri, 2-5, & Sat 10-12 & 2-5, mid April to mid July. Admission charge. Wheelchair access to ground floor.***

The Wells & Walsingham Railway (*01328 856506*) on the eastern outskirts of the town (off the A 149) is the longest 10.25" narrow gauge railway in the world hauled by a unique Garratt locomotive, built especially for this line. Between Easter and September, a full daily timetable is run. Wells is also famous for its whelks, found in the black sand along the Wash.

Walk 9:Wells and Warham

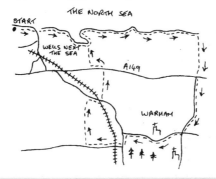

Directions:
1. From Wells Quay, go east along the B 1105 and where it bends sharply round to the right go straight ahead into a minor road. 2. Bear left onto a track past the fishermens' huts and so out to the sea bank. Walk along this bank and as it leads you round a tidal creek to Warham Greens. Follow this as far as a sign reading Nature Reserve-Holkham(East). 3. Go right here along Cockelstrand Drove to the A 149. Cross the road and follow the lane which leads up the hill to Warham. 4. At the crossroads with All Saints Church, turn right and follow the lane past St. Martin's Church and round to the right to the B 1105. 5. Turn left here for a short distance, then first right on a track towards Gallow Hill. 6. Go right again just before a barn and follow the track back to the B 1105. Go right here and then left into a track once you have crossed the railway bridge. 7. At the A 149 turn left for a short distance and then first right along a track back to the sea bank. Turn left here to retrace your steps to Wells Quay.
Start: Wells Quay Approx. Distance: 7 Miles
Approx. Time: 3 Hours Map: Landranger 132

Walsingham

A few miles inland from Wells is Walsingham. For over 900 years pilgrims have made their way here to England's National Shrine, and in Medieval times it was the most important pilgrimage site in northern Europe. It all began around 1060 when the Virgin Mary is said to have appeared in a vision to Richeldis de Faverches, the Lady of the Manor, and commanded her to establish a *Santa Casa*, a replica of the Nazarene House of the Annunciation. Story goes that Richeldis hesitated between two sites for the building and that work began on one but with little result by the end of the day. The following morning, it is said, the timber-built, religious house stood complete on the alternative site. A well sprang from its grounds and, thereafter, miraculous cures were claimed. The shrine Richeldis built was added to by the Augustinians between 1360 and 1390 and following a bequest by the Countess of Clare (Suffolk), and although Henry VIII was later to make a pilgrimage here he, nevertheless, ordered its Dissolution following his quarrels with the Papacy. Today, only the ruins of the Priory can be seen in the gardens of Abbey House, especially the piers of the west tower, the east gable end, and the 15th Century gatehouse at the north end of the main street. The site of the original Holy House can be found in the grass north of the nave and is marked by a small wooden plaque. *The grounds are open variously between April and September (Wednesday is the safest bet), 2-5. Small admission charge. Wheelchair access.*

Not to be outdone, the Franciscans built their Friary (Greyfriars) at the southern end of the village in 1347. Again, a victim of the Dissolution, only the ruins survive and these now form part of a private house. The most impressive remains are the former Guest House with its tall upper-storey and gable ends, the walls of the kitchen, and the little cloister. These are occasionally open to the public; the times of opening being marked on the outside gate.

Walsingham Church Priory, East Window

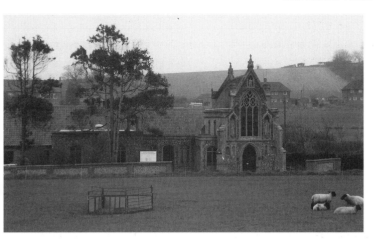

The Slipper Chapel, Houghton St. Giles

Following Dissolution, Walsingham remained all but dead for many generations until the early 1830's and the beginnings of the Oxford Movement; founded by a group of intellectuals following Catholic emancipation, in 1829, and who were set on reforming Church procedure. With this, handfuls of pilgrims started to return and despite the fact that much of what they found was in ruins. Zealous appreciation though was to see Catholic convert Charlotte Pearson Boyd buy the derelict *Slipper Chapel at Houghton St. Giles* in 1895 with its restoration work not completed until 1934. Earlier pilgrims had once stopped at Houghton St. Giles, the last wayside Shrine before Walsingham, removed their footwear and walked the last mile and a half barefoot; hence its name. Others, however, view *slippe* as meaning narrow passage. This is now the Catholic National Shrine with its Holy Ghost Chapel which is *open daily*.

Elsewhere, other restoration work was also afoot, led by local man Alfred Hope Patten, later a priest at Walsingham from 1921-58. He was responsible for rebuilding Richeldis' Chapel as the new *Anglian Shrine of Our Lady* in Walsingham in 1931, and reputedly discovering the 11th Century well in the process. The building's exterior is somewhat disappointing, but inside is the Annunciation Altar - a carving depicting Mary receiving news of her soon-to-be virgin-born child - and 15 side chapels, representing the mysteries of the Rosary. *Services and prayers are held regularly each day,* some outside, and baptismals are performed by the Holy Well. Additionally, the Shrine Garden outside is marked by the Stations of the Cross.

Other religious buildings also abound with the Catholics, Anglican, Methodist and Russian Orthodox all having their own churches. Additionally, the *Shrine Office* will arrange pilgrimages and accommodation for those who require assistance *(01328 820255)*. Even if you are not of a strong religious bent, the processions here, especially during Easter Week, are interesting in their own right. Summertime, candlelit processions are usually held on Saturday evenings starting around 8p.m. and the Annual National Pilgrimage on Spring Bank Holiday is attended by thousands, concluding in the Priory Gardens.

Walsingham is unique in that it was planned and built along a grid-iron system (as at New Buckenham) specifically to cater for these pilgrims. Consequently, many other fine Medieval, timber-framed buildings have survived, their jettied upper-storeys projecting over their ground floors. Around Common Place, for example, there is a range of fine 15th and 16th Century buildings including *The Shirehall (01328 820510)*. Originally built to house important visitors to the Priory, a Georgian facade was added in the 1770's and from then until the 1860's the Quarter Sessions were held here, the Petty Sessions continuing until as late as 1971. Today, it is a *Museum* housing the original courthouse, prisoners cells alongside other exhibits on Walsingham's history. *Open daily, 11-1 & 2-4, Easter to September, and also Sat & Sun during October. Admission charge.*

Close to the Shirehall is *The Walsingham Estate Co. (01328 820259)*, the place to go for snowdrop bulbs, lifted from the Estate woods. Occasionally aconites are also available. Although it is primarily a mail-order nursery, it is also *occasionally open between April and September* with Wednesday once again the best bet but sometimes also during the weekends.

Food & Accommodation

The Black Lion Hotel *(01328 820235), Walsingham.* This is one of the oldest buildings in the village and is named after Edward III's wife, Queen Philippa of Hainault. The northern end was specifically built for Edward II (1327-77) who made several pilgrimages here. It was not until the 1600's, however, that it became a coaching inn, and during the 1700's until 1861, the Petty Sessions were held here. **Wheelchair access.**

The Old Bake House *(01328 820454), Walsingham.* A well-respected restaurant and once the old bakery where the original ovens have survived, and offering limited but good value accommodation for B & B guests. The smallish cellar bar is contrasted by the lightness of the main dining room. Good stable food and service.

The Old Rectory *(01328 820597), Great Snoring.* This brick built rectory was once part of the manor house established around 1525 for Sir Ralph Shelton; although renovation in Victorian times changed it from its former hexagonal shape, the polygonal turrets, mullioned windows and friezes of moulded brick remain as distinguishing features. Standing in two acres of secluded garden, a restful stay is assured. The accommodation is of a high standard and there is a choice of self-catering or main building B & B styled facilities. No choice main course dinners are distinctly English in orientation. No children under 12 years old.

Off-centre, within Common Place, is the 16th Century octagonal Pump, once the village's main water supply. Unfortunately, overladen with bunting, its pinnacle snapped off during some celebration or other and in its place is a 'brazier' lit only on State occasions. Friday Market is a fine, oblong area crowded with interesting buildings, including the Black Lion Hotel and the Catholic Hospice. Edward III granted the Friary the right to hold a market on Fridays and on other special occasions; this continued until the 19th Century. John Wesley is known to have preached here, the Methodist Chapel nearby thought to be the oldest such religious building still in use. Of the shops, most are geared towards religious pilgrims; here you can buy anything from an ikon to the *Book of Common Prayer* to pilgrims' badges and candles, the latter made in Walsingham.

Heading out of Walsingham (Little) towards Great Walsingham you will cross the beautiful, Medieval, pack horse bridge over the River Stiffkey. Although the village here is dwarfed by that at Little Walsingham, it still has its own charm and interest. In the centre of the village is Berry Hall, early Tudor in origin, and complete with Saxon moat (not open to the public). To the south of the Hall is St. Peter's Church, described by Nikolaus Pevsner as "... a singularly beautiful church because its architecture is all one." The clerestory windows here are rare since there are few such original examples intact. The bells here are also some of the earliest known to have been cast, around 1330. Finally, note the 13th Century scratch dial in the churchyard.

Walk 10: England's Holy Shrines

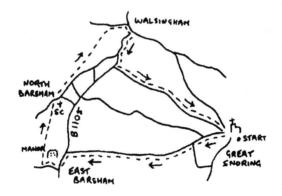

Directions:

1. From your park near the phone box in Great Snoring, walk up the road towards the Church. Go through the little church gate and along the path beside the wall to a stile. Once over the stile continue along the meadow until you reach another stile. Go over this and turn right to a junction, and then left along the road. 2. Where the road forks, go left heading towards East Barsham along another country lane (about one and a half miles). 3. At the junction with the B 1105, go left (note the imposing East Barsham Manor on your right behind the wall and not open to the public), and follow the road up the hill. Go past the pub and then take the lane on your right which leads to West

Barsham. 4. After a short distance, at some brick pillars, climb up the bank on your right to reach the dismantled railway. Continue along this bank in a northerly direction for about one mile. Where you see a road below you and where the former bridge over it is no longer, you will have to scramble down the bank and up the other side to the next missing bridged link. Again go down to the road and then turn right. 5. Continue along the lane to the Slipper Chapel and just after this turn left up a track to rejoin the bank on your right. Continue along this embankment until you arrive in Walsingham. Turn right into the village and explore as you will. 6. Leave Walsingham by the B 1105 heading in a south westerly direction towards Houghton St. Giles (ignore the fork in the road on your right leading to the Slipper Chapel and North Barsham though). As the road bends right, go left instead (with the lodge on your left) along a track through the trees. 7. Carry straight along this track and then into a green lane (i.e. ignore the track when it forks left into a field). After about one mile you will reach the road where you turn left into Great Snoring. At the next junction, go right along the road past the Church and so to your start.

Start: Great Snoring Church
Approx. Distance: 8 Miles
Approx. Time: 4 Hours (allow longer if you intend to explore
Walsingham in any real depth)
Map: Landranger 132

Fakenham

Yet further inland is Fakenham which began life as a 6th Century Saxon settlement. By 1250, it had its own market and several centuries later, in 1784, Messrs Gurney, Birkbeck, Buxton and Peckover established the first bank in the Market Place. Prior to this last development, a fire destroyed most of the properties in the Market Place in 1738 and, hence, most buildings can only be dated after this. It was left to the railways, however, to facilitate the town's real expansion. Basically, there is not much to see here, the Victorian maltings and flour mill are still evident as are two inns; the 18th Century red-brick Red Lion, and the early 19th Century, white-washed Crown Hotel, together with a handful of Georgian houses. Market day is Thursday, and an auction-cum-flea-market is run by *Hugh Beck Auctions (01328 851557)* in the old cattle market buildings on the same day. In the Church of St. Peter & St. Paul can be found the arms and monograms of the Lancaster family; the manor of Fakenham once belonging to John of Gaunt. The west tower is remarkably tall -115 feet high - and lavishly decorated. And for entertainment *The Racecourse (01328 862388)* runs a seasonal programme of horse racing events.

To the south of the town is *The Museum of Gas and Local History (01328 851696)*. This is the oldest gasworks in the country and it produced coal gas from 1846 -1965; thereafter, its industry was made redundant by the discovery of gas in the North Sea. *Open Tue, Thur, Sun & Bank Hol Mon, 10.30-3.30, end May to end September. Admission charge.* For opening times beyond 1995 contact the Tourist Information Centre.

Pensthorpe Waterfowl Park (01328 851465) can be found one mile east of Fakenham. The Nature Reserve occupies over 200 acres of wetland and former gravel workings on the banks of the River Wensum. One of the largest collections of waterfowl, well over 100 species, can be found - from Arctic long-tailed ducks to harlequins and the tiny, tropical pygmy geese. A new exhibition gallery equipped with large video-screen ensures good viewing as do the changing shows of wildlife photography, paintings and wood carvings. There are a number of nature trails, woodland, meadow and waterside, on the Reserve. *Open daily, 11-5 mid March to early January, (10-6 end July to beginning September). Admission charge. Wheelchair access.*

Also just east of the town is *Old Barn Studios (01328 878762), Kettlestone* which exhibits work by both local and visiting artists - paintings and sculpture. Additionally courses are run throughout the year.

Food & Accommodation

The Boar Inn *(01328 829212), Great Ryburgh.* An ancient and very popular inn close to the banks of the River Wensum. A beamed bar and cosy open fires in winter make for a warm welcome. Best to book the restaurant at busy times though. **Wheelchair access.**

The Crown *(01328 862172), Colkirk.* A traditional, English country pub maintaining games of skittles, shove ha'penny and dominoes. Well presented bar food and a decent selection of wines and ales.

Manor Farm *(01328 829353), Sibbard Road, Fulmodeston.* A traditional Norfolk farmhouse offering sound B & B accommodation amidst acres and acres of arable land. Although well furnished and decorated, the atmosphere is very much informal. Evening meals by prior arrangement only.

Sculthorpe Inn *(01328 856161), Sculthorpe.* A sister inn to that at Thornham, the Mill enjoys an unspoilt location, straddling an island on the River Wensum. The views over the River are especially satisfying. Good bar food, real ales, morning coffee and afternoon teas. **Wheelchair access.**

The Raynhams

Finally we head west to the Raynhams. Raynham Hall (East Raynham) is one of the most attractive country houses in Norfolk built in the 1620's for Sir Roger Townshend. His successor, the 2nd Viscount Townshend, was popularly known as 'Turnip' Townshend as a result of his revolutionary introduction of crop rotation methods, and his pioneering farming of turnip, until then considered only as a garden root crop. The Hall itself is not open to the public but the walk outlined below skirts the edge of the Hall and Stableyard Farm. The Church of St. Mary, close to the Hall, dates from as recently as 1868 but, nonetheless, provides a quiet grace to the surrounding countryside.

Nearby West Raynham is an attractive village, its Church, St. Margaret's, now a ruin and heavily clad in ivy but still attractive. The three villages, East, West and South Raynham, nestle either side of the River Wensum and the surrounding countryside is peaceful and undisturbed. If you do follow the walk described below, do stop by 14th Century, St. Martin's Church. Inside you will find what is thought to be a very early, probably 13th Century, stone mensa, or communion table.

Walk 11: The Raynhams

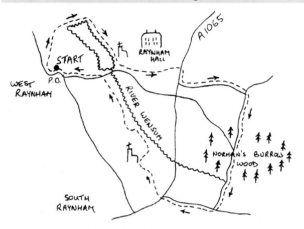

Directions:

1. From the Post Office walk further up the lane, past the pub and take the right turn at the junction (signed Helhoughton). After about 200 yards, turn right at the footpath (signed) which runs along the edge of the playing field and cross over to the right of Round Plantation. Follow this to a stile. 2. Turn right and follow the green waymarkers along the edge of the wood to a kissing gate. 3. Go right towards the farm, through the farm yard and immediately left after the Church. At a field, continue straight ahead along the edge of that field. At the wood, go right towards a group of laurels and once with a walled garden in front of you go left until you reach the gate to the lodge. 4. Go right at the road, A1065, and then after a while take the left hand road signed Colkirk, just before a phone box. Continue along this lane for about one mile until you see a track on your right which runs along the crest of a hill. Stay on this track past Corn Bill Coppice, Webb's Covert and Norman's Burrow Wood. At the minor road, turn right towards South Raynham. 5. At the A1065, go left and just before the petrol station take the path on your right, across a meadow, followed by two more meadows, a series of wooden planks to a gate and a minor road. Go right to the Church 6. At a gate, once you have past the Church, cross the meadow diagonally right and then along the edge of another field (a stream on your right) to a stile. At the road, turn left along the road to West Raynham. At the junction, go right to return to your start.
Start: West Raynham Post Office (It can be a muddy walk)
Approx. Distance: 5.75 Miles Approx. Time: 3 Hours
Map: Landranger 132

The Central Coast

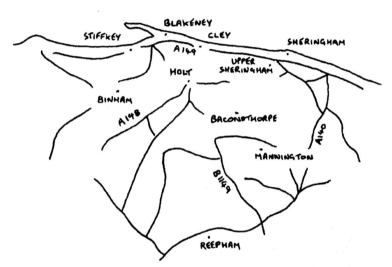

O ur tour of the Central Coast begins in the village of Stiffkey and concludes in the village of Booton. This is an area replete with attractive,
predominantly flint-built small villages, many of them with a distinctive character all their own. Included amongst this last category would be Cley-
next-the-Sea, Blakeney, Glandford, Binham, Letheringsett, Upper Sheringham
and Heydon. Three towns also fall into this area, namely Holt, Reepham and
Sheringham, the former classic county towns and the latter a smallish but
attractive seaside resort.

Stiffkey

Even though the main road runs through Stiffkey, the village remains one of
Norfolk's most charming and picturesque corners. At one time it was dominated by the Hall (not open to the public), built by Nathaniel Bacon in 1578, but
much of this was destroyed by fire in the 18th Century. Originally, it was U-
shaped with long, projecting wings, and a number of circular towers. Only the
west range, part of the north, and the gatehouse of 1604 are still intact, but these

69

are, nevertheless, still attractive when you catch a glimpse of them. Close by is the Church of St. John the Baptist. The earlier Church of St. Mary's was built in 1310 with the current edifice added in the 15th Century; each with its own rector. By 1558, St. Mary's was demolished and St. John's allowed to flourish.

Like Cley, further along this stretch of coast, Stiffkey once had its own quay and harbour but it is now separated from the sea by its salt marsh (you can walk along the edge of the marsh to Morston). Nonetheless, 'Stewkey Blues' (Stewkey being an earlier spelling, probably 16th Century, of Stiffkey) or cockles are still known for their excellence.

One interesting retail outlet to investigate is the *Stiffkey Lamp Shop* *(01328 830460)* which stocks a good range of original antique lamps and light fittings, and where these are sympathetically blended with modern reproductions. At the Chapel, next door, and part of the same operation, old and new bathroom fixtures and fittings, door knobs and related furniture can be had.

Food & Accommodation

Morston Hall Hotel *(01263 741041)*, *Morston*. A 17th Century brick and flint house, enclosed in gardens, and offering stylish accommodation and cuisine. Evening meals are on a no-choice, one-sitting basis, but are consistently of a high standard; to avoid disappointment, it is best to phone and check the menu suits your tastes. The wide and open entrance lounge is tastefully decorated with antiques and strong fabrics, and is dominated by a large inglenook fireplace. **Wheelchair access to restaurant.**

The Red Lion *(01328 830552)*, *Stiffkey*. Re-opened in 1990, the Red Lion has built up a steady following, both with locals and regular visitors alike. The simple, rustic furniture and furnishings are carefully deployed to make you feel at home in the country. Good bar food and real ale, and it is best to book the restaurant if you intend eating here over the weekend.

Just south of Stiffkey, Cockthorpe Hall is thought to have been the birthplace of Sir Clondisley Shoves, an Admiral serving under both Myngs and Narborough and who assisted in the 1704 capture of Gibralter; until 1994 it housed a decent toy museum. The nearby Church of St. Andrew & All Saints is now redundant, though maintained by the Norfolk Churches Trust.

Onto **Morston** where good walks can be enjoyed along the Quay and its surrounding marsh (under the protection of the National Trust). Additionally, depending upon the weather and tide, boats will take you out to the sandbanks, and to Blakeney Point: contact *John Bean (01263 740038), 12 High Street, Morston* or *Temple's Seal Trips (01263 740791)* based at the village pub. For those seeking out local delicacies, try *Scaldbeck Farm (01263 740306)*, which is noted for its oysters; the beds, however, can only be viewed by appointment.

Morston Quay

Walk 12: Cockthorpe and Stiffkey

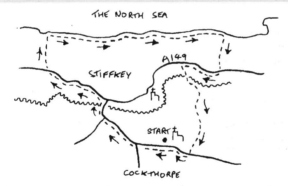

Directions:

1. From All Saints Church, walk the country lane down the hill into Stiffkey. 2. At the junction with the A 149, go left and walk along the road for a short distance. Take the second right-hand lane leading down to the marshes. 3. At the end of the lane, just in front of the marshes, turn right to walk along the well-defined path through Stiffkey Greens (about one mile). 4. At the end of here, follow the path round to the right, between the river and fence, to White Bridges. 5. At the A 149 again, turn right and follow the verge for about half a mile until you see a path on your left. 6. Follow this path as its runs alongside the River Stiffkey, over two footbridges and onto Cockthorpe Common. 7. Walk over the Common until you come to a gate and once through this, turn right to return to All Saints Church.
Start: All Saints Church, Cockthorpe Approx. Distance: 5.5Miles
Approx. Time: 2.5 Hours Map: Landranger 132

Blakeney

A must for every visitor to Norfolk is Blakeney's colourful waterfront crowded with yachts, cruisers and dinghies. Its streets are comprised predominantly of brick and flint houses with some of the ancient warehouses and granaries still intact. At intervals, lokes or alleyways lead into yards where former fishermens'cottages huddle together away from the ravages of the wind and sea. In 1849, 60% of the population were either fishermen or occupied in allied trades such as sail making: an annual Fish Fair was an important occasion for all. Many of these cottages are now holiday homes but the Blakeney Housing Trust, formed after World War II, ensures that some at least are maintained for use by local residents.

Blakeney was first noted in *Domesday* as one of a small group of ports around the River Glaven estuary. By the 13th Century, it was prosperous enough for the Carmelite Friars to found a Priory on the eastern side of the port. The *Guildhall* on the Quay side, with its vaulted roof, may have had some connection with the Friars but its origins remain uncertain. Throughout past centuries, the Guildhall has been used for a variety of purposes by merchants and mariners and one time it was even a morgue for drowned sailors. It is now in the care of English Heritage, *open all year, free of charge.*

Blakeney's importance during the 13th Century can further be gauged by the fact that it was fourth on a list of ten English ports required to provide ships to carry the King and his retinue to Flanders. In 1326, it was listed as one of the country's 59 ports permitted to trade in horses, money and precious metals; this required the presence of a merchant who had sworn his allegiance to the King. Later, the 1580 census recorded the Port with a population of 360 and owning 12 ships with tonnage ranging from 16 to 100.

Blakeney Quay

The Port's demise, however, was sadly assured by local landowner, Sir Henry Calthorpe, who built a bank across the River Glaven in 1637. Silting up began soon afterwards and was further compounded by the 1824 Enclosures Act. More embanking was undertaken to join Blakeney to Cley by road with the net result that the channel between Cley and Wiveton ceased to be navigable. Blakeney continued to ship coal and grain until World War I but, thereafter, the onslaught of the railways and larger shipping vessels meant the village's already dwindling trade came to an end.

Food & Accommodation

Blakeney Hotel *(01263 740797)*, on the waterfront, offers one of the finest maritime outlooks in the country. Much of the accommodation has undergone improvement and refurbishment in recent years, and the restaurant affords fine food and uninterrupted views. Category A+ rooms are well worth the extra expense. **Wheelchair access.**

The King's Arms *(01263 740341) Westgate, Blakeney*, is situated just off the Quayside. It is one of the most popular pubs in the area and was once three, narrow fishermens' cottages. Tasty, if standard, pub food and good beer are available, as is self catering accommodation. **Wheelchair access.**

The White Horse *(01263 740574), Blakeney*, is a 17th Century, flint and brick-built inn and has also recently been renovated and refurbished. It offers stylish pub food and accommodation (for sea views ask for the Harbour Room), together with a good choice of wines and ales. **Wheelchair access.**

The Church of St. Nicholas stands well away from the Quay. It was originally built in the 13th Century, but about 100 years later the nave was rebuilt and a tower added. A second tower was also built for the specific purpose of guiding ships into the harbour; its light is still lit at night.

Samphire, also known as 'poor man's asparagus', is a particular feature of this part of the Norfolk coast. Although it is often pickled in vinegar, it is more usually boiled or blanched and served with melted butter. The crop is picked during late July and August, and only the stringless green tips are eaten. It can be bought locally or pick your own off the salt marshes.

Blakeney provides a superb natural harbour with a unique mix of dunes, saltings, mud flats, salt marshes and creeks, all protected from the open sea by Blakeney Point. Owned by the National Trust since 1912, Blakeney Point is a shingle ridge of over 1, 000 acres. It can be reached, usually by ferry, from either the Quay - details are posted on the board at the Quay - or from Morston. More than 270 species of birds have been recorded here, as have over 190 species of flowering plants. An observation hide is in constant use outside the nesting season. Additionally, *Blakeney Point Sailing School (01263 740704)*, offers instruction on small boats in the harbour. Tennis is also available on Langham Road *(01263 741106)* where racquet and balls can also be hired.

Walk 13: Blakeney & Cley Marshes

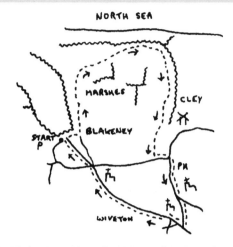

Directions:

1. From Blakeney Quay car park follow the path on top of the bank which runs along the right hand side of the car park as you face the Quay. Follow this for about half a mile and bear to the right taking the central path (the left hand path leads to mud flats and the far right will take you back to Blakeney). Follow this path towards Blakeney Eye.
2. Continue along the bank and Cley Channel around Blakeney Eye to a stile. Take the path inland, on your right, towards Cley village. Follow this for about three quarters of a mile until you reach the road.
3. At the road, turn left and follow to a sharp-left hand bend where you turn right and follow the Wiveton road until you come to Cley village green. Turn right along the edge of the green, just before the pub, following the road. At a junction, turn right and follow the road over Wiveton Bridge. 4. At another junction, go straight across keeping the Bell public house on your right. Follow the road until you come to Blakeney Church. 5. Cross the main road and take the left hand of two lanes leading down into Blakeney proper, and returning to the Quay at the bottom of this lane.

Start: Blakeney Quay car park
Approx. Distance: 7 Miles
Approx. Time: 3 Hours
Map: Landranger 133

At *Langham Glass* (01328 830511), a couple of miles or so inland from Blakeney, you can watch traditional hot lead-crystal glass making and blowing in this historic barn complex. The flint Long Barn was built in 1722 and now houses the factory shop and tea rooms. *Open daily throughout the year, 10-5. Admission charge.*

Just a mile inland from both Blakeney and Cley is *Wiveton;* built in 1922 and still in use, the stone bridge near Wiveton marks the head navigation point of the River Glaven. In earlier centuries, Wiveton rivalled both Blakeney and Cley in its fishing and sea trading: it was the first of the three to suffer demise from 17th Century land reclamations.

A census of 1580 recorded this now small and peaceful village as having 13 ships, among them 'men-of-war', the smallest having a tonnage of 40. Parish records name actual vessels including the *Gyles* part-owned by Robert Paston. The Church of St. Mary the Virgin, built at the end of the 13th Century, was sited at the harbour's head but now overlooks the village green, and beyond from the other side to Cley. Although some of the brasses here have been stolen, a number, nevertheless, remain, including a 21 feet long skeleton in a shroud, dated to around 1500, and another to George Brigge (d. 1597) and his wife; you will need to look under the bits of matting for these. A close search of the interior pillars and stonework also reveals mason's marks; among these a three-master ship of the hoy-type in the chancel, and the remains of a small merchantman or 'man-of-war' near the lectern.

There are a number of pathways over the nearby and undisturbed Wiveton Downs. This 17 acre picnic site affords excellent views over the coast.

A little further south from Wiveton takes us to *Glandford,* an estate village belonging to nearby Bayfield Hall. The Flemish gabled *Shell Museum,* built by Sir Alfred Jodrell in 1915, houses his fine collection of shells, fossils and semi-precious stones. Specially noteworthy features include a walking stick made from shark vertebrae, a giant tortoise carapace, and a heavily inscribed nautilus shell. The Museum is *open Mon-Thur, 10-12.30, and Fri-Sat, 2-4.30. Admission charge. Wheelchair access.*

Rebuilt in 1906, St. Martin's Church is a copy of the former Medieval structure which once occupied the site. Look out for the richly carved screen and choir stalls made from local oak and cedar. A Church carillon can also be heard playing hymns at regular intervals throughout the day.

Although nearby Bayfield Hall is not open to the public, *Natural Surroundings (01263 711091)* which occupies an eight-acre site on the Estate is. Organically grown herbs, flowers, and trees can be purchased, and demonstration gardens, a wildflower meadow - with over 100 different species in spring and summer, including orchids - and woodland can be walked around. *Open daily, 10-5.30, March to October. Otherwise Thur-Sun, 10-4. Admission charge to gardens only.* A regular programme of events and planting/conservation courses are run

Cley-next-the-Sea

Cley, pronounced 'Cly', is a pretty and predominantly flint-built village which now rests one mile from the sea. Like Blakeney, it was also once a busy port centred around the Church at the mouth of the River Glaven, and the countless

Flemish gables remind one of prosperous trade with the Low Countries.

In the 14th Century, Cley accounted for almost half the export of north Norfolk's wool. Grain and flour were also heavily traded from the wharves at Newgate and the former post mill (no longer in existence). In 1406, Cley seamen captured a Scottish ship taking Prince James of Scotland to France. Smuggling and piracy were then common practice and even though England was not then at war with Scotland, the Prince was held hostage by Henry VI for 17 years; soon after his release he succeeded to the throne. During the early 18th Century, the Customs House, which still stands, and other prominent houses and wharves were built by the present Quay. This was due mainly to the silting upstream, the result of Calthorpes' disastrous reclamation efforts, which determined that larger vessels could no longer pass through the Glaven. More recently, serious damage to property was caused during the 1953 floods - the worst for 400 years.

St. Margaret's Church which overlooks the green and the Glaven Valley dominates one end of the village, and is testimony itself to Cley's former importance and wealth; in 1612, an incredible 117 houses near the Church were destroyed by fire. Cinquefoil windows dominate the upper walls of the nave, and the south porch - built after the Black Death - has 16 armorial crests including those of the de Vaux family. They were responsible for much rebuilding of the Church at the end of the 13th Century and commissioned Ramsey, Master Mason of Norwich Cathedral, for this purpose. The misericord seats in the chancel are thought to date from the 16th Century and are carved with the initials JG; representing the merchant's mark and arms of John Greneway's grocery company.

Built as a cornmill in 1713, Cley's other well-known landmark is its Windmill. The best known of all its occupiers was Steven Barnabus Burroughs who worked the Mill from 1840-1919, after which it fell into disrepair. Bought as a holiday home in 1921, it was renovated to its current form in 1983. The sails, fanstage and galleries were replaced five years later. The Mill is open to visitors for a small charge from Whitsun to the end of September. Better still, stay there and enjoy an enchanting evening, waking up to spectacular views across the marshes; full details are given below in the food and accommodation entry.

Cley Smokehouse *(01263 740282)*, is noted for its excellent fish - smoked salmon, mackerel and herring. The smoking process can usually be viewed.

A few doors down is **Made in Cley** *(01263 740134)*, a showroom/working studio for five potters and a jeweller. Finely glazed porcelain and more everyday functional ceramics can be bought here.

The Old Butchers Bookshop & Gallery *(01263 741212)*, is also worth a look for its interesting collection of secondhand and some antiquarian titles. The gallery adjoining it usually displays work by local potters, sculptors and painters.

Cley Mill

Cley Nature Reserve, situated on the seaward side of the Cley to Salthouse road, occupies 400 acres of salt marshes and is protected from the sea by a shingle bank thrown up after the 1953 floods. The land was bought by the Norfolk Naturalists Trust in 1926 and is now a Bird Reserve of international importance. Indeed, the path along the East Bank has been called 'the most famous birdwalk in Britain.' The bird list for the Reserve numbers 330 species and includes many summer visitors and nesting birds such as avocet, bittern and common tern. Brent geese, widgeon, teal and mallard all winter on the Reserve in great numbers. Exceptional flora include the yellow horned poppy, sea sandwort, campion, and aster. The public footpath along the East Bank has eight permit-only hides, one for the disabled and two for everyday public use. *Permits and parking can be obtained from the Norfolk Naturalists Trust Visitors Centre (01263 740380), just off the roadside, open April to October.*

Food & Accommodation

Cley Mill *(01263 740209)*, offers unusual and good standard B & B and self-catering accommodation. No evening meals but nonetheless an evening to remember in the round guests room which is suitably and comfortably furnished.

The George and Dragon *(01263 740652)*, is a fine pub - good food, ale and bar staff - which also provides accommodation. The Norfolk Naturalists Trust was founded here and a 'bible' on the lectern records bird sightings. The proprietor has recently added a bird-watching hide in one of the top floor rooms, mainly for residents use, and this affords fine views over the open marsh. *Wheelchair access.*

The Three Swallows *(01263 740526)*, has recently been renovated and refurbished (1994) and occupies a superb site on the village green, next to the Church. Good food and ales. *Wheelchair access.*

Whalebone House *(01263 740336)* is a mid 18th Century flint building offering solid B & B accommodation with a busy tea room below. Everything is home-made and plentiful.

A little further east to *Salthouse*; in Medieval times, known for its salt and evap-orating pans, hence its name. Even before Roman fortification of the coastline around here, it was certainly an important settlement of the early Britons. Barrows and earthworks can still be found on the Heath above the village and those that have been excavated have revealed the ashes of the dead. Take the trouble to go up on the Heath which can be a mass of gorse or heather depend-ing upon the time of year, and fine views across the surrounding marshland are guaranteed. The marshes around Salthouse were reclaimed in the 16th Century by Dutchman, Van Hasedunck. This later prompted Sir Henry Calthorpe's fatal efforts to build a causeway between Cley and Blakeney and, in so doing, deprive Wiveton of its access to the sea.

Kelling Heath which adjoins that of Salthouse is a complex mix of woodland, heath and gravel pits. A nature-trail, identified by squirrel waymarkers, will take you around this beautiful area. Alternatively, try the rather longer walk described below which sees you through some of the best heathland, coastland and rhododendron wood in this part of the county.

The deep waters of Weybourne Hope just beyond the low watermark has made *Weybourne* an attractive site for foreign invasion. An old adage from the 18th Century ran as follows:
> *"He who would ol' England win*
> *Must at Weybourne Hope begin."*

The first actual defensive operation to be placed here was during the Napoleonic Wars, although earlier plans had been considered at the time of the Spanish Armada. The most significant stationing began in 1935 with Weybourne Camp acting as an anti-aircraft gunnery school; the army proper moved in four years later putting up pill boxes and huts, and digging trenches. The Army stayed until 1958. From then until 1988, when it was taken over by Berry Savory to house his ever-increasing military collection, the camp remained pretty well unused. Now called the *Muckleburgh Collection (01263 588210)*, after a nearby hill, Savory's Museum houses over 120 military vehicles - most restored here -and in excess of 1, 500 other related exhibits, dating from 1759-1991, some even from the recent Gulf War, for example, Iraqi anti-aircraft guns. The old NAAFI has also been restored and forms the centre of this, the largest private collection of its kind in Britain open to the public. *Open daily, 10-5, mid March to end October. Admission charge.*

Weybourne Priory and All Saints Church, their buildings tightly interwoven, cannot be separated. The Augustinian Priory, founded by Sir Ralph Meyngaryn as a dependency of West Acre Priory, was built between 1200 and 1216; the Canons must, however, also have made use of some existing Anglo-Saxon buildings. Dominating the scene is an impressive central tower with its pilaster strips - raised bands of stone imitating timberwork - intact and typical of late Saxon decoration. The windows are also characteristically Saxon. Disagreements with West Acre during the 14th Century allowed the Weybourne Canons some degree of autonomy but the Order here was never significant enough to stand on its own feet. In 1530, the Prior and last Canon sold everything moveable and thereafter the empty buildings, including the Church they had earlier absorbed, fell into decay. Restoration was not begun until the mid 19th Century and took over twenty years to complete; thereafter Weybourne could again enjoy its parish Church though the Priory was to remain in picturesque ruins.

On the east side of the village, is a privately owned and well-restored, five-storey tower mill complete with cap and sails. It is best seen from the path which runs beside it down to the cliff edge, but once again take care along this shoreline as considerable erosion has occurred in recent years. The beach fishing, incidentally, is reputedly very good for mackerel and cod.

Sheringham

Our last major coastal stop in this Chapter is at Sheringham, a popular if small resort but it was not until the end of the last Century that this became so. Prior to that, Sheringham was very much a fishing town, its fishermen known as Shannocks, and especially noted for its catch of lobster and crab. *White's Directory* of 1836 records a considerable fishing community here involving six curing houses, 26 herring boats and a number of smaller boats. By 1875, *Kelly's Directory* documents 200 boats, 23 of which were equipped for deep-sea fishing. Furthermore, prior to the 1930's, beach auctions were a colourful if noisy affair where boxes of fish - cod, skate, mackerel, herring and shellfish - were laid out on the west gangway. Thereafter, as still happens, the fishermen market their own catches, lobster being a local speciality. The town never developed into a trading port, as at Cromer, although there was occasional traffic in coals; Henry Ramey Upcher himself owning two schooners.

> As there is neither harbour nor jetty at Sheringham, boats are launched down a slipway under a concrete bridge which joins the East and West Promenades. At high tide, all that can be seen of the beach is a ridge of flint pebbles and granite, the latter imported from Norway as part of the 1994/95 additions to the town's sea defenses, but at low tide, the extensive sands here are revealed. With an especially low tide, the second sands can also be seen.

During the winter months, flint picking from the beach provided employment for the fishermen and their families. These flints, once milled down, were used as body ingredient for the Stoke-on-Trent pottery industry. By the late 1960's, however, the practise was considered detrimental to the town's sea defenses and was, therefore, ceased.

Nor has sea defence works been the only problem at Sheringham; like all coastal towns, it too has been mindful of the threat of invasion from its shores. In 1673, for example, the Lord Lieutenant of the County was petitioned for arms and ammunition to repel any landing by the Dutch. It is thought the gun still to be found on the corner of Gun Street was offered in response to this request. The dangers of air attack though have not been so easy to deflect, for on the 19th January, 1915, a German Zeppelin dropped the first air bomb on British territory; it crashed through the roof of a cottage in Whitehall Yard, near Wyndham Street, but, thankfully for the occupants, failed to explode.

Lifeboats have played an important part in Sheringham's history since 1838 when the Hon. Mrs Charlotte Upcher of Sheringham Hall gave the town its first such boat, the *Augusta*. This was replaced in 1894 by the *Henry Ramer Upcher* which saved over 200 lives in its 41 years of service; it can still be seen in its original shed on Westcliff. More recently, in 1994, Sheringham's traditional boat has been replaced by a faster, more lightweight craft which can be found on the far west end of the Promenade.

A small *Museum*, housed in a former fisherman's cottage, can be found in an alley off Station Road. The displays concentrate on the town's history and especially on that of its fishing community.

Food & Accommodation

Crofters *(01263 822151), High Street.* A charming bistro-styled restaurant with an emphasis on fresh sea food. Main course portions are especially generous. The only slight nuisance is having to go through the kitchen - very clean - to use the toilets.

The Lobster *(01263 822716).* Probably the most traditional of Sheringham's pubs and patronised by local fishermen and the lifeboat crew (the latter may well burst into song, having formed the *Shanty Men* to raise money for charity and achieving quite a reputation, nationally and internationally, for themselves). Odd bits of fishing memorabilia decorate the walls of the saloon bar and the open fire in winter is very welcoming. Avoid the public bar if it is busy as the pool table is awkwardly placed in the centre of the room. **Wheelchair access.**

The Two Lifeboats *(01263 822401).* Substantially renovated in recent years and although the sea bar is plushly decorated it is somewhat out of keeping with its setting overlooking the sea. The front bar is much more traditional and in-keeping with the building's period style. Extensive bar and restaurant menus can be chosen from, and there is usually a decent range of bottled wines. The accommodation above airs on the small side but is nonetheless crisp and clean. **Wheelchair access to lounge bar.**

Other than being predominantly flint built, Sheringham has little to offer in the way of architectural interest save the odd Flemish-gabled building on Westcliff. Nor are its churches especially interesting, except the excellent knapped flint work on the exterior of St. Peter's Church built in 1895. But do look at the fine stained glass windows in the public toilets in 'Marble Arch', under the West Esplanade. They are quite beautiful, despite their ungainly, if necessary, setting.

The rail connection first with Cromer and from there to London was begun in 1906 and the service to Norwich is still continued. But for those with a taste for the past, try the restored locos and carriages of the **North Norfolk Steam Railway** *(01263 822045)* running the 'Poppy Line' via Weybourne and Kelling Heath to Holt (roughly a ten mile round trip). During the summer months a regular timetable is offered. Additionally, the East Coast Pullman dining car runs on Saturday evenings and Sunday lunchtimes.

For interesting shopping try **Westcliffe Gallery** *(01263 824320), Augusta Street,* known for their regularly changing exhibitions of local painters (including the newly formed Norwich School) as well as highly respected international artists of the likes of Robert Heindel. For crabs, try the small kiosk on the corner of Gun Street, and the two fishmongers for other local catches including lobster. Also note two combined but interesting operations on the High Street; **Downtide Marine** *(01263 823183)* cater for water sports enthusiasts, especially jet skiers, and the adjoining shop specialises in pianos, both traditional and electronic. Both are owned by a former fishing family, the Wests. As for entertainment, try **The Little Theatre** *(01263 822347).* Performances by touring professional companies as well as local amateur dramatic and operatic societies are of a good standard and are heavily attended.

Bicycles can be hired at **A1 Cars** *(01263 822228), 21 St. Peter's Road.* **Swimming** can be enjoyed at **The Splash** *(01263 825675), Weybourne Road,* and **Golf** at **Sheringham Golf Club** *(01263 823488)* also on *Weybourne Road.* Set on the cliff edge, this is an attractive downland course with much gorse. Visitors are welcome but do take your handicap certificate. As for *fishing*, this is good from the west beach at high water. Late evening being good for dab, plaice, and sole.

Now adjoining Sheringham is the parish of Beeston, and the village was once on the pilgrimage route to Walsingham; tradition has it that the Augustinian Priory was founded in the early 1200's. A turbulent history followed and it was eventually dissolved by Henry VIII, in 1539. The remains are nonetheless extensive, if only difficult to explore being overgrown with weeds. Nearby, All Saints Church stands alone on the cliffs above the sea, except for the caravan site that is. Unusually, the porch here is paved with knapped flint and the sanctuary paved with the black ledger-stones of the Cremers of Cromer and Felbrigg.

Upper Sheringham

A mile to the south of Sheringham is the delightful and typically flint-built village of Upper Sheringham, much of it still owned by the National Trust. In the square by the Church is a well given to the village by Abbot Upcher in 1814 to celebrate European peace following Napoleon's exile to Elba, and until the 1950's servicing, via the hills behind, the villagers' water requirements. All Saints Church itself dates from 1300 and contains a fine monument to Abbot Upcher (d. 1819).

Upper Sheringham Well and Church

The main attraction though is **Sheringham Park**. The Hall, however, is not open to the public but was built 1812 -17 for Abbot Upcher to Humphrey Repton's design. Repton's *Red Book* is still kept at the house; these *Red Books* contain his building and garden design specifications for most major projects he undertook and are highly regarded by scholars of both disciplines. The Hall, is relatively modest and can only be visited by prior arrangement with the tenant (written requests only); the National Trust acquired the property in 1985 and lease the Hall out. Not to worry for it is the Park here which is a must and is best visited mid-May and June when the rhododendrons and azaleas are in full bloom. So impressive are these that they would rightly deserve the accolade of 'Europe's Himalayas'. A series of paths and wooden boardwalks (suitable for wheelchairs) allow visitors to see these to best advantage and the views from some seated areas across the fields and woods to the sea are unforgettable. A raised observation platform in the centre of the Park and another gazebo on its edge are well worth the effort it takes to climb them. No wonder Repton considered Sheringham his favourite work. The National Trust has recently begun a restoration programme at the Park which will facilitate the clearing out of much of the overly abundant 'purple' rhododendron (this is, in actual fact, a weed) and the re-establishment of the 50-plus true strains of azalea and rhododendron. *The Park is open all year, dawn to dusk,* and is managed by the National Trust *(01263 823778)*; a charge is made for the car park only.

Food & Accommodation

The Red Lion *(01263 825408), Upper Sheringham.* Two smallish bars characterised by rather simple pine furniture but with a warm welcome. The food is home-cooked and wholesome and a good range of ales and malts is always to hand. Accommodation is also available.

The National Trust *(01225 791199)* manages a pretty detached cottage on the edge of Sheringham Park. (Sleeps 4.)

Walk 14: Kelling Heath and Sheringham Park

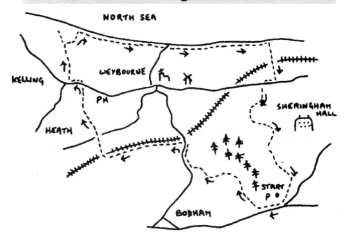

Directions:

1. From the National Trust car park walk back to the main road, and turn right walking along the side of the road for a few hundred yards.
2. Go right into Pinewood Leisure Park and walk through the site, keeping to the left hand main track. Where that track swings sharp right, go left between the caravans to cross a stile into the woods.
3. Go left onto the footpath which skirts the edge of Weybourne Wood following that path round to the right. At a gate, keep left to the road and then turn right down Sandy Hill Lane. 4. Just before Weybourne Railway Station, turn left along a footpath (signed) which stays close to the railway track for just over one mile. After climbing a small hill, the footpath broadens into a wide track and continue along here until you reach a crossing point at a cottage on the opposite side of the track. 5. Go across the track and follow the path which leads in a north-easterly direction over Kelling Heath for about three quarters of a mile. (At the top of a slight incline you will notice a red roofed building ahead and just to your right, and similarly to your left the top most elements of Kelling School.) Aim left towards the School. 6. Once you reach the main road (A 149), turn left and after the Police House on your right, take the right hand lane which leads down to the coast. Turn right at the Quaq, and follow the path round the Reserve onto Kelling Hard. 7. Rather than walk the tiring shingle, look for a narrow path on your right which runs just behind the shoreline. Continue along here for approximately two miles first to Weybourne, then round the edge of a group of coastguard cottages, perched precariously on the edge of the cliff, and until you see a track on your right leading to a bridge. 8. Take this track, cross the bridge, and at a gate onto the main road (A 149) bear right along the edge of the field for a few yards to an opening. Cross the road, ignore the drive leading to a house, and instead skirt the edge of Oak Wood. This path leads into the grounds of Sheringham Hall via a gate. For

those with energy to spare, note beforehand the steps cut into the mound on your left which leads up to a gazebo affording great views of the open countryside around. 9. Once in the Park, at a junction of paths just before Sheringham Hall, go right. Follow this path for one mile as it leads through the rhododendron wood to your start.
Start: National Trust car park at Sheringham Hall, off the A 149
Approx. Distance: 10 Miles
Approx. Time: 4.5 Hours
Map: Landranger 133

Just beyond Sheringham, and also on the coast, is *West Runton*, an attractive, small village once forming one parish with East Runton but now the two have their own separate identities. Much of the village is flint built and affords excellent access to the good beaches here. Recently, part of a pre-historic elephant's skeleton was revealed in the cliffs; efforts to uncover the rest of this giant's remains are underway, and the dig is documented more substantially in the Cromer Museum. Runton once acted as a natural over-spill for holiday makers finding the resorts of Sheringham and Cromer already full. Camping and caravanning - originally made popular during the two World Wars - have become the village's economic mainstay and somewhat disappointingly these sites mar the clifftop - perhaps some careful planting and landscaping would make the area altogether more palatable and sympathetic.

The Shire Horse Centre (01263 837339), is a working Museum and Show Centre for draught horses. Regular demonstrations are given of pre 1950's drilling, ploughing, harrowing and shoeing techniques using the Centre's own Shire Horses. A Museum of farm equipment and a smithy are amongst the facilities, as are horse-drawn rides in a cart around the village. The West Runton Riding School operates alongside the Centre. *Open Sun-Fri & Bank Hol Sat, 11.15-3, end March to end October. Admission charge.*

Walk 15: The Roman Camp and the Runtons

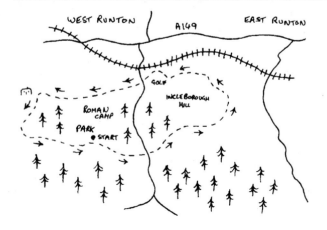

Directions:
1. From the National Trust car park at the Roman Camp walk eastwards along the track until you arrive at the road. Cross over the road and take the footpath which leads straight ahead, ignoring the first track to the Caravan Site on your left; a little further along ignore additional left hand forks. The path descends through Edwards Plantation weaving its way through the root and branch systems of what seem like giant-sized rhododendrons. 2. At the bottom, take the path over the field and at a junction of paths take the right fork, keeping the hedge on your right, past Congham Hill, through two gates to Abbs Common. 3. Go left here, and left again to East Runton Old Hall. 4. With the Hall on your right, go in a westerly direction to skirt Incleborough Hill making sure the path splits into three, near a footpath sign, to take the right hand fork through the field. 5. At the surfaced road, go right to skirt the Golf Course and at the road turn left to walk past West Runton Common. 6. Turn right into Calves Well Lane which soon becomes little more than a bridleway running along the edge of the wood, and continue along here until you go left just before a bungalow. 7. Look out for two 'National Trust - Beeston Regis Heath' signs and after the second, follow the path into the wood and on up the hill. 8. At the top of the hill, follow the path which runs alongside a fence for a little while and then the first left-hand path which goes through a plantation will lead to a track passing a Cairn and so return you to the Roman Camp.

Start: The National Trust car park at the Roman Camp
Approx. Distance: 4 Miles
Approx. Time: 2 Hours
Map: Landranger 133

Holt

The central coastline is now left behind as we travel a few miles inland to the pretty county town of Holt. In the time of Edward the Confessor, Holt was a royal demesne, the word *holt* being Anglo-Saxon for wood. Today, it is a smallish but very stylish place attracting visitors from all over the country savouring its off-beat shopping. The main street is lined with Georgian buildings, mostly built after the 1708 fire which raged through the town - evidence of the inferno can still be seen on the floor in St. Andrew's Church.

Architecturally, there is little of real importance in Holt excepting Gresham School. This was originally begun as a grammar school by John Gresham in 1555 after he bought the Manor House there; the School remained relatively small until 1900 when it was made a Public School and moved to its current site. The Greshams themselves were an interesting family, John being Lord Mayor of London when he founded the School, and his brother, Thomas, founded the Royal Exchange. Further eastwards from the School is the North Norfolk Steam Railway which connects Holt with Sheringham on the coast. *The Holt Flyer* (01263 712283) is a horse-drawn bus service operated by The Railway Tavern and runs between the pub and the North Norfolk Railway terminus at Holt. Even if you are not using the steam train, you may still enjoy the round trip.

Interesting shops abound in the town and it is best just to wander around to see what takes your fancy. For antiques, however, try **Heathfield Antiques** *(01263 711122)* with their bias towards restored, Continental pine, **Maura Henry** *(01263 711240)* for antique porcelain or **Baron Art** *(01263 713906)* for Art-Deco ceramics, and **Richard Scott Antiques** *(01263 712479)* for some very unusual eclectic items including ancient Chinese artefacts. Other interesting outlets include the **House and Garden Shop** *(01263 711586)*, **Gough's Antiquarian Booksellers** *(01263 712650)*, and the flower shop at **No. 2 Chapel Yard** *(01263 713933)* who create extravagant yet simple arrangements of both fresh and dried flowers.

Holt Country Park, just outside the town, covers an area of circa 100 acres, mainly coniferous woodland planted 1958-60. It is believed to have been the site of Holt Races, an important county event during the 18th Century. There is an observation tower which provides excellent views over the Glaven Valley and a Visitors Centre in the main car park where details of the walks to be enjoyed here can be had.

Food & Accommodation

Byfords *(01263 711400)*, *Shirehall Plain, Holt*, offer an interesting mix of delicatessen, cafe and restaurant with occasional jazz evenings as another feature. The home-cooked food here is of a consistently high standard.

The Hunny Bell *(01263 712300)*, *Hunworth, nr. Holt.* Standing on one side of the picturesque village green, this is a typical country pub serving traditional ales and bar food.

The John H. Stracey *(01263 860891)*, *Briston, nr. Holt.* A 16th Century inn named after the former world welterweight champion. A wide choice of reasonably priced food is available both in the bar and the restaurant, the latter converted from old stables. Accommodation is also available.

The Kings Head *(01263 712691)*, *Letheringsett.* Originally built in the early 19th Century and once adjoining the old brewery buildings, reasonably priced bar food, a good range of malts and ales can be had here. The main bar has some unusual wall decorations including a signed poem by John Betjeman. A very spacious garden is occasionally host to traditional jazz weekends.

Yetman's *(01263 713320)*, *37 Norwich Road, Holt.* Informality and good food are the overriding qualities of this cosy and cheerful restaurant; it cannot be missed for its bright yellow paintwash. The emphasis is on local, seasonal ingredients; the fish bought from nearby Weybourne or Lowestoft and the meat and vegetables from local organic producers. Home-made breads including olive and walnut are a speciality. A simple but elegant dining room and small, prettily furnished lounge create a fresh and relaxing environment.

At nearby **Letheringsett Water Mill** *(01263 713153)*, restored in 1982, over two and a half tonnes of wholewheat flour a week are produced, much of it sold on the premises for animal and pet food though also used in locally produced breads. You can visit the Mill's working floors for a small admission charge. Otherwise it is **open for sales all year, Tue-Fri, 9-1 & 2-5, Sat 9-1, and in summer Sun 2-5.**

Records of 1384 document John de Keyly and William de Gastele buying 48 acres of land and a watermill. Over the centuries this found its way to John Brereton, who also owned what was to become Letheringsett Hall and a brewery. But by 1754, the Mill had had to be rebuilt due to a fire , and again in 1802. It was finally closed just after the end of World War II.

St. Andrew's Church, with its round tower, is predominantly Saxon in style though built shortly after *Domesday*. Final completion and additions are 13th Century done under the guidance of the Priors of Binham. Look for Johnson Jex's gravestone in the churchyard; although Jex was the local blacksmith, he studiously taught himself the art of watchmaking. The Castle Museum in Norwich holds some of Jex's very finely crafted timepieces and tools.

Further west is Thursford, an attractive village in its own right, but best known for the **Thursford Collection** *(01328 878477)* of showmens' engines, fairground and barrel organs, fairground Gondola ride (worked daily) and the Wurlitzer organ. The collection was first begun by George Cushing and is now a charitable trust for the preservation of steam. A resident organist gives afternoon recitals on the Wurlitzer, and the Christmas Carol Concerts here attract thousands upon thousands of visitors every year. There is also an extensive gift shop complex and a narrow gauge railway in the grounds. **Open daily, April to mid November, 1-5, and occasionally also between 11-1 (phone first). Admission charge. Wheelchair access.**

Binham

Now to Binham where Peter de Valoines, a nephew of William the Conqueror, founded **Binham Priory** in 1091 as a cell of the Benedictine Abbey of St. Albans; work continued on the complex for the following 150 years. Built of local flint and Barnack limestone, the latter was brought from Northamptonshire by sea and river barges along the River Stiffkey. The surviving Norman nave now serves as the parish Church of St. Mary and the Holy Cross with the extensive ruins of the former monastic buildings surrounding it - including the chapter house, warming room, rectory and kitchens - and are managed by English Heritage.

The Priory enjoyed something of a chequered history due in great part to the unscrupulous behaviour of its Priors. William de Somerton, Prior from 1317-35, is credited with having sold much of the church plate and squandered the proceeds on his alchemical attempts to turn base metals into gold. Thereafter,

Binham Priory

Henry VII demolished the Priory in 1540, selling what was left to Thomas Paston in 1542. *The Paston Letters* actually record the receipt in 1553 of rubble from the Priory to build a house in Wells. Furthermore, Edward Paston himself, planned to build a house in Binham using further stonework and he would probably have succeeded had not falling masonry killed one of his workmen; other workers viewed this as an evil omen and all further demolition work was subsequently halted.

Of particular interest in the Church are the Norman triforium clerestory and wall passage, the seven-sacrament font, and the Tobrok Cross, shaped from shell cases to commemorate those who died in North Africa during World War II. *The Priory is open all year during daylight hours, free of charge.*

Food & Accommodation

Lower Green Windmill *(01328 878110/ 0181 8838137), Hindringham.* Although now minus its sails, this is nevertheless a most attractive Tower Mill affording off-beat, self-catering accommodation.

English Heritage also manages the stump of the Market Cross on the village green, marking the site of the annual four-day fair to which Henry I granted his Charter, beginning on the Vigil of St. Mary, and a weekly Wednesday Market. These continued until the 1950's, but are sadly no longer.

Baconsthorpe

Although not a particularly attractive village, Baconsthorpe is nevertheless typically rural and boasts the remains of a once fine *Castle* on its outer rim. The ruins of this and the three-storeyed, knapped flint gatehouse are now managed by English Heritage, and *can be visited throughout the year, free of charge.*

The Castle was originally built by the Heydon family as both a manor house and wool-processing factory. Sheep were brought into the Castle via a turnstile at the northern end of what was probably called the 'long room' and here they were shorn. The end line for their fleeces being the weavers room on the first floor. The Castle itself, was begun in 1450 and completed in 1486 but unfortunately John Heydon failed to comply with the necessary Royal License to fortify his property. By 1600, the family's fortunes were at a low ebb and by the end of the Civil War, the greater part of the Castle had been demolished. The Heydons subsequently occupied the Castle gatehouse which they converted into the smaller dwelling of Baconsthorpe Hall; the staircase and inner archway of this still stand.

Food & Accommodation

The Black Boys *(01263 768086), The Green, Aldborough.* On the edge of the lovely village green, you cannot miss the pub in summer with its mass of flowering tubs and hanging baskets. If you are lucky you can also enjoy local league cricket matches held on the green. An uncluttered, unfussy environment providing decent food and good ales. *Wheelchair access.*

The Hare and Hounds *(01263 713285), Hempstead, nr. Baconsthorpe.* A charming, rural, freehouse simply furnished but with a warm atmosphere. A good range of reliable bar food and traditional ales can be had including a fruity bitter brewed for the pub by Woodforde's.

Margaret's *(01263 577614), Chestnut Farmhouse, The Street, Baconsthorpe.* For an afternoon tea to remember go here; all the cakes, scones, pastries and jams are homemade. B & B accommodation is also available. *Open Tue-Sun, 10.30-5.30, beginning of March to end October. Also open Bank Hol Mon and Mon during July and August.*

Soon after the Norman Conquest, William de Warenne was granted the estates at neighbouring *Gresham.* Henry III granted the village a Charter for a market but this was not taken up. Sir Edmund Bacon built Gresham Castle here in 1319, and at the time he was granted a license to crenellate. In 1429, the Castle was bought by the Pastons but they were forced to evacuate it after Lord Moleyns laid seige to it with a thousand strong force. Moleyns drove out the Paston family and promtly razed the Castle to the ground. (See *The Paston Letters* for explicit details.) It is thought the Castle was similar in shape to that at Baconsthorpe but as the remains are so scanty and hidden under dense undergrowth it is impossible to identify precisely. The village was once also the ancestral home of Sir Thomas Gresham, founder of the London Exchange and his brother John founder of Gresham School, Holt. Interestingly, Geoffrey Chaucer's son once owned Chaucer's Farm in the village. Today, the village is a motley collection of housing, spread out over quite a considerable distance. But do look up potters *Andrew and Joanna Young (01263 577548), Common Farm, Sustead Road, Lower Gresham,* who make practical but distinctive everyday pots in a regular range which has become very collectible.

Mannington

A little to the south-east, set in lovely rolling countryside is *Mannington Hall*. Although an order to crenellate was granted the owners in 1450, the house was not begun until 1460, and apart from the ornamental moat, the house was not actually defended. The original plan for the Hall is difficult to separate from the later work and particularly that done by the 2nd Earl of Orford who commenced his alterations in 1864. It is thought that the great hall ran the entire height of the building and that the layout was designed along Medieval lines. The structure is a mix of brick and flint with a touch of terracotta - possibly the earliest use of terracotta in the country. A noticeably odd feature, which the architectural scholar Nikolaus Pevsner attributes to the Earl of Orford, is a sequence of misogynist inscriptions in Gothic script on the front and rear walls of the Hall. One of these runs as follows:

> *'A tiger is something worse than a snake, a*
> *demon than a tiger, a woman than a demon,*
> *and nothing worse than a woman.'*

Today owned by Lord and Lady Walpole, the Hall is only open by prior appointment but the gardens and surrounding woodland are accessible to the public. The lawn runs down to the moat which is crossed by a drawbridge to herbaceous borders. The moat also encloses a secret, scented garden planted in a design which follows the ceilings of the Hall. Within what were the kitchen gardens, a series of rose gardens (over 1,000 different varieties) follow gardening design from Medieval to modern times, have been created. A number of follies - including a Doric Temple - and a Saxon Church stand in the grounds. A range of country walks (over 20 miles of waymarked paths) around the surrounding woodland and countryside have also been made available. There is also a garden shop here with close links with Peter Beales Roses. *The gardens (01263 584175) are open on Sun, 12-5, Easter to October, and on Wed, Thur & Fri,*

Mannington Hall

The Grim Reaper as depicted in Little Barningham's Church

11-5, May to August. Admission charge. The walks and car park are open daily, 9-dusk, for which there is a small admission charge.

Although neighbouring Barningham Hall built for Sir Edward Paston in 1612 using red brick and stone dressings is not open to the public, the Church of St. Mary in the Estate grounds can be visited. The former chancel, with a Victorian addition, now serves as the parish Church, but the Perpendicular nave and west tower are ruins only; nevertheless the setting is most picturesque. Go to Little Barningham if only to visit another Church and see for yourselves the unusual wood-carved grim reaper.

Horace Walpole, younger brother of Sir Robert Walpole, had **Wolterton Hall** built for himself between 1727 and 1741, and it continues to be held by the Walpoles, the same as at Mannington Hall. Designed by Thomas Ripley, as was Houghton Hall, there are similarities between the two buildings though naturally Wolterton is more modest. Shortly after additions by George Stanley Repton were completed, the Hall was abandoned in favour of that at Mannington. Restoration work did not begin until 1989 and guided tours of the Hall are only available by prior application. Some rooms in the Hall however, are available for hire for receptions and conferences.

The Hall however, is home to the **Hawk and Owl Conservation Trust** *(01263 761718)* and visitors can enjoy the bird of prey conservation trail in the grounds to the park. This circular walk (approximately two miles in length), passes through a variety of habitats and many different birds of prey - kestrels, sparrowhawks, barn owls, tawny owls, red kites, rough and common buzzards - can be seen. An interpretive exhibition, documenting the conservation of birds of prey, can be found in the Trust's Centre housed in the stables here. Note that the Centre itself neither keeps nor displays live birds but rather encourages an understanding of their natural habitats which is where the birds themselves can be seen. **Open Wed, Fri, Sun & Bank Hols. 12-5, April to end October. The** *grounds to the Hall, including the nature trail, are open daily, 9-dusk. A charge for the car park only is made.*

Food & Accommodation

The Earle Arms *(01263 587376), Heydon.* A charming pub on the village green which has a very modest public bar but a much more comfortable, recently refurbished, lounge bar. The menu is short but excellent; anything from shark fish to locally caught crab. A good range of meat and vegetarian dishes are also available.

The Walpole Arms *(01263 587258), Itteringham.* Taking its name from Britain's first Prime Minister (the Walpoles still live and own Mannington and Wolterton Halls) and standing astride the Weavers Way, this is a characterful and friendly pub - exposed brickwork, beams and open fires - much used by locals. The food constantly improves but do aim to eat earlier rather than later at least in the evenings. **Wheelchair access.**

The National Trust *(01225 791199)* has two semi-detached holiday cottages for let in Itteringham. (Sleeps4;4.)

Normally a quiet backwater on the Holt to Norwich road, *Corpusty* is home every year to one of Norfolk's best Guy Fawkes celebrations, attended by thousands, on the Saturday immediately after November 5th (or November 5th itself if this falls on a Saturday). A huge bonfire is lit after a somewhat macabre torch lit procession through the village- fancy dress and military styled drumming are the pattern. A good firework display follows the mock execution of Guy Fawkes; the whole event is free but please give generously to the many collectors you will see about, for without such donations the whole occasion will fall apart.

An unusually attractive and serene village, *Heydon* is accessed by only one route, and the village has been much used in period television dramas and films. At one end, the village is dominated by the Hall, the centre of which was built for Henry Dynne, an Auditor of the Exchequer, in 1581. Further additions have been made over the centuries, but the polygonal chimneys still dominate the roof line. The Hall is home to the Bulwer-Long family (it is not open to the public) and they continue to own much of the village, including the houses around the green, the pub, store and smithy. The Church of St. Peter & St. Paul, built 1469, houses a number of recently uncovered wall paintings.

Reepham

An unexpectedly charming but small market town with its mix of Georgian houses and half-timbered and plaster buildings. The square is dominated by the red-brick Brewery House (built 1700) known locally as Dial House because of its well-preserved sun dial. A curious anomaly is St. Michael's Church which faces the Market Place - strange because it is not Reepham's parish Church but rather that of nearby Whitwell. The chancel does, however, connect with

Reepham's own St. Mary's Church via the vestry and a stone staircase. In St. Mary's look for the fine, important monument to Sir Roger de Kerdiston (d. 1337) with its beautiful carving. Against the tomb are eight small figures - probably mourners or weepers. St. Mary's was for many years the mecca for pilgrims who came to worship at the shrine of the Madonna here.

Another interesting place to visit here is **Reepham Station Museum** *(01603 871187)*. Opened in 1994, this is an unusual, privately owned Museum showing thousands of historic British shop exhibits; anything from tinned and bottled foodstuffs to other household products and advertising signs. ***Open daily, 10-4, April to October, and in winter by prior arrangement. Admission charge.***

This is an area noted for its fine churches and the magnificent, complete, Perpendicular Church of St. Peter & St. Paul at Salle, which can be accurately dated to 1405-20, is no exception. (The arms of Henry V providing this date can be found by the west doorway of the tower.) Built from Barnack stone, the Church stands alone, remote in the Norfolk countryside, but cannot be missed thanks to its beautiful 126 feet high west tower. Look for bosses along the ridge of the chancel roof with their scenes from the Life of Christ including the Annunciation, Nativity, Magi, Entry into Jerusalem, The Last Supper and so on to The Ascension. The many brasses here are also worth seeking out, including that in the nave to Geoffrey Boleyn (d. 1440) and his wife. It is also reputed that Ann Boleyn was herself laid to rest here, her family once occupying nearby Blickling Hall.

Then there is **Cawston** where St. Agnes Church was begun by Michael de la Pole (Earl of Suffolk) in 1350 but building continued for another 150 years. The Parish fortunes fell into decline soon after the Church was completed and even its stained glass windows were sold off to cover outstanding debts. Its richly appointed hammerbeam roof though is still intact. In the north aisle stands a plough - a relic from a ritual observed on the first Monday after Epiphany - which was hauled through the village for alms to be given and spent in the local inn. Later, the Guildhall at Sygate in Cawston became the Plough Inn; and when this closed in 1950, the brewers presented its sign to the Church where it now hangs in the north wall. Another inscription in the Church commemorates this somewhat odd tradition:

> *"God spede the plow*
> *And send us all corne enow*
> *Our purpose to make*
> *at crow of cok ye plowlete of Sygate*
> *Be merry and glade*
> *Wat Goodale yis work mad."*

Booton is also known for its twin-towered Church, begun in 1875 and complet-ed in 1891. Built from knapped-flint and stone, its originator was a descendent of John Rolfe, who married the North American Indian Princess Pocahontes (see the entry on Heacham for further details of this interesting story). St. Michael

& All Angels is an unorthodox building, with rather large and high doors. Inside, one unique feature is the enormous window above the chancel arch which is in the form of a spherical triangle. Other features include the exquisite wood carvings on the doors, pews, stalls and panelling.

Nearby ***Booton Common*** is under the care of the Norfolk Naturalists Trust and provides a diversity of habitats from dry heath to alder carr and mixed coppice. This is best visited in late Spring or early Summer when the wild orchids, meadow thistle and marsh helleborine can be seen. A footpath winds around the southern edge of the Common and a short trail leads through the Reserve.

Food & Accommodation

Grey Gables *(01603 871259), Cawston.* Formerly the rectory adjoining Brandiston Church, and now a pleasant, rural hotel. The atmosphere is homely and relaxed rather than elaborate or lavish. Good, straight forward English and French cuisine.

The Ratcatchers *(01603 871430), Cawston.* Although a pub the emphasis is very much on the restaurant end of things and The Ratcatchers is renowned for its excellent fare which uses only the best of local produce. The kitchen is a regular winner of both regional and national awards. You ***must*** book first though as it does get extremely busy.

The North-East Coast

Norfolk's north-east coast begins for us at Cromer and ends with a tour around one of the county's principal towns, Great Yarmouth, and its dormitory village of Caister-on-Sea. There is much to be seen along this stretch of coast, just as there is within its immediate hinterland, especially the National Trust's holdings at both Felbrigg and Blickling. Much of this coastline was popularised as *Poppyland* by Clement Scott during the late 1800's and, for the most part, it remains pretty well unspoilt today.

Cromer

After Great Yarmouth, Cromer is the most interesting and popular resort along Norfolk's most easterly coastline. The principal period of Cromer's development belongs to the 1890's and the coming of the railway. Before then, as a holiday resort, it was patronised only by the gentry and its main industries were sea-trading and fishing. In particular, the town was known for its exports of wheat, barley and malt, and for the coals brought in on colliers from Sunderland and which landed directly on the beach. Sea trade continued in this way until competition from the railways no longer made it viable; the *Ellis* and her cargo made her final voyage from Cromer in 1887.

The last of the wooden jetties reaching out from Cromer's shore was erected in 1846 and was just 70 yards long. It provided a focus for the Victorian gentlefolk who regularly promenaded along it. This was dismantled in 1897 and a new metal Pier built in its place in 1900. Today, the old Edwardian *Pavilion Theatre (01263 511245)* remains, as does the freestanding Lifeboat Station of 1923, and despite repeated damage to the Pier in 1953, 1980 and more recently in 1993 when a significant portion of the structure was swept away. Furthermore, the Pavilion Theatre continues its reputation as one of the best end-of-Pier venues in Britain (summer season only) for first-rate performances. The recent TV serial *September Song* was to use Cromer Pier as its main story line and location.

> The once prosperous town of **Shipden** situated north of Cromer, finally fell foul to the sea, disappearing completely in the late 14th Century. A large rock, several yards out to sea from the Pier, can occasionally be seen at low tide and marks the remains of St. Peter's Church, Shipden.

Probably the town's most famous son was Henry Blogg, the heroic lifeboat coxswain, awarded the RNLI's Gold Medal on no less than three occasions. After his death in 1954, a memorial bust to him was erected on the cliff path to the east of the town. Blogg was coxswain for a remarkable 38 years, including those years between 1935 and 1945 when he coxed the *H.F.Bailey* answering 128 calls and saving an incredible 518 lives. In 1991, Peter Cadbury (of chocolate manufacturing fame) presented the boat to *The Lifeboat Museum.* Other craft are also on show at the Museum which can be visited on the eastern edge of the Promenade *daily from May to September*, and occasionally also at other times.

Cromer as seen from the East Promenade

Cromer Pier

In 1719, a brick lighthouse was erected on the hills to the east of the town - until then the Church served to warn sailors of the perils along this shore. But then, as now, the sea's advance threatened its safety and another was built further inland, on the western edge of what is now Cromer golf course.

Good, sandy beaches are one of Cromer's endearing features. The cliffs behind revealing much evidence of forest bed deposits. Visitors are advised not to climb these cliffs as considerable erosion has taken place over the years, especially during the winter of 1993/94, thus making them very unsafe. This advise is offered along with one of Edward Lear's charming limericks:

> *There was an old person of Cromer*
> *Who stood on one leg to read Homer;*
> *When he found he grew stiff,*
> *He jumped over the cliff,*
> *Which concluded that person of Cromer.*

The brightly painted, small, double-ended, clinker built boats with their straight keels are lined up at the end of the working day at the eastern end of the beach. Ideal for crabbing, these boats enable the fishermen to shoot lines of baited pots onto the rocky ground off shore. These shanks are hauled by hand the following day, the crabs removed and the pots rebaited; the whole operation requiring some not inconsiderable strength and skill. Cromer crabs are a notable delicacy, one not to be missed during the March to autumn season, after which the storms make this farming too dangerous a practice to continue. Cromer crabs tend to be smaller than those from other parts of Britain. They are also fleshier because they do not change their shells as frequently as those caught off other shores. If you want to try your own hand at fishing, this is available from the beach (best around the third breakwater east of the Pier) and the Pier itself.

The Church of St. Peter & St. Paul dominates the skyline boasting the tallest church tower in Norfolk, at over 160 feet high, surpassed only by Norwich Cathedral. It is a magnificent and majestic flint structure, much of it knapped.

Half way up the steps to the top of the tower is Harry Yaxley's Hole, named after the boy who dangled from the opening while he collected birds' eggs. His legs were held by a friend inside the tower but when the latter demanded a greater share of the yield and it was refused, young Harry was let drop. Remarkably, he survived.

As noted already, the main period of building in Cromer belongs to the 1890's - tall houses with bay windows, gables and dormers and occasionally domed angle turrets. The main architect was Skipper of Norwich and he is responsible for, amongst others, the Hotel de Paris (1895). Cromer Hall, on the outskirts of town, is a magnificent knapped flint building of the 19th Century. In Gothic style, it is adorned with turrets and battlements and was once the seat of the Wyndhams (relatives of those Wyndhams of neighbouring Felbrigg Hall); unlike Felbrigg, however, Cromer Hall is not open to the public.

In search of the picturesque, renowned artists of the Norwich School of Painters, notably Dixon, Cotman and Bright, regularly chose Cromer as the subject of their paintings during the latter part of the 19th Century. In their way too, they, indirectly, helped to popularise the beauty of both the town and the surrounding countryside.

Dr. Edward Bach (1886-1936), who was to devise a natural method of healing through the personality, using wild flowers and their essential properties, spent much of his later years in Cromer. In and around the town, he found and prepared most of the12 remedies referred to by him as 'The Twelve Healers'; the name by which his system of herbal medicine is now known is the **Bach Remedies.** He was also to treat, at his Cromer practice, many local people including the fishermen for whom he had a strong intuitive regard. Today his remedies, available locally and worldwide, provide an inexpensive alternative to prescribed and over-the-counter drugs, and enable patients to treat themselves according to their own analysis of their personality and the ailments from which they are suffering.

Much of the town's history is ably displayed in the *Cromer Museum, (01263 513543),* found near the Church on Tucker Street. Making use of former Victorian, fishermens' cottages, and retaining their old cooking ranges and gas lamps, the Museum tells the story of Cromer's crab fishermen, its geology and its development as a fashionable resort. Of particular note is the *Poppyland* collection. The poet and journalist Clement Scott helped popularise Cromer and its easterly coastal villages by identifying the region as *Poppyland* (solid fields of dainty-petalled, red poppies are still a wonderful sight to be seen here). He immortalised the ruined, cliff-edged Church at Sidestrand in his poem *The Garden of Sleep*; the sea finally claiming the last of the tower in 1915. Thanks to his efforts, new Cromer industries were begun including the manufacture of Poppyland crockery and perfume. The Museum is *open daily, Mon-Sat, 10-5, & Sun 2-5. Admission charge.*

THE GARDEN OF SLEEP
On the grass of the cliff, at the edge of the steep,
God planted a garden - a garden of sleep!
'Neath the blue of the sky, in the garden of corn,
It is there that the regal red poppies are born!
Brief days of desire, and long dreams of delight,
They are mine when my Poppy-land cometh in sight.

In music of distance, with eyes that are wet,
It is there I remember, and there I forget!
O! heart of my heart! Where the poppies are born,
I am waiting for thee, in the hush of the corn.
Sleep! Sleep! From the Cliffs to the Deep!
Sleep, my Poppy-land, Sleep!

CLEMENT SCOTT

Sadly, Cromer has lost some of its Victorian charm, though perhaps increased renovation efforts underway will shortly see some return to its former glory. The shopping here is everyday functional rather than offering anything unusual, but do try those crabs, available locally from both fishmongers and the fishermen direct.

Food & Accommodation

The Bath House *(01263 514260)*, on the east Promenade is a pleasant pub offering good, traditional bar food, regular guest beers and friendly service. Accommodation is available.

As for sports, tennis and squash enthusiasts can find excellent, hourly, facilities at the **Cromer Lawn Tennis & Squash Club**, *(01263 513741), Norwich Road*. Alternatively, the **Royal Cromer Golf Club** *(01263 512219), 145 Overstrand Road* welcomes visitors but evidence of membership of your own club is required.

Action of rather a different sort can be found at nearby **Carting Action Sports** *(01263 720509), The Avenue, Northrepps*. Three miles south-east of Cromer, the site can be found just off the A 149, opposite the Service Station in the village. Here, fast action, grass-carting can be had for all those over 12 who enjoy the thrills of motor sport. Full safety-features, from roll cages to harnesses are ensured on these carts.

The Weavers Way is a 56 mile long distance path between Cromer and Great Yarmouth, and uses a mix of public footpaths, lengths of disused railway line and some minor roads. Additionally, a number of car parks along several points along its length, allow day visitors access to the route. Its name is derived from the hugely successful weaving industry in this area between the 12th and 18th Centuries. The Way passes through a variety of landscapes, from undulating mixed farmland and woodland to extensive Broadland river valleys and marshes.

Walk 16: Poppyland

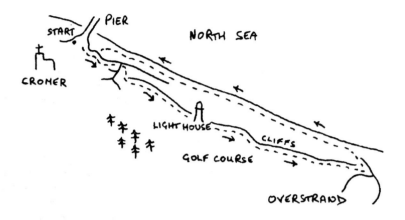

Directions:

1. From Cromer Pier, walk eastwards along the Promenade to the Old Lifeboat Shed. 2. Go right, up the slipway, and near the top of the hill take the left hand path (signed) as it skirts the gardens. Continue along this path for about half a mile as it climbs steadily up towards the Lighthouse. 3. Once at the top, bear left away from the Lighthouse to the cliff edge and walk close to the cliff edge around the perimeter of the Golf Course. (Note, although this is traditionally a public right of way, years of cliff erosion means that walkers and golfers are close to loggerheads. Remember the Golf Course is private property, and stay as close to the cliff side as is safe.) Continue along here, the path ahead obvious. 4. Once at Overstrand, keep left to the road and either take the opportunity to wander around the village, in which case follow the road round to your right, or go down the slipway path on your left, turning left onto the beach to return to Cromer. Remember when walking along the beach to allow enough time to safely avoid incoming tides. If this is not possible, return along the cliff top in the same way as your outward journey.

Start: Cromer Pier
Approx. Distance: 4.5 Miles
Approx. Time: 2 Hours
Map: Landranger 133

Overstrand

A short distance east of Cromer sees us in Overstrand, originally a fishing village, and whilst fishing still continues on a small scale, Overstrand itself has become something of a quiet holiday resort endowed with good, sandy beaches. Overstrand itself literally means 'above the beach' and the once thriving fishing community, affectionately known as Beckhythe, occupied the buildings on the cliff edge. Do be extremely careful on these cliffs as they crumble and fall away easily, as demonstrated during the winter of 1993/94 when a large area of land gave way endangering many nearby properties. Such damage in this area is not new: in the 14th Century the Church here fell into the sea requiring a new one, St. Martin's, to be built. A mile further east, at Sidestrand, the 15th Century Church was in danger of succumbing to the same fate, so in 1881 it was taken down, stone by stone, and built on its current site. Its former tower was later to be made famous by Clement Scott's poem but it too finally gave way in 1915/16.

The village was originally made popular by Clement Scott in his writings of *Poppyland*; a term he coined to celebrate the vast quantities of poppies which grew, and still grow, in the area. Through Scott's writings, Overstrand was to become a favourite watering hole of the rich and famous, many of whom built elaborate second homes here. For example, Edward Lutyens was commissioned by Lord and Lady Battersea to convert two villas into a grand residence. This became 'The Pleasaunce', its extensive grounds and gardens designed by Gertrude Jekyll; it is now a Christian Fellowship Holiday Home. Over the years, these gardens have been much neglected but a project is reportedly underway to restore them to their former glory.

Other Lutyens buildings include Overstrand Hall, designed for Lord and Lady Hillingdon and now a Convalescent Home, and the unusual 19th Century Methodist Church - thought to be the only non-conformist church he designed - with its peculiar plain brick lower floor, and flint and glass clerestory above. Towards the west end of the High Street, is a large and impressive building known as 'Sea Marge', built and designed by Arthur Bloomfield in extravagant mock-Tudor style for Sir Edgar Speyer between 1908 and 1912. At the time of writing the property is empty, but the gardens, once heavily ornamented, would originally have been laid out in high Italian fashion.

If you continue along Coast Road as it joins the main Mundesley Road, turn left and walk the few hundred yards to Mill House, now called 'Four Winds', on the left. Again this was made famous by Clement Scott as it was here that he stayed with the Miller and his daughter, Louie Jermy; a TV movie about the same was released some years ago. The mill itself no longer stands but it was originally on the hill almost opposite the house. Another well-known author to live in Overstrand was Florence Barclay who wrote many well received novels between 1908 and 1920 from her home at Danum House, Paul's Lane.

Felbrigg

Just inland from Cromer is **Felbrigg Hall** *(01263 837444)* now managed by the National Trust. The first owners of the Hall were Simon de Felbrigg and his wife - he a standard bearer for Richard II and she cousin to Richard's Queen, Anne of Bohemia. In 1459, it was sold to Sir John Wyndham. The current structure, began as a modest Jacobean house in 1620, was enlarged in 1675, and the interior remodelled in 1750, and again during the 1840's. The castellated stable block was built in 1825. In the 19th Century, the house was sold to John Ketton, a wealthy local merchant. His daughter married Thomas Wyndham Cremer, a direct descendant of the Sir John Wyndham who had the Hall built in 1620. Even though the wheel had come full circle, the line was destined not to survive, and so the Hall passed into the hands of the National Trust in 1969.

The imposing south front is framed by heavy chimney stacks, and the words *Gloria Deo In Excelsis* are set in the stone parapet; an unusual motif for houses in England. Inside, the house retains its original 18th Century furniture, an outstanding library, as well as the paintings collected by William Wyndham II during his Grand Tour of 1740. The Hall is one of the best documented houses in the country thanks to its last private owner, R.W. Ketton-Cremer, and his book *The Story of a House.*

If time permits, visit the walled garden which retains its traditional potager character, richly planted with a combination of fruit, vegetables and flowers to a formal design behind neatly clipped box hedges. In early autumn, don't miss the display of a wide variety of colchicums; the National Collection is housed here. The brick-built Dovecote in the garden is especially attractive and once housed over 2, 000 white doves, many of them destined for the Hall's dinner

Felbrigg Hall

table! Felbrigg Hall is **open Mon, Wed, Thur, Sat & Sun, 1-5, March to October (Bank Hols 11-5). The gardens are open the same days from 11a.m. Admission charge. Wheelchair access to the ground floor and to the gardens.** Additionally, a number of evening concerts are also staged during the summer months; phone for details.

The Church of St. Margaret, within the grounds of the Estate, is usually open and is well worth a visit. Dedicated to St. Margaret of Antioch, the Church attained its current form during the first half of the 15th Century when it was largely rebuilt by Simon de Felbrigg. There is an impressive series of brasses, commissioned by him, and dedicated in Norman French to the memory of his family. There is also a fine collection of Wyndham monuments, including a bust by Nollekens. The statue of St. Margaret and the dragon above the south porch was donated by the last private owner in 1968. At one time, the village of Felbrigg - the name derives from the Danish meaning *a plank bridge* - surrounded the Church but at an unknown date (perhaps as a result of the Black Death) it was rebuilt some considerable distance away. The Church now stands isolated in the Park.

The full beauty of Felbrigg's environment is best appreciated if you follow the walk described below. This takes in the Church, the Great Wood and the ornamental lake, merged from a group of ponds in the 1750's to form a single sheet of water. Fishing is permitted here from June to September and permits can be obtained from **Holt Tackle and Bait** *(01263 712855), Cromer Road, Holt,* and from **Tatters Tackle** *(01692 403162), Market Place, North Walsham.*

As for the Great Wood, this is now a nationally important site for fungi and lichens and has now been granted the status of an SSI. Note the many large sweet chestnuts with their spiral patterned bark and which date from the 1860's. It is thought that much of the planting of the Great Wood, however, was done by Nathaniel Kent, a well-known land and agricultural improver of his time. Kent firmly believed that owners should take full advantage of the timber-growing potential of their estates and so bring their woods into a proper planting and felling rotation. His thoughts can be read in his *Hints to Gentlemen of Landed Property* published in 1775, shortly after he had undertaken the management of the Felbrigg Estate.

Today, much of the wood is being cleared from obtrusive undergrowth and the like, and no doubt we shall soon be able to enjoy an even more spectacular sight than the one which already greets us. Also to be found in the woods is a traditional charcoal furnace, where wood from the Estate is prepared in authentic fashion, and which can be bought to flavour your own barbecues at home. Finally, the last stretch of the walk takes in one of the most beautiful country lanes in Britain, affectionately named *The Lion's Mouth*; it is very much like entering the jaws of a huge beast as it winds its way between ancient chestnut and beech tree trunks before concluding just after one of the Felbrigg Estate's former entrance gates.

Walk 17: Felbrigg Great Wood

Directions:

1. Go through the kissing gate at the bottom of the Lion's Mouth (just before a T junction) and follow the path through the field which bears diagonally left to a stile. Once over the stile go straight ahead for a few yards only (the charcoal furnace in front of you) and then bear immediate right to a path which runs between fencing along the edge of two fields. 2. The path weaves its way round to the right, over a planked bridge and through a gate into a meadow. Follow the path around the meadow and so to the shores of the lake. Continue around the lake's edge, through a gate and onto the next gate where you go left with a large seven-trunked beech tree - all that remains of a substantial belt that extended northwards in the 1840's. 3. Follow the edge of the field as it bends to the right to arrive at the Church. From the Church, follow the track which leads through the open parkland to a gate, near to the entrance to the hall itself. 4. Once through the gate, go left over a cattle crossing and onto the next grid where you turn immediate right once over it, to enter the Great Wood. 5. At the first meeting of paths, after about 100 yards and at the top of the slight incline, bear left. Continue along here until the main track swings round to the right. Follow this round to the right and after a few yards take the left hand path. Go down Foxburrow Valley and up through a tunnel of red cedar conifers. Where this meets another track go right to pass the ice house also on your right. 6. After about 100 yards you come to something of a clearing, ignore the Estate waymarkers and instead turn left here and continue using the left hand track until you come to another junction. Here you go straight across and down to where you meet the road, The Lion's Mouth. 7. At the road, turn left and follow this lane to return to your start, approx three quarters of a mile away.

**Start: At the very bottom of the Lion's Mouth, just before a T
junction, but not the entrance to the Estate itself.
Approx. Distance: 4 Miles Approx. Time: 2 Hours
Map: Landranger 133**

Mundesley

About nine miles east of Cromer is Mundesley. Formerly a prosperous fishing village which once attempted to develop into a second Cromer, it is now a quiet holiday resort with a safe and sandy beach. Although the waters here are shallow, the tides have nevertheless eroded away much of the cliffs and surrounding land; at times, houses too have been lost to the ravages of the sea. One or two interesting buildings still stand, notably two Victorian hotels, the Mundesley Royal (1892) and the Manor Hotel (1900).

A very recent attraction is the **Mundesley Maritime Museum**, *The Old Mundesley Coast Guard Station, Seafront Gardens,* and probably the smallest Museum in the country; housing a coastguard lookout gallery of the 1930's and 1940's reached by the original spiral staircase, a telescope-radio set, and charts and records depicting Mundesley's maritime and commercial connections. *Open weekends, 10-4, May to September. Small admission charge.*

On the outskirts of the village is **Stow Mill**, also known as Paston Mill, built in 1827 and abandoned during the 1930's. It was bought for private restoration in 1971 and the owner has done much excellent work including the repair of the Mill's cap and sails. *The Mill is occasionally open for a small admission charge.*

One and a half miles south-east of Mundesley is the small hamlet of **Paston.** The influential Paston family made their home here and are especially remembered for their collection of letters, dated 1422-1509, which provide a vivid account of the violence, intrigue, and daily living during the reigns of Henry VI, Edward IV and Edward V, Richard III and Henry VII. The letters also reveal how the Pastons were able to increase their own standing and power by a series of marriages and by making careful decisions about which side(s) to join during the civil strife of that time. *The Paston Letters* are among the earliest known writings in English, and were retained by the family until 1732. They passed through a number of hands before being bought by John Fenn of East Dereham. In 1787, he published 155 of the letters and their related documents and within the space of just one week, this first edition was completely sold out.

The Paston's home no longer stands but the current hall has been built on the same site. The family's steep-roofed barn, built in 1581 from brick and thatch, remains on the outskirts of the village. It is an especially fine building, enhanced inside with alternate tie-beams and hammerbeams. The Church of St. Margaret is probably early 14th Century, certainly of the Decorated style and heavily thatched. As should be expected, there are many monuments inside to the Paston family, and the three plain tomb-chests are also undoubtedly theirs. Anyone interested in churches should not miss the nearby Church of St. Peter & St. Paul at **Knapton.** Here the early 16th Century double-hammerbeam roof is considered one of Norfolk's best. A total of 138 angels adorn the roof's members and others are strategically carved on the wall-posts. Nor should the 13th Century font and its later 1704 cover be missed.

A little further along the coast at *Bacton* one outstanding structure deserves brief attention. Broomholm Priory - sadly, not open to the public, but still visible from the road-side - was originally founded as a cell of Castle Acre in 1113, and then came under the direct control of the Cluny Order at the end of that Century. Although its early life was quiet and one would guess poorly endowed, it nonetheless gained considerable status when a relic of the Holy Cross was claimed to be held there in the 13th Century; Henry III being a frequent visitor at that time. For those of a literary bent, you will find reference to the Priory in Chaucer's *Canterbury Tales* when the Miller's Wife exclaims: *"Helpe, Holy Cross of Bromholm."* The ruins are pretty impressive and include parts of the Gatehouse, and parts of the north and south transepts.

The only other thing to note at Bacton, and let's face it it cannot be missed, is the huge North Sea Gasworks. Development of the same was made prosperous in the mid 1960's when gas of this shoreline was first drilled.

Happisburgh

Happisburgh, pronouced 'Haisboro', a few miles beyond Bacton, is an interesting village sitting along the edge of a dangerous stretch of coast. Dominating the horizon is the imposing red and white *Lighthouse* built in 1791 and Britain's only private working light. Even this was scheduled for closure in 1988 but was rescued by the Happisburgh Lighthouse Trust in 1990. *Open to the public, the hours of opening posted at the bottom of the entrance way. Admission charge.*

The Church of St. Mary also stands high on the horizon having served as an additional landmark along this stretch of coast for the last 500 years. Its graveyard bearing ample testimony to the ravages of the sea - amongst the many graves to shipwreck victims there is also a mass grave commemorating 119 seamen from *HMS Invincible* which was wrecked on the sands here in 1801. As for the village itself there is a row of thatched cottages, in Walcott Road, which have retained some interesting Medieval fragments, including two brick-arched doorways. A short walk away is Happisburgh Manor, built by Detmar Blow in 1900, and considered one of his best works.

Food & Accommodation

The Hill House *(01692 650004)*. An unusual pub retaining much of its Tudor origins including a priest's hole in the restaurant ceiling. Sir Arthur Conan Doyle was a regular visitor here and is known to have written *The Dancing Men* during one visit. A good range of food and traditional ales can be enjoyed in the garden, at least in summer, which overlooks the sea. **Wheelchair access.**

Cliff House *(01692 650775), Beach Road.* Great for home-baked breads, cakes, pastries, scones and so on. Open for cream teas during summer 8.30-7. Out of season, weekends only, 10-5.

Aylsham

We now leave the coast for a while to explore those towns and villages inland. In 1372, John of Gaunt, the youngest son of Edward III and the father of Henry IV, became Squire of Aylsham, thus, at the time, making Aylsham the main Norfolk town belonging to the Duchy of Lancaster. Later, Sir Thomas Erpingham took over as Lord of the Manor and, today, Aylsham continues to thrive as a small market town though naturally its townsmen are no longer legally bound to practice archery on Sundays at the Butlands (now the town centre car park) as they were until the 18th Century.

The height of the town's own industry can be placed between 1350 and 1800 firstly with linen and canvas manufacture, and later with worsted. Indeed, the influence of the Flemish weavers who came to Aylsham during the 1700's is much evident in the town's architecture, many buildings boasting fine Flemish styled gable-ends.

St Michael's Church is heavily flint-faced with a 14th Century tower which houses a fine ring of 10 bells. Humphrey Repton (d. 1818), the famous landscape architect, is buried in the churchyard, Repton writing his own fitting epitaph as follows:

> Not like Egyptian tyrants consecrate
> Unmixed with others shall my dust remain.
> But mold'ring, blending, melting into earth
> Mine shall give form and colour to the Rose.
> And while its vivid blossoms cheer Mankind
> Its perfumed odours shall ascend to Heaven.

Roses do indeed grow around his grave, but not so the nearby grave of the last man to be hung for sheep rustling in Norfolk.

Wherries traded up the River Bure to Aylsham until 1912, when a great flood pretty well destroyed the locks making the water unsailable. *Domesday* records a watermill, which was subsequently rebuilt in its present form in 1798; until 1960 it was used as a provender mill.

Food & Accommodation

The Ark (*01263 761535*), *Erpingham*. A cottage restaurant with good standard accommodation as a recent addition. Above average cooking takes advantage of seasonal produce and draws upon Elizabeth David for inspiration. Of particular renown is the home-made brown-bread ice-cream. **Wheelchair access.**

The Spread Eagle *(01263 761591), Erpingham*. A busy rural pub parts of which are Tudor in origin. Beer was brewed here until the 1850's and since Woodforde's moved here in 1983 the tradition has been continued. Lord Haw Haw is reputed to have stayed here just prior to World War II and his spurious propaganda broadcasts on behalf of Hitler's Germany. **Wheelchair access.**

More recently, the **Bure Valley Railway** *(01263 733858)*, a narrow 15" gauge line, opened. Visitors can now travel the nine miles from Aylsham to Wroxham on the Broads. A regular timetable is run May to September inclusive, and also during Easter Week. On some days a special Broadland Boat-Train service is available which includes a one and a half hour cruise on the Broads.

Market day is on Monday and although it is no longer held in the town centre, it is only a short walk away. Furniture and household effect auctions are heavily attended on this day as are the less frequent but more specialist fine art and antique furniture auctions. Contact **G.A. Keys**, the auctioneers *(01263 733195)*.

Midway between Cromer and Aylsham and set back from the A 140 is **Alby Crafts** *(01263 761702)*; a working complex for a variety of local craftsmen and women producing a whole range of goods from quality furniture to reproduction Tiffany lamps. The centre also holds a **Lace Museum** (closed Sat) and **Bottle Museum**, the latter claimed to be unique in Britain with over 2, 000 bottles on display. The centre is **open Tue-Sun & Bank Hols, 10-5, mid March to mid December, and weekends only from mid January to mid March.**

Buxton is an attractive village south-east of Aylsham, with its Watermill recently rebuilt following a disastrous fire during the mid 1980's. The Mill provides a varied shopping and refreshments centre with furniture and furnishing specialists to the fore.

Blickling

Blickling, a couple of miles north west of Aylsham, is noted for its imposing Hall built between 1619 and 1627 in Jacobean style with Flemish gables, square corner turrets with ogee caps, polygonal shaffed chimney stacks and a dominant clock tower. Centuries before the Hall was built by Robert Lyminge (designer of Hatfield House), the Manor of Blickling was held by the Saxon King Harold. After Harold's defeat at Hastings, it passed to William the Conqueror's Chaplain and then through the hands of many families including the Erpinghams, Fastolfs, and Boleyns to Sir Henry Hobart, Lord Chief Justice, who commissioned the home we now see. In 1940, after the death of Lord Lothian, the Hall passed to the National Trust.

The most magnificent room is the 123 feet long gallery, housing one of the finest libraries in the country, with over 12, 000 leather bound volumes, many published before 1500 and some dating back to the Anglo-Saxons. The fine, moulded Jacobean, plaster ceiling symbolises the 'Five Senses and Learning'.

The Gardens to the Hall have been laid out in a basic Jacobean style but with a blend of features from all periods thereafter up to the 20th Century. Remarkably, the massive and splendid yew hedges date from the earliest period of planting. The complicated flower beds and herbaceous borders are a must in spring and summer and can be combined with good walking through the

Blickling Hall

landscaped Parkland (the Weavers Way crosses through the Park). Samuel Wyatt's Orangery of 1782 houses half-hardy plants, and a statue of Hercules by Nicholas Stone, and in the corner of the northern block is the 'secret garden', the remains of an 18th Century garden for which Humphrey Repton made his recommendations; this is now a lawn with a central sundial and surrounded by high beech hedges. Other features include the lake, formed before 1729 and subsequently enlarged, the Gothic Temple of 1773, and in the heart of the Park a 45 sq. feet pyramidical Mausoleum of 1796 for the Earl and Countess of Buckinghamshire.

The House *(01263 734077)* is ***open Tue, Wed, Fri, Sat, Sun & Bank Hols, 1-5, from the end of March to the beginning of November. Admission charge. Wheelchair access to ground floor and Gardens. The Gardens, Shop, Plant Centre and Restaurant are open the same days as above, 11-5; during July and August these are also open daily. The parkland is open all year.*** Coarse fishing can be enjoyed from the lake and day tickets are available from the Water Bailiff as he makes his regular rounds. The National Trust also stage a regular programme of open air events during the summer; best to phone them direct for current details.

Food & Accommodation

Buckinghamshire Arms *(01263 732133)*, *Blickling*. A handsome, Jacobean freehouse which can get very busy in the summer. Wherever possible, local produce is used in the kitchen and traditional ales, especially Adnams of Southwold and Woodforde's of Norwich, are available on tap. Accommodation is also available.

The National Trust *(01225 791199)*, has two period cottages for holiday lets nearby: one at Silvergate and the other, a former Mill, at Moorgate. (Sleeps 3;6.)

Walk 18: Blickling Park

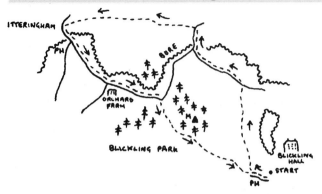

Directions:

1. From the National Trust car park, turn left towards the Hall and immediate left along a tarmac lane past the Buckinghamshire Arms. After a short distance, look for a narrow path on your right as it runs alongside a wall. Go through the gate and head towards the lake. 2. Follow the path along the western edge of the lake until it joins a copse. At this point you will need to walk along the edge of a field, keeping the woodland on your right. At the end of the field, you join the road to Moorgate. Turn left here and follow this quiet road as it goes through gentle countryside for about one mile. 3. Where the road bends sharply to the left, go right into a tree lined track which runs alongside the River Bure. Cross the wooden bridge and continue along the lane. Where the lane joins a road, just after a sharpish bend, go left along a wide track between fields. Once past a couple of cottages, ignore a footpath to the left continuing westwards. 4. The path tends to wind somewhat and where it turns left continue straight ahead instead at the field edge with the yellow waymarker. Once over the stile, continue along another field (keeping the hedge to your left) to a stile. Cross the meadow and over another stile. You will then join a wide, tree-lined lane leading to a gate and across another meadow. 5. Go through the farmyard gate keeping the old farmhouse on your right. Once at the road, turn left and left again (signed Aylsham) following the road over the River Bure again and on past the Walpole Arms. 6. At the fork here, keep left (signed Moorgate). Continue along this quiet minor road, passing first Itteringham Mill and then Orchard Farm, for about one mile. 7. Where the road bends sharp left, take the footpath through and along the edge of the Great Wood. Continue along this clearly defined path, ignoring another which runs off to the right for another mile. (Towards the edge of the woodland, approximately half a mile, a path to the left can be followed to the Mausoleum, but retrace your steps if you take this option.)Woodland eventually gives way to open parkland through the Blickling Estate. At a T junction of tracks, go right through the gate and along the lane back to the walk's start.

Start: National Trust park at Blickling Approx. Distance: 6 Miles Approx. Time: 2.5 Hours Map: Landranger 133

Close to Blickling is *Ingworth,* a pretty village set around oak woods, meadows and a mill stream. The thatched Church of St. Laurence's is Saxon in origin, though it lost its round tower in 1882; what is left of this is also thatched in keeping with the rest of the roof. Inside, the early 18th Century box pews are considered some of the oldest in the country, and do look out for the exceptionally well carved arms of William III.

The village is also home to *The Black Sheep Ltd.* which rears the world renowned black Welsh Mountain Sheep for its fleece. Originally begun in 1966 with only six sheep, the flock at Ingworth now exceeds 1, 000. A shop in the village, open daily except Mon, (01263 734078), and another at Aylsham, open Mon to Sat, *(01263 733142),* stock a sizeable range of knitwear and woollen accessories.

North Walsham

Another interesting market town is North Walsham, where an unusual three-tiered market cross has stood at the foot of this charming Market Place since the 16th Century. It was renovated after a great fire spread through the town in 1600 and destroyed many of the timber-framed houses. It has eight timber pillars supporting a roof with dome and lantern; this forms the pivotal point for the Thursday Market.

St. Nicholas' Church is of Saxon origin but has been substantially rebuilt and modified over time. It remains, however, one of the largest parish churches in Norfolk. Inside, look for Sir William Paston's tomb of 1608; made from alabaster, Sir William lies comfortably propped up on his elbow exactly as he had specified. The carved arms of Edward III and of John of Gaunt can be found in the pinacled Church porch.

Food & Accommodation

Green Farm Hotel & Restaurant (01263 833602), *Thorpe Market.* Standing back from the road, this fine flint and brick, 16th Century farmhouse is typical of properties in the area. The interior decor is rather plain and simple, but the bedroom accommodation does benefit from better antique furniture; if you are staying do ask for one of the larger rooms. Welcoming touches for residents - chocolates, flowers and fruit in the bedrooms are appreciated. The best value food is to be had in the bar and the choice is excellent.

Toll Barn (01692 403063), *Norwich Road, North Walsham.* Very high standard B & B accommodation and service are the key here. Additionally, with five acres of grounds and open countryside beyond, a peaceful stay is assured. Although 18th Century in origins, Toll Barn has been thoughtfully renovated and without loss of charm; exposed beams and brickwork abound. Packed lunches available. No evening meals.

Sir William was responsible for founding the town's Paston School in 1606 though much of the building dates from 1765. Horatio Nelson is counted among the School's early pupils. The town was clearly prosperous in Georgian times, probably due in part to the North Walsham & Dilham Canal, even though this was ill-fated, and which temporarily connected the town to the Broads. More likely, much of the wealth was conceived in Tudor times and carefully managed at least for a while; North Walsham was after all a wool-weaving town of high regard. Today, the town's fortunes are not so obvious but it is nevertheless an interesting gateway to the Broads.

A recent addition to the town's attractions is the **Norfolk Motor Cycle Museum** *(01692 406266), Norwich Road*. This collection of motorcycles, dating from the 1920's to the 1960's, includes many rare examples all restored by owner George Harmer. There is also an interesting display of die-cast toys dating from the 1940's. *Open daily, 10-4.30. Admission charge. Wheelchair access.*

At nearby Gunton, the **Gunton Park Sawmill**, a particularly rare water powered Sawmill, can be seen. *Open on the 4th Sun of the month, 2-5, April to September.*

Worstead

Although now a relatively quiet village just south of North Walsham, Worstead was once a thriving town which gave its name to a type of cloth made from a closely twisted yarn of fine wool. The manufacture of worsted (note the different spelling) was first introduced by Medieval Flemish immigrants but not recognised as a distinct cloth until the reign of Edward II. Its manufacture was to continue as a cottage industry until the Industrial Revolution which saw trade move to the mills of Yorkshire and Lancashire, and Worstead fall steadily into decline. Geoffrey the Dyers House, on the corner crossroads, is named after Geoffrey Litester who led the local Peasants' Revolt against the then Poll Tax; the house is in fact a row of former weavers' cottages.

Clothier's riches undoubtedly contributed to the grand 14th Century Church of St. Mary (this was originally just one of three churches in the town) with its 109 feet high tower, box pews and hammerbeam roof. The chancel-screen dates itself as 1512. On the dado are four panels each with four well-preserved saints painted on them. Part of the Church is, today, given over to local spinning and weaving efforts and work in progress can be seen on many of the looms. Outside the Church is an attractive square - until 1666, a weekly Saturday market was held here - of Georgian and Queen Anne houses known as Church Plain; many of these would naturally have been weavers' homes, the weaving done in the upper floors on 12 feet high looms.

If further evidence of Worstead's former importance is needed, then mention should be made that in 1334 it was listed as the nineteenth most wealthy town in Norfolk, and in 1449 its inhabitants are recorded as collectively paying more in the way of taxes than those living in nearby North Walsham.

Dilham Canal

Happisburgh Lighthouse (previous page)

Effective Crop Protection on the Broads

Horsey Windpump

The Cliffs at Overstrand (above)

The Cliffs at Hunstanton

tannia Pier, Great Yarmouth

Trinity Guildhall, King's Lynn (above)

The former servants' quarters at Blickling

West Street, Cromer

Wymondham's Octagonal Market Cross

Henry Blogg of Cromer

Norwich's colourful Market Place

The Church of St. Peter & St. Paul, Cromer

Pilgrim's Sign for The Hospice of Our Lady, Little Walsingham

Processional Crosses made for Easter Week, Little Walsingham

The 'high church' Altar-Screen of Wymondham Abbey

The Chancel-Screen at St. Mary's Church, Worstead

St. Mary Magdalene Church, Sandringham

Sandringham House and Gardens

The Dovecote, Felbrigg Hall

Access to the town would once have been through one of many Medieval gates, and the hamlets which survive beyond the village - Lyngate, Briggate and Bengate - are witness to such earlier glories.

Briggate Mill, once three-storeys high and one of the largest Watermills in Britain is now little more than ruins. Originally built to grind corn, it was later, in 1908, converted to a grist mill for animal feeds. Fully operational until 1970, it was later, in 1975, the subject of an arson scandal, five people being found guilty during the ensuing trials.

Walk 19: Worstead

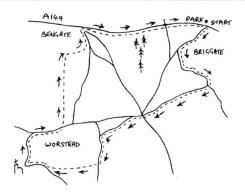

Directions:

1. From the Weavers Way car park, go back to the road and turn right to Briggate Bridge which crosses the former North Walsham & Dilham Canal. 2. Once in Briggate, turn left into White Horse Lane and just before Briggate Farm, go right along a bridleway. 3. Go straight across the road (signed Worstead) and after a short distance, just before the first house, take the left fork along Barnards Road. 4. At the junction with Lyngate Cottage, turn left and where the road bends right continue straight ahead along a bridleway to a red brick barn. 5. Opposite the barn, go right along a path through the field. At the gate, go straight on, along the road, to the centre of Worstead village. 6. Go right into School Road and at the village-green head right to go past a pond and onto the road. 7. Once you've past a cottage (red brick) with a plaque saying GBB 1821 on the wall, go left through the first field onto a footpath leading to Bengate. 8. Just before the village, turn right into a farm track which takes you to Yarmouth Road. Go left here to the bridge under the bypass, and then go right along a path which leads up the embankment to the old railway line. This is now the Weavers Way. 9. Continue along here for about one mile, passing an old cornmill (built 1850), now a private house, over an old wooden bridge straddling the Canal, and over another bridge, this time over the dyke, to return to Honing Station.
Start: Weavers Way car park at Honing's former railway station
Approx. Distance: 3.5 Miles Approx. Time: 1.5 Hours
Map: Landranger 133

Great Yarmouth

Great Yarmouth, the main town along Norfolk's eastern flank, takes its name from its situation at the mouth of the River Yare. It was made a free borough in 1208, and made 'Great' in 1272 by a Charter granted by Henry III. It was obviously an important place prior to this for in 1123 Bishop de Losinga of Norwich established St. Nicholas' Church here.

For centuries, fishing was Great Yarmouth's main industry, and herring its principal catch. The Annual Herring Fair which continued for over 600 years was a right originally granted by Edward the Confessor. Even in 1900, Great Yarmouth was still the premier herring port in the world and during the season the town's population would be swelled by as many as 10, 000, with the Scottish fishermen, fishergirls, curers and coopers forming the bulk of this phenomenon. Even after World War I, the herring catch at Great Yarmouth continued to rise with a record number of boats, 1, 149, fishing from its shores. Thereafter, decline can be attributed to a number of factors, not least the requisitioning of boats and men for World War II, and the gradual dying away of the Scots vanguard. Over-fishing and competition from other nations' fleets also contributed to the decline of Yarmouth's fishing industry. Today, its fleet is smaller than neighbouring Lowestoft's but trade in other commodities has taken over.

> **The Great Yarmouth Herring Fair** which went on for 40 days each year was first held in 1270, and was continued well into the 19th Century. Steamships increased the yield considerably and for many generations the herring supply seemed inexhaustible. Today, the catch is strictly controlled but herring remains a feature of the Yarmouth fishing industry and they can be bought in many places locally either fresh, salted or smoked. With bloaters (smoked herring) the ungutted herring are soaked in brine before being placed in the smokehouse. There they are cooked over a slow fire of oak billets and dust for 24 hours. As the smoke cures the herring, they also swell and so become bloaters.

In earlier days, trade with the Baltic countries and other parts of Britain, notably London and the North-East, was especially prosperous. In 1702, for example, 211 colliers were registered in Yarmouth (greater than London's fleet) specifically deployed for carrying coal from the North. Today, the harbour still bustles with coasters, oil and gas supply ships.

Along South Quay there are some very fine period houses including the Customs House, built in 1720 for John Andrews 'the greatest herring merchant in Europe.' Most wealthy merchants lived along South Quay and their resplendent houses once gave Great Yarmouth the air of a Baltic waterfront.

As a resort, however, Yarmouth did not become popular until the 19th Century, recommended by the Victorians for those with a weak habit, and further growth

Great Yarmouth's Quay as it once looked around the 1920's

followed the arrival of the railway. Today, the sea-front provides two Piers packed with entertainment, gardens and a Marina Centre.

Substantial parts of the old town wall, including 11 towers, begun in 1260 still survive (it once had 16 towers and 10 gates), and formerly it once enclosed over 140 'rows' or narrow alleys between two and a half feet and six feet in width, where the poorer elements of the population lived. Old Yarmouth grew up on a sand drift and consequently there was little room for wide streets - hence the 'rows' which are thought to date from the 16th Century. In Tudor times, an especially narrow horse-drawn cart was devised for hauling goods and nets through these alleys. To begin with the 'rows' were named. For example, one near the churchyard was called Snatchbody Row after those unsavoury characters Murphy and Vaughan who had once been active in resuming the bodies of the dead. Another, measuring only two and a half feet across, was once called Kitty Witches Row. To avoid the inevitable confusion which often arose, however, the rows were numbered rather than named at the beginning of the 19th Century. Charles Dickens once likened the rows to the bars of a grid iron and whilst others would disagree with him, nonetheless, very few have survived, most pounded by German bombers in 1942.

> Great Yarmouth is also renowned for its *tripe* which can be bought locally on the Market. **Chitterlings** are another speciality - pig intestine boiled and eaten either hot or cold or baked in pastry with apples and currents! Again, you can sometimes find this on the Market.

Today, the Market Place remains very much the centre of town - Market Days are Wednesday and Saturday, and also Friday during the summer season - and leading off it King Street is still the main shopping centre. All in all, Yarmouth has much to offer the visitor and whilst it is very much a brashish holiday resort, its charms and features are well worth the time spent exploring them.

Places to Visit

Museums:

Elizabethan House Museum *(01493 855746), 4 South Quay.* Built in 1596, this is a fine Jacobean merchant's house with heavily panelled rooms and a 19th Century frontage. It was here that the Cromwellians arrived at their decision to behead Charles I. Today, it houses a Museum of local social and domestic life; period furniture abounds and there is also an especially fine plaster ceiling. *Open Mon-Fri & Sun, 10-5, Whitsun to end September. Also open during Easter Week. Admission charge.*

The Maritime Museum for East Anglia *(01493 842267), Marine Parade.* The building dates from 1860 and was once a home for shipwrecked sailors. The displays cover the county's maritime history including that of the Broads. A rare Broads boat - a racing lateener - built in 1827 is one of the more unique vessels preserved here. *Open Mon-Fri & Sun, 10-5, Whitsun to end September. Also open during Easter Week. Admission charge.*

Old Merchants House, Row 111 House and Greyfriar's Cloisters *(01493 857900), all on South Quay,* are managed by English Heritage. The Old Merchants House has beautiful wooden mullioned windows and is home to a collection of 17th and 18th Century domestic ironwork. At Row 111, you can visit two houses in the 'row' style unique to Great Yarmouth. Remarkably, the fixtures of these are intact and additionally there is a display of architectural fittings salvaged from the horrendous bombings during 1942 and 1943. At Greyfriar's, the rare vaulted cloister is all that remains of a Franciscan Friary founded in 1226. *All are open daily, 10-6 (last admission at 5pm), April to September; entry by guided tour only. Admission charge.*

Tolhouse Museum *(01493 858900), Tolhouse Street.* The mid 13th century Tolhouse is one of England's oldest municipal buildings and was used as a court and jail until the late 19th Century. Although its usual inmates were either vagrants or criminals, records, nonetheless, show that in 1645 16 women were held here prior to their execution; like hundreds of others before them they had been convicted of practising witchcraft by that infamous Witch-Finder General, Matthew Hopkins. A handful of the original cells can be viewed here. *Open Sun-Fri, 10-5, end May to end September. Also open during Easter Week. Bookings at other times. Wheelchair access difficult but planned.*

Ecclesiastical and Public Buildings:

St. Nicholas' Church, St. Nicholas' Street, is the largest parish Church in England.

Dating from the 12th Century, it was once attached to the Benedictine Priory here. Much restoration has continued throughout its history and especially during the 17th and 18th Centuries and more recently as a result of the serious damage during the bombings of 1942. The general effect is one of space but confusing because of its mix of architectural styles.

The Fisherman's Hospital, Market Place. Although not open to the public, take a few minutes to view this building from the outside. Founded in 1702 to house retired fishermen and their wives, the Hospital, actually a Charity, was built around three sides of a square. The building is single-storeyed with dormers and gables. In the middle of the courtyard stands an imposing, majestic Statue of Charity.

Piers. Great Yarmouth boasts two Piers, the Wellington built in 1853 and the Britannia following in 1901. Both now house the usual seaside amusements and theatres.

Food & Accommodation

Old Station House *(01493 732022), North Road, Hemsby, nr. Great Yarmouth.* An early 20th Century house set in a peaceful environment. Comfortable B & B accommodation, and guests have their own sitting room. No evening meals.

The Red Herring *(01493 853384), Havelock Road, Great Yarmouth.* A Victorian oddity built around 1860 which provides a homely and cosy though not plush environment. Traditional pub games are a feature and, in 1990, the pub hosted the World Marbles Championship. Exotic sausages, sourced the world over, are a must from the menu. Good traditional ales. *Wheelchair access.*

Seafood Restaurant *(01493 856009), North Quay.* A busy restaurant converted from a former Victorian pub. The range of seafood on offer is wide and the cooking simple but good; the cold cabinets display the day's catch. To avoid disappointment, book in advance.

Entertainment:

Boat Trips. For a regular programme of Broads trips during the summer months go down to Haven Bridge just beyond the old city walls where you can choose between two pleasure steamers.

Great Yarmouth Butterfly and Tropical Gardens (01493 842202), *Marine Parade.* Exotic plants and butterflies under glass.

Great Yarmouth Pleasure Beach (01493 844585). Over 70 fairground rides, sideshows and the like.

Greyhound Racing: contact *Great Yarmouth Stadium (01493 720343)* for details. The Stadium also manage stock-car, hot-rod and banger racing events.

Horse Racing: contact the *Racecourse (01493 842527)* on *North Denes, Great Yarmouth.*

Pleasurewood Hills Theme Park *(01502 508200),* on the A12 between Great Yarmouth and Lowestoft. Although based in Corton, Suffolk, it is so close to Great Yarmouth to warrant inclusion. Entertainment for the whole family whether it be the circus, Punch and Judy, or the myriad of rides, from juveniles to white-knuckle roller-coasters. *Open daily mid May to mid September, and some weekends during April, late September and early October.*

Sea Life Centre *(01493 330631), Marine Parade* for a sea world experience of a difference.

Theatres: a number of theatres offer a varied programme including **Britannia Theatre** *(01493 842209)* and the **Wellington Pier Theatre** *(01493 842244).*

Sports Venues:

Cycle Hire: contact *Lawford Cycles (01493 842741), 224 Northgate Street, Great Yarmouth* for details.

Horse Riding: *Crossways Riding Centre (01493 781531), Lound Road, Browston.* BHS approved and providing instruction in riding and jumping.

> **The Angles Way** is an 80 mile long distance path through the Waveney Valley, beginning at Great Yarmouth and ending at Knettishall Heath (Suffolk). It is a fine walk meandering its way through parts of the Norfolk Broads, the more southerly marshes and riversides and concluding in the Suffolk Brecks. Many historical sites can be visited along the way including Burgh Castle and Bungay. At Knettishall Heath, the Way joins two other long distance footpaths - The Peddars Way and the Icknield Way. For further details contact The *Norfolk & Suffolk Area Ramblers' Association* who publish a booklet entitled *The Angles Way,* which is also available locally.

Sea Fishing: various sea angling trips are arranged by *Bishop Boat Services (01493 664739), 48 Warren Road, Gorleston-on-Sea; M. Dyble (01493 731305), 13 St. Margaret's Way, Fleggburgh, Mr. Read (01493 859653), 17 Wellington Road, Great Yarmouth,* and *NJC Fishing Tackle (01502 589556), The Boulevard, 6 Yacht Station, Oulton Broad.* Permits and licenses are not required from the beaches but a small charge is made for fishing off Wellington Pier during the winter as it is off Britannia Pier.

Tenpin Bowling: *Regent Bowl (01493 856830), Regent Street, Great Yarmouth.*

Walk 20: Great Yarmouth

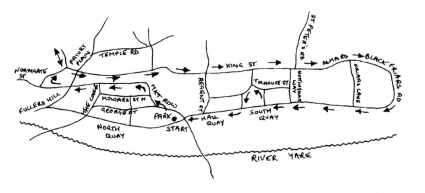

Directions:

1. From the car park off Hall Quay, walk towards Hall Quay and turn left along George Street, and cross the Stonecutter's Way and then go right into Broad Row, and then Market Row. 2. Go left along the Market Place to Fullers Hill, and cross into Whitehorse Plain. 3. Cross Northgate Street to visit St. Nicholas' Church. Go left into Priory Plains (Anna Sewell's birthplace on your left), and just before Temple Road, turn right into St. Nicholas' Road to rejoin the Market Place (Fishermen's Hospital on your right). Go left along Market Place and then along the full length of King Street. 4. Turn left into Alma Road and go through the ruins of Garden Gate in the old Town Wall. Then turn right into Blackfriars Road to South-East Tower (once a smoke house for curing fish). 5. Go right into Mariners Road and then right along South Quay. 6. Just after the Old Merchant House, turn right into Gaol Walk to visit the Tolhouse Museum. 7. Just after Tolhouse, go left into Yarmouth Way, and then left along it to rejoin Hall Quay. 8. Turn right into Hall Quay passing The Elizabethan House on your right, before returning to your start.

Start: Hall Quay car park
Approx. Distance: 2.75 Miles
Approx. Time: 2 Hours

Caister-On-Sea

Once an important Roman station and naval base, Caister is now little more than a dormitory village of Great Yarmouth. With the decline of Britain's fishing fleets, traditions linked with that once 'great' industry have given way to the needs of tourism, modern housing and transport. The caravan parks are endless, affording the holiday maker immediate access to Caister's wide and sandy beaches.

The site of the rectangular walled roman harbour town - thought to be in use until the 4th Century - lies mainly to the north. Covering an area of 30 acres, excavations during the 1950's and 1960's have revealed a ten feet thick flint wall which replaced a former, ramparted, wooden palisade. Something in the order of 150 poor men's boat burials of the later Saxon period (circa 650-850 AD) have also been found outside these walls. The town is considered to have been evacuated during the first Danish settlements towards the end of the 800's. Managed by English Heritage, *Caister Roman Site is open all year, free of charge.*

The remains of *Caister Castle* (01572 787251) built for Sir John Fastolf upon his triumphant return from Agincourt, can also be visited. Built of pink and yellow brick, and once surrounded by a moat, it was one of England's most substantial 15th Century castles. In the south corner is Caister Hall, with its Georgian embellished tower. After Fastolf's death around 1459, incidentally Shakespeare used Fastolf as a model for his character Falstaff in *Henry IV,* his property and lands were inherited by the Paston family. Today, it is also home to a large collection of steam cars and motor vehicles including an 1893 Panhard-Levassor. *Caister Castle Motor Museum is open Sun-Fri, 10.30-5, mid May to end September. Admission charge.*

Food & Accommodation

The Fisherman's Return *(01493 393305), Winterton-on-Sea.* Close to Winterton's sandy beach and converted from former fishermen's cottages, the atmosphere at this pub is relaxed and welcoming. Old maritime photographs and prints provide added context and interest. Good home cooking, and a good choice of wines, champagne, malts, ales and cider. Accommodation is available.

Tower Cottage *(01493 394053), Black Street, Winterton-on-Sea.* Opposite the Church and built towards the end of the 18th Century, this is a charming flint cottage where beams and exposed walls add further to the B & B's charm. Most of the bedrooms are in the main house though one with its own sitting room and bathroom is in the adjoining, converted barn. Packed lunches available. No evening meals.

Norwich

orwich began life as three small Anglo-Danish settlements on the banks of the River Wensum. Evidence, however, of a defensive market and something resembling a political centre - called Northwic - have been identified from coins dating from as early as 920 AD, and which bear Athelstan's inscription. Even before the arrival of the Normans, Tombland, in the city centre, had a market supported by Norwich's international tradeport and a variety of industries had already been established - pottery manufacture, for example, in Pottergate, and iron-smelting north of the River. Today, Tombland is a mainly Georgian square but it is nonetheless named after the Saxon *toom* meaning open marketplace. The population at the end of the 11th Century has been estimated as being as high as 5, 000, and for many decades Norwich was second only to London as England's largest city. Building of the Cathedral began in 1096, the Castle followed shortly afterwards presumably with the great stretch of wall around the city put up at around the same time.

Norwich Cathedral, building of which began in 1096

As early as 1144, the Jewish element of the population began its banking practises in Norwich; unlike other European cities, Norwich did not impose restric-
tions on the Jews and, untypically, nor were there any Jewish ghettoes in the
city. Perhaps it is not unreasonable to assume, therefore, that Norwich was a
city where trade, in all its various guises, was paramount in the minds and lives
of its people. Indeed, Norwich and Norfolk as a whole have something of a long
tradition of free-thinking or dissent, however you want to term it, *viz* the likes
of Boudicea, Cromwell and Kett. The city's adoption of the Jews was in essence
no different from the liberal attitude it displayed towards others in danger -
whether they be Dutch Protestants, French Huguenots or Flemish weavers.

> Specific Norwich non-conformists have included **Harriet Martineau**
> (1802-76) who was born to a family of manufacturers of Huguenot
> descent in Gurney Court, just off Magdalen Street. Elizabeth Fry, the
> Quaker prison reformer was also born here. Harriet Martineau began
> her literary career writing moral tales for children but her true pen-
> chant was as a populariser of economic subjects and as a propagan-
> dist for social reform, especially wage reform. *Illustrations of Political
> Economy* was published in 1832, and she also wrote regular columns
> for the *Daily News, Westminster* and the *Edinburgh Review*. Despite
> her puritan, unitarian background, her views were increasingly of an
> atheist bent as is best gauged in her *Letters on the Laws of Man's
> Social Nature* (1851).
>
> Around the same time and holding rather different views was a group
> of intellectuals who used the Octagon Chapel in the city as their
> meeting place. Prominent among these was **Amelia Opie** (1769-
> 1853), author of *Father & Daughter* (1801), and an ardent supporter
> of French Revolutionary ideals. **William Taylor** (1765-1836), another
> member of this group, was similarly a supporter of the French
> Revolution and was later to introduce the works of radical German
> thinkers such as Goethe to English readers; his *Historic Survey of
> German Poetry 1828-30* being particularly instrumental in this
> respect.

Over time, Norwich capitalised on its importance as a trading centre - it was
granted the status of City in 1403 by Henry IV - and this is evidenced by the
number of subsidiary markets established here. For example, Rampant Horse
Street was the site of a lively horse market, and St. John Maddermarket an area
for the sale of dyestuffs produced from the madder plant. In his work *Lavengro*,
George Borrow (1803-81), provides us with a lavish account of the Norwich
horsefair:

> *"...indeed horsefairs are seldom dull. There was shouting and whooping, neighing
> and braying; there was galloping and trotting; fellows with highlows and white
> stockings, and with many a string dangling from the knees of their tight
> breeche, were running desperately, holding horses by the halter, and in
> some cases dragging them along; there were long-tailed steeds, and
> dock-tailed steeds of every degree and breed; there were droves of wild ponies
> and long rows of sober cart-horses; there were donkeys, and even mules.*

Yet, gradually, Norwich's staple industry became the manufacture of cloth, and this was further supported by the settlement of Flemish weavers - many of them refugees - from as early as the 11th Century through to the 14th Century. Worsted cloth being their primary product. Interestingly, story has it that these weavers brought with them their pet caged birds and that it is from these that Norwich City Football Club gets its affectionate name, *The Canaries*.

> **Norwich shawls** were once an important item of manufacture for the city, and grew from the region's already prominent textile industry, and its importance as a centre for international trade. Among the goods imported were the fine and beautiful Kashmiri shawls woven from silky Tibetan goat wool. Norwich shawls attempted to copy these hugely expensive originals but at a much more affordable price. The first to begin such weaving was Alderman John Harvey in Colegate, followed by P.J. Knights who was successful with the 12 feet wide seamless Norwich shawl counterpane. A dozen such shawl manufacturers were recorded in the city in 1802, and further improvements in its weaving followed in the 1830's with the introduction of the Jacquard loom. Shawl production, however, peaked in the 1850's when there were around 28 manufacturers. Thereafter, decline set in principally as a result of changes in the style of women's dress. The last Norwich shawls were made in the 1930's by Gout & Co. but all examples of the art remain very collectible; the Bridewell Museum, incidentally, has a number of these on display.

In 1723, Daniel Defoe in his *Tour Through The Eastern Counties* estimated that as many as 120, 000 people in and around Norwich found employment in the wool and silk industry and that the merchants associated with these owned upwards of 1, 000 ships; worsted being exported worldwide to Russia, China, India and the American colonies. Textiles at this time clearly being England's main export and Norwich's pivotal role revealed by its continued status as England's second largest city, London again still premier. Textiles continued as Norwich's main product base until the early 19th Century when other industries began to take this lead away, and as Britain's primary textile manufacture moved to the newly industrialised north.

Shoemaking, which once employed thousands in the city during the 19th Century, still continues; Bally (now Swiss owned), Bowhill & Elliott, and Start-rite still leading the British contingent. Although excavations have revealed fragments from a 10th Century and 11th Century shoemaking industry, it was not until the end of the 18th Century that it became a prominent feature of the Norwich industrial scene; Chase's *Norwich Directory* of 1783 recorded 45 shoe manufacturers and ten pattern-makers. In 1792, James Smith began his factory and although the site and company name have changed several times since, the company nonetheless still survives as Start-rite, specialist manufacturer of children's shoes. Another manufacturer, David Soman, first began making caps in 1799 but quickly shifted to footwear recognising the huge potential it afforded; in 1933, after passing through a number of generations, the business finally became part of Bally, the Swiss manufacturer's operation.

Why Norfolk became so important a shoemaking centre is not clear but perhaps the decline of the textile industry inadvertently contributed to the rise of another industry requiring a similarly skilled workforce. Bridewell Museum houses a large collection of tools and machinery associated with the industry as well as a great many examples of Norwich-made footwear. Additionally, from 1900 to 1916, the Museum was once Thomas Bowhill's shoe factory base: Bowhill & Elliott's retail outlet can now be found just around the corner in London Street.

The breweries also flourished during the late 18th Century and thereafter; in 1845, there were an incredible 505 pubs in the city and so demand for ale and beer was assured. All local breweries were successful enough until the 1950's but from then on sadly lacked the necessary capital and power to expand nationally; Watney's stepped in taking over most of those breweries still extant in Norwich. More recently, there has been some revival in smaller, specialist breweries as seen by Woodforde's very successful efforts begun in 1981 from premises in Drayton on the outskirts of the city, but now operating from Woodbastwick on the Broads.

The railway arrived in Norwich in 1845, and this was especially instrumental in J.J. Coleman's decision to commence a mustard mill in the city itself. Coleman's shop in Bridewell Alley, in the centre of the city, being opened in 1973 to celebrate Coleman's 150th Anniversary of mustard manufacturing in Norfolk. At the time of writing, Coleman's is on the market although a suitable purchaser has yet to be found. It is to be hoped that whoever does take Coleman's over will do so in a way in which preserves the county's, probably the country's, most favourite relish.

Even banking owes much to Norwich's early position as a centre for national and international trade. Although the Jewish community had in earlier centuries been the most instrumental in money-lending practises, it was, nevertheless, a local family, the Gurney's, who established the first formal banking operation in 1775. Later, in 1896, they were joined by three other banking families and founded the first, soon to be countless, Barclays Bank. Norwich Union has continued this ability within the financial sector and today, despite the substantial and recent relocation of many staff to Sheffield, continues as the city's largest employer.

R. H. Mottram (1883-1971) was born at Bank House, Bank Plain, a former Georgian house and head office of Gurneys Bank (the present building houses Barclays Bank, formed from an amalgamation with Gurneys) for his grandfather was responsible for carrying bank notes between Gurneys Norwich Bank and London. Mottram lived there until 1900 and later himself worked for a bank; his *Our Mr. Dormer* recounts the story of the rise of a banking family and although it is set in an imaginary *Easthampton*, it clearly draws upon Norwich and the Gurney's. He was to return to the same theme in a later book *Castle Island* (1931).

One of the most impressive views of Norwich can be gained just north-east of the city centre at Mousehold Heath, an ancient tract of heathland. From here, on a clear day, you can identify all of Norwich's 30-plus Medieval churches, although the greater proportion are now redundant; many have found alternative uses ranging from antiques centres to a puppet theatre. You may also be able to imagine the plight of Robert Kett, leader of the Peasants 'Revolt against 16th Century land enclosures, who held the heath and its surrounding area until his troops, desperately short of food and water, were impelled to move closer to the city; they were subsequently dispersed by men loyal to the Earl of Warwick and Kett's fate was sealed. He was hung from the ramparts of Norwich Castle in 1549.

Mousehold Heath also provided a favourite vista for many of the Norwich School of Painters whose work is well represented in the Castle Museum. In 1803, the Norwich Society of Artists was founded by a group of local painters, most were landscapists drawing much of their inspiration from the Norfolk countryside. Although they did not develop any common style as such, their collective identity and influences upon each other has led them to be regarded as a School. Foremost amongst these artists were John Crome, John Sell Cotman, John Thirtle, Joseph Stannard and Robert Dixon.

The Society's first exhibition was held in 1805 and these continued pretty well yearly until 1833; at that time they were unusual in being some of the first exhibitions to be staged outside London and unique in showing work by local born artists. Today, with greater interest in and appreciation of English watercolour and landscape painting, the quality of the Norwich School's work - especially that of Crome and Cotman - is more widely recognised than it was over a century ago.

> **Edward Seago** (1910-1974) was born in Norwich, the son of a coal merchant. Despite a life-long heart complaint he became involved in pre-World War II undercover espionage on behalf of the British government. He was later to join a travelling circus, and *Circus Company,* a vivid and fun account of this experience, was published in 1933. Although he wrote a number of other books, he is best remembered for his superb paintings of the East Anglian landscape - especially Norfolk and Suffolk - in all its many moods. His works today are highly collectable and rightly command significant prices at auction.

Norwich has never lost its individual character and maybe this can best be attributed to its relative isolation from the rest of the country - on the one hand it is cut-off from the Midlands by both the Fens and the Wash, and on the other it is quite a considerable distance from London. Early and substantial trade with the Continental Low Countries has also found its reflection in much of Norwich's vernacular architecture - Flemish gable-ends being a characteristic feature. But nowhere has the city's charm been lost - let's hope today's developers do not become the exception- from the cobbled streets of Elm Hill with its quaint and colourful buildings flanking the River Wensum on one side, to the permanent market, Mondays to Saturdays, in the city centre. This is one of few such surviving sites replete with its colourful array of canopies and many of the 200-plus traders selling first-rate local produce - from fruit and vegetables to the latest sea catch and speciality sausages. Although the original market was held in Tombland, it was removed to its present site by the Normans and remains one of the best and most picturesque in England. Although it would be pretty difficult to miss the market when in Norwich, do take the opportunity to walk through the many alleys separating the stalls; you will not be disappointed.

Elm Hill, Norwich

Places to Visit

Museums:

Bridewell Museum (01603 667228), Bridewell Alley. An interesting local history Museum with excellent sections devoted to Norwich's once important textile industry, and also to its shoe-manufacturing, and food and brewing industries. Additionally, there is a good replica of a well-stocked pharmacist's shop, and another exhibit to be found is the first wire netting machine to be made in the world; Charles Barnard, a Norwich man, being responsible for its invention in 1844. His product proved a resounding export success - the Australian market especially buoyant. More elaborate items manufactured by that company have included the wrought-iron gates at Sandringham. The building housing the Museum was originally built in 1370 by the father of William Appleyard, the first Mayor of Norwich. *Open Mon-Sat 10-5. Admission charge.*

Castle and Castle Museum (01603 223624), Norwich Castle. Replacing an earlier earth and wood structure, Norwich Castle is 12th Century Norman with the fifth largest keep in England. In 1834, the building was refaced with Bath Stone. Perhaps surprisingly, as early as 1220 the Castle was demilitarised and until 1887, when it was turned into a museum and art gallery, it served as the county jail. The open bailey, however, was for centuries used as the site for the great livestock market - this was moved to the southern outskirts of the city in 1960. More recently, extensive archeological excavations have been undertaken, and in 1993 the Castle Mall Shopping Centre opened nearby.

> **Elizabeth Fry** (1780-1840), daughter of the wealthy banker John Gurney, was born in Norwich and devoted much of her life to prison reform both at home and abroad. Although raised a Quaker and endowed with their humanitarianism, it was not until she visited Newgate prison, in 1813, where she found over 300 women, both tried and untried, huddled together with their children in the most squalid of conditions that her real fight for such reforms first began. She went on to found hostels for the homeless and to assist countless other charitable organisations.

The Museum within the Castle concentrates on local history - natural, agricultural, artistic, trade and commercial. Some of the best collections include those of the Norwich School of Painters - especially Crome and Cotman - and of Lowestoft Porcelain. Look out for 'Old Snap', a comic porcelain dragon which is a relic of the Guild of St. George. From the 15th to the 19th Century, a dragon like this accompanied processions around the city, snapping its jaws at the crowds as it went by. Additionally, the collection of stuffed birds includes rarities such as Norfolk's last Greater Bustards. Finally, the Castle Dungeons can also be visited. *Open Mon-Sat 10-5 & Sun 2-5. Admission charge. Wheelchair access.*

John Jarrold Printing Museum *(01603 660211), Jarrold Printing Co., Whitefriars.* The Museum occupies three floors (across two buildings) of printing works and the displays include a range of letterpress type, platen and hand presses, and hand and mechanical binding equipment. **Open Wed 10-12 noon & 7-9 p.m.,** *otherwise by prior arrangement. Admission charge for adults; children free.*

The Mustard Shop *(01603 627889), Bridewell Alley.* Norwich leads the world in mustard manufacture, Colman's having begun its Norfolk practise in 1814 partly due to the demand for compliments to the local herring catch. Colman's Mustard Shop is a combination Mustard Museum and Retail Outlet, opened in 1973. Some of the varieties sold here are generally not available elsewhere. Perhaps one of its most popular strains, however, is the hot English mustard produced from seed grown in the countless brilliantly yellow fields which surround Norwich. **Open Mon-Sat 9.30-5. Free of charge.**

Sainsbury Centre For Visual Arts *(01603 456060), University of East Anglia, Norwich.* Opened in 1978, the permanent collection here includes strong holdings of Oceanic, African, native North American and Pre-Columbian art, together with works by well-known 20th Century artists - among them Moore, Epstein and Giacometti. In addition, there are regular, important travelling exhibitions shown here. **Open daily, excluding Mon, 12-5. Admission charge. Wheelchair** *access.*

Strangers Hall *(01603 667229), Charing Cross, St. Benedicts.* Once a Medieval merchant's house now a Museum where the rooms are furnished in a variety of period styles, from Tudor to late Victorian. **Open Mon-Sat 10-5. Admission** *charge.*

The Royal Norfolk Regiment Museum *(01603 223649), Britannia Barracks.* The Museum draws upon the Regiment's history from 1685 to 1985, and includes exhibits of uniforms, paintings, campaign medals and Regimental silver. **Open** **Mon-Fri 9-12.30 & 2-4.30. Closed public holidays. Free of charge. Wheelchair** *access to ground floor.*

Ecclesiastical & Public Buildings:

Norwich Cathedral (01603 764385) The Cathedral was first begun in 1096 by Bishop de Losinga on the orders of the Pope; the Bishop had been found guilty of simony (he had paid William Rufus the princely sum of £1,900 in return for the Norwich bishopric - he had formerly been Abbot of Ramsey) and this was his required penance. Much of the building was finished after de Losinga's death, although the present 315 feet high spire - second only to Salisbury's - is 15th Century, the original timber structure destroyed by a hurricane in 1362. In its original parts, the Cathedral is built from Barnack and Caen stone with flint forming its core walls. The cloisters begun in 1297 and finished circa 1430 are the largest in England and the library above, one of the best in the country, holding more than 7, 000 works of reference.

The cloisters themselves contain over 400 coloured, carved bosses, each depicting a different story from Christ's Passion to the Book of Revelation, and a further series focusing on the lives of the Apostles and Martyrs. Inside the Cathedral proper, a similar treat is in store - in the nave, and the north and south transepts. Here the carved bosses tell the Biblical story from the first days of Creation to the Last Judgement. In the nave, these are split into two lots of seven bays - the first set depicting the story from the point of view of the Old Testament and the second using the New Testament. Perhaps my favourite has to be that bay which recounts the Israelites' escape from Egypt and then on to a promised land.

Of almost equal note are the 60 plus 15th Century carved misericords to be found in the choir stalls. These stalls mostly belong to two dates - either 1480 for those under the tower or 1420 for those nearer the screen. Everyone has their favourites and included amongst mine would be Sloth (Chaucer's kitchen chaos) and Wrestlers & Seconds.

There is so much of interest to be found in the Cathedral that to do justice to it in this volume would be impossible. The best advise, therefore, is to take your time exploring its many features and use the Cathedral's official guide publication to give you whatever extra information you need. On this note then, one last thing worth looking out for is Bishop de Losinga's throne which is sited in its original position in the apse behind the high altar. It is the oldest in England, possibly 8th Century, and probably one of the most sumptuous.

Cathedral Close is best entered via a choice of two magnificent gates, although there are others. St. Ethelbert's was built by the town's people as a penance for one of their periodic assaults, probably justified, against the monks. Erpingham Gate, intended as a memorial to Sir Thomas Erpingham, is an exceptionally fine Perpendicular monument depicting the 12 Apostles, 12 Virgin Saints and Sir Thomas himself. Sir Thomas it may be recalled is described in Shakespeare's *Henry V* as *"... a good old commander and a most kind gentleman"*; he is now buried in the Cathedral choir. In Shakespeare's dramatisation, Henry V meets Sir Thomas on the morning before the Battle of Agincourt:

> KING HENRY: *Good morrow, old Sir Thomas Erpingham;*
> *A good soft pillow for that good white head*
> *Were better than a churlish turf of France.*
>
> ERPINGHAM: *Not so, my Liege: this lodging likes me better*
> *Since I may say, Now lie I like a King.*

Henry then borrows Sir Thomas's cloak, and so disguised, makes his rounds of the English troops gauging their morale before commencement of the Battle.

The Medieval precinct within the Close still retains its Old Bishop's Palace, although this now forms part of King Edward VI's School buildings. Nearby is the grave of Edith Cavell, executed in Belgium, in 1915, for helping British pris

St. Ethelbert's Gate

oners escape from the German Army of Occupation. A monument to her can be found outside the main entrance to the Cathedral. During the Middle Ages, upwards of 60 Benedictine monks lived in Cathedral Close; today, it is a delightfully quiet precinct (no vehicles except for access) with some Medieval buildings such as the Deanery still in tact. The rest are Georgian elegance.

Walk through the Close, down to the River Wensum and you will find Watergate with a house known as Pull's Ferry joined to it; although there is now no ferry, pleasure craft can be hired from further along the banks of the River. Nearby Cow Tower, managed by English Heritage and open free of charge all year, is a circular brick tower which once formed part of the city's 14th Century defenses

St. Andrew's Hall & Blackfriar's Hall, *St. Andrew's Plain.* St. Andrew's Hall was once part of the church of the 'Sackites" (so called because its members dressed in sack cloths) or Friars of the Penance of Jesus Christ. The order was suppressed in 1307 and the building was then granted to the Dominicans or Blackfriars. They did not fare too much better and were suppressed in turn, in 1538. The building, though, is especially valued as it is the only English Friar's Church still standing. The current structure was begun in 1440 and the nave and aisles are over 265 feet long. Becket's Chapel, with its brick vaulting, stone pier and its barrel-vaulted crypt, still survives under the present building. A particularly fine hammerbeam roof also survives in the Hall itself. Today, St. Andrew's Hall is home to a regular programme of concerts and events, ranging from beer festivals to antique and book fairs, to classical music evenings.

St Giles, *Giles Street,* has an imposing tower, 120 feet high, topped by a pretty little cupola. Much of the 14th Century Church remains but later additions are obvious. Again, a beautiful hammerbeam roof dominates the interior, this enhanced with angels.

St. Peter Hungate, *Elm Hill,* is now a centre for ecclesiastical art and brass rubbing. There is also a good collection of musical instruments here and the Church holds part of a manuscript of the Wycliffe Bible. Once again, there is a good hammerbeam roof.

> **Julian of Norwich** was one of the great mystics of the Middle Ages, living the life of a recluse in a cell near the Church of St. Julian, from which she took her name. Story has it that aged 30, in 1373, she fell ill and claimed to have received a vision. Soon after this she wrote her *Sixteen Revelations of Divine Love* - one of the first works by a woman in the English language. Although the original manuscript is sadly lost. the oldest surviving copy is 15th Century (now in the British Museum) but it was not until 1670 that the first printed edition was made available. In essence, St. Julian saw the hazelnut as incorporating the whole of God's creation: "*... In this little thing I saw three truths: the first is that God made it; the second is that God loves it; and the third is that God sustains it.*" Julian lived in her cell at Norwich for 40 years - to the right of the altar in the present-day Church of St. Julian. Somewhat controversially, she talked of God as 'Mother' and for this she is often referred to as one of the first feminist theologians. In 1942, the original Church of St. Julian was destroyed by a bomb but in the early 1950's the building was reconstructed, rebuilt on the foundations of the Medieval structure where it can be seen today.

St. Peter Mancroft, *Market Place,* too has a fabulous hammerbeam roof, the hammerbeam here concealed by fan-vaulting. Best of all is the rare timber baptistry, one of only three in England. Also of particular note is a 16th Century (1572) tapestry and some superb stained glass. The Church was first begun in 1430 and consecrated in 1455; this is Norfolk's parish church *par excellence.*

The Great Hospital, *Bishopsgate,* was founded, in 1249, by Bishop Walter de Suffield to house 30 aged or infirm chaplains. Furthermore, 13 of the poor's sick were allowed one meal per day and permitted to warm themselves by the fire in winter. Only parts of the original building survive, and unusually for a building of this kind, part of it was constituted as a parish church - St. Helen's-and this is still the case. To the north of the Infirmary Hall is the cloister built circa 1450, and to the west of the range is the Master's Lodging. In 1383, the Hospital was visited by Richard II and his wife, Anne of Bohemia; they assisted in a rebuilding programme and, in honour of their efforts, the roof has 252

Pull's Ferry

gilded panels with a black, monarchical, double-headed eagle on each. Today, the only easily accessible part of the Hospital is St. Helen's Church.

The Guildhall, Market Place. The city's Guildhall was built in the first half of the 15th Century but by 1634 its structure was pretty well undermined by overly avid saltpetre diggers. A dungeon beneath the Guildhall once held a 15th Century heretic, imprisoned there before being burned at the stake. Story goes that on the eve of his execution, he put his finger into the flame of a candle so as to prepare himself for the full horror of the following day.

The Music Room, King Street, is probably the oldest surviving, private dwelling in England and was once known as 'The Jews House'. Although the stone facade is mainly 17th Century, most of the remains are actually 12th Century. The timbered interior roof is reportedly magnificent. Both Sir John Paston and Sir Edward Coke lived here at some point, and in Elizabethan times it was the meeting place of the City Waits, hence its name.

Live Entertainment:

Maddermarket Theatre (01603 620917), St. John's Alley. This a delightful replica of an Elizabethan playhouse reconstructed after World War I from a former chapel and warehouse. An adventurous programme is always scheduled here. The repertory company has been the first to return to a Tudor apron stage, and although the actors are amateurs, with a tradition of anonymity, the works are performed under the guidance of professional producers. Will Kemp, the Elizabethan actor, is reported to have morris danced from London to the Church of St. John in the Maddermarket. It is said to have taken him nine days to complete the journey but quite why he did so remains unanswered! Some believe the old adage 'nine-day wonder' stems from Kemp's exploits.

> The man responsible for the Maddermarket Theatre, founded by him in 1921, was **Nugent Monck.** Although earlier in 1910, Monck had produced a revival of the Norwich 'Paradise Play', a mystery play regularly acted by the Grocers' Company in the Middle Ages, at the Maddermarket he went on to produce over 280 plays before retiring in 1952. His story is well accounted for in R.H.Mottram's *History of the Maddermarket Theatre,* as it is in David Holbrook's *A Play of Passion.*

Norfolk & Norwich Festival (01603 614921), Box Office, 1 Merchant's Court, St. George's Street. Norwich has been holding an Arts Festival since 1772, and it is the oldest city festival in the country. Until 1989, it was held on a tri-annual basis but increasing success has now assured an annual event. The Festival's aim is to make it an occasion for everyone and the venues (countywide) reflect this achievement. The programme is always well balanced between classical, chamber, jazz and rock music with new works commissioned specifically for the Festival being a strong feature. Poetry recitals, theatre, films, walks and children's events are also well represented - many of them are free and staged in the open air. Artists and performers range from those with truly international reputations to those with local backgrounds but nonetheless talented. All in all it is an event to write into your October diary; it runs for approximately two weeks during that month and full details can be had from the Box Office.

The Puppet Theatre (01603 629921), St. Jame's Church, Whitefriars. Begun by respected puppeteers Ray and Joan daSilva in 1980, and using a formerly redundant church, the Norwich Puppet Theatre - one of few such companies in the country - offers a varied and interesting programme throughout the year. Most of the shows draw upon traditional children's stories such as *Jack & The Beanstalk* and *Peter & The Wolf* but all the puppets and sets are designed by the company themselves. Choose from the main auditorium or the Octagon Studio for the under fives.

Sports Venues:

Ballooning: Anglia Balloons (01603 880819), Peacock Lodge, Marlingfield.

Boat Hire: Norwich Boat Hire (01603 701701), The Yacht Station, Riverside Road, Norwich.

Football: Norwich City Football Club (01603 761661), Carrow Road, Norwich.

Go-Karting: Norwich Indoor Kart Centre (01603 486655), Vulcan Road North, Norwich.

Horse Riding: Salhouse Equestrian Centre (01603 782749), The Street, Salhouse. BHS Approved.

Swimming: *Norwich Sports Village (01603 788912), Drayton High Road, Hellesdon.* A competition sized pool.

Tennis: *Norwich Sports Village (01603 788912), Drayton High Road, Hellesdon.* Indoor, outdoor and table tennis.

Tenpin Bowling: *Crome Bowl (01603 700203), Telegraph Lane East, Norwich.*

Gardens:

The Plantation Garden, *4 Earlham Road, Norwich.* The entrance to the garden can be found between two hotels near St. John's R.C. Cathedral. This is a surprisingly tranquil and impressive three-acre Victorian town garden created in what was once a Medieval chalk quarry, and is only a few minutes walk from the city centre. Although restoration work is ongoing, two particularly remarkable features are the Italianate terrace - 60 feet in length - and the 30 feet Gothic fountain. ***Open Sun 2-5.30, April to October. Admission charge***

Interesting Retail Outlets:

Bowhill & Elliott *(01603 620116), 65 London Street.* Continuing Norwich's shoemaking tradition and known worldwide for their exclusive slippers.

Churchills *(01603 626437), 32 St. Andrew's Street.* Norfolk's leading tobacconist with an extensive range of loose tobaccos and smoking accessories.

Country & Eastern *(01603 631407), 6 Bridewell Alley* and at *8 Redwell Street.* Stockists of a wide range of quality goods imported from India and the Far East - anything from candlesticks to oriental rugs and furniture.

Crome Gallery *(01603 622827), 34 Elm Hill.* A gallery selling good quality, local and national art as well as offering a restoration and framing service.

Elm Hill Stamps & Coins *(01603 627413), 27 Elm Hill.* If you are a collector of stamps, coins or postcards then this is a good spot to explore. Regular auctions are an added feature.

Philip Milne *(01603 667441), 2 Wright Court, Elm Hill.* Stuffed animals, birds and insects sold under DOE licence. A complete taxidermy service is also offered.

The Mousetrap *(01603 614083), 2 St. Gregory's Alley.* Stocks an extensive range of traditional British and Irish farmhouse cheeses as well as a good choice of French regional specialities.

Norwich Heather & Conifer Centre *(01603 39434), 54A Yarmouth Road.* Over 700 varieties of heaths and heathers are grown here, plus over 400 varieties of conifers. *Open daily, excluding Thur, 9-5 & Sun 2-5. Wheelchair access.*

Pickering & Son *(01603 742002), 30 The Street, Old Costessey.* Pickering's make over 40 different types of sausages all without artificial additives. Some of their more popular recipes include Norfolk Pork (with lemon and Bramley apple), Grandad's Recipe (with nutmeg) and Aunt Edna's (with sage). Other food stuffs they are well known for include Black Pudding and naturally produced Bacon. Look for their stall on Norwich city centre Market Place if Costessey is too out of the way for you.

Food & Accommodation

Hotels:

Dunston Hall & Country Club *(01508 470444), Ipswich Road.* Only a ten minute drive from the city centre this is Norwich's answer to a distinctive hotel but it is nevertheless heavily geared as a conference centre (opened 1994). However, set in over 100 acres of garden and woodland, and restored to a high standard (the Hall itself is neo-Elizabethan in style), the facilities here ensure a relaxing stay regardless of the visitors purpose. Extensive leisure facilities include a heated pool, steam room, sauna and gym. A ten-hole golf course, tennis and squash courts are also planned. The Restaurant and Carvery further extend the options. *Wheelchair access.*

Close to Dunston Hall is the site of **Venta Icenorum**, once the market town of the Iceni tribe in 70AD, and which was subsequently added to by the Romans. Standing beside the River Tas, it was an important administrative and trading centre, pre-dating Norwich's importance by several centuries. Although there is no official access to the site, permission to view the remains may be granted by the owners of Old Hall Farm, Caister St. Edmunds. If you are lucky, you will be able to explore well over 1,000 feet of outer walling built from a mix of brick and tile and supported by flint coping. This once enclosed over 35 acres, although the town itself is thought to have been much larger than this. Roman occupation continued until the 5th Century - evidence of a Roman glass-making industry abounds here. Thereafter, the Anglo-Saxons moved in; their burial mounds remain a feature of the surrounding landscape.

St. Edmund's Church, celebrating the memory of the East Anglian King Edmund, is reached by crossing the former moat of Venta Icenorum. Although built in both the 13th and 14th Centuries, there is nonetheless a wealth of earlier materials (Roman) in its structure.

Hotel Nelson *(01603 760260), Prince of Wales Road.* A five minute walk from the city centre. The River Wensum washes against the Hotel's front and leisure craft can be hired only five minutes walk away. High standard, friendly service and accommodation. The Riverside Lounge takes full advantage of the Hotel's situation. *Wheelchair access.*

Stakis Norwich Hotel *(01603 410544), Norwich Airport, Cromer Road.* Found on the northern outskirts of the city this a recent establishment with smart and practical accommodation. Other features include a Carvery, the French styled 'Walbro' Restaurant, indoor pool, sauna and gym. *Wheelchair access.*

Bed & Breakfast:

Foxwood *(01603 868474), Fakenham Road, Taverham.* If you are looking for a B &B establishment, then just ten minutes from the city centre a quiet stay is ensured in this 1930's house set in approximately 20 acres of parkland. Comfortable, well furnished accommodation. Evening meals available.

Restaurants:

Adlards *(01603 633522), Upper St. Giles Street.* Occupying an 18th Century building, Adlards is a good, steady centre of excellence where everything - from ambience to quantities - are discreet. Well-balanced menus, calling on a full European range, are a notable feature. *Wheelchair access.*

Brasted's *(01603 625949), St. Andrew's Hill.* A warm and intimate atmosphere pervades this restaurant. The menu has a bias towards seafood but not to the exclusion of meats, and none are overly elaborate; classic English and sophisticated European fare are the norm.

By Appointment *(01603 630730), St. George's Street.* Converted from two former shops in buildings which date back to around the 16th Century, the atmosphere here is one of genuine conviviality. The menus are chalked on a blackboard but the food and service are both good and stable. *Wheelchair access.*

Greens Seafood *(01603 623733), Upper St. Giles Street.* As its name suggests, Greens is heavily geared towards seafood - there is very little choice for meat eaters, though rather more for vegetarians - and it is consistent in its quality. Dishes of the day are usually a fresh local catch and are often the better for it. *Wheelchair access but toilet facilities are difficult.*

Hectors House *(01603 622836), Bedford Street.* A combination cafe, bar and restaurant with something of a bohemian air. Equally good for a coffee, beer, glass of wine, snack or full meal. The music can be pretty loud but the range is refreshingly eclectic - anything from classical to rock. Occasional jazz evenings are another feature. The cheerful, friendly service is a plus.

Marco's *(01603 624044), Pottergate.* A long established restaurant with a sophisticated Italian bias, both in its menu and wine list. A favourite for its quiet charm and unhurried atmosphere. *Wheelchair access; toilet facilities difficult.*

St. Benedicts Grill (01603 765377), *St. Benedicts*. A homely restaurant which has steadily gained a considerable reputation for itself (established 1991). Menus are chalked on wall mounted blackboards, and the furnishings are typically coun-trified. Here you get food the British sometimes really want to eat, including bangers and mash, and at very accessible prices. The proprietor was trained by the Roux brothers so do not be misled by the simplicity on offer. The owners have also taken over the next door restaurant, Pinnochio's, but St. Benedicts Grill is easily the winner. *Wheelchair access but toilet facilities difficult.*

Pubs:

The Adam & Eve (01603 667423), *Bishopsgate*. Norwich's oldest pub, parts of which date from 1249, and which once served as a refreshment house for the Cathedral builders and masons. Even though it gets extremely busy, the service is always friendly. Traditional bar food, a good range of ales on handpump and unusually a good choice of wines is to hand.

St. Andrews Tavern (01603 614858), *St. Andrews Street*. A former 16th Century merchant's house, but with a distinctly Victorian interior - interesting brewing and related artefacts adorn the walls. Known for its real ales and also for its live music - usually on Tuesdays and Thursdays. *Wheelchair access.*

The Ugly Bug (01603 880794), *High House Farm Lane, Colton*. Only a ten minute drive east of the city, the Ugly Bug was converted as recently as 1991 from a for-mer house and enjoys a reputation for consistently good, if simple, food and ales. Day fishing permits for the River Yare can be had from the proprietors. *Wheelchair access.*

If you go out to the Ugly Bug, it is worth taking the route via **Bawburgh** (six miles east of Norwich). Documented in *Domesday*, Bawburgh Mill, standing astride the River Yare, was a working Mill until 1967. Behind the Mill is the **Church of St. Mary & St. Walstan,** the latter the patron of agricultural and farm workers. The villagers still pay their annual homage to St. Walstan, the service at the Church being followed by a procession down to the well, its curative waters no longer drawn, and thereafter a ploughman's lunch enjoyed in the grounds of Church Farmhouse.

The Old Post Office buildings date from the 1400's and behind these is Hall Farm housing development which has successfully incorpo-rated into its planning the **18th Century Slipper House and Dovecote.** Both are protected Ancient Monuments and once stood in the grounds of Elizabethan Bawburgh Hall, now demolished.

Walk 21: Norwich

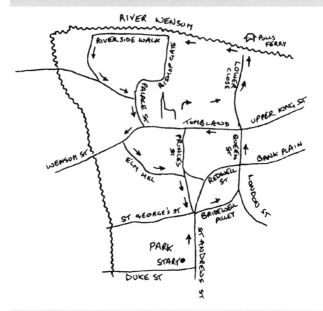

Directions:

1. From the Car Park on Duke Street, return to the Park's main entry point and turn left into Duke Street, up a slight incline to a junction. 2. Turn left into St. Andrews Street, cross the road and take the second right into Bridewell Alley. (Both the Bridewell Museum and Colman's Mustard Shop can be found along here.) 3. Turn left at the top of the Alley, and follow the road round to your right as it joins London Street - go left here to a junction. 4. Cross straight over and go along Queen Street. 5. Go left at the junction, the area here known as Tombland, crossing the road into the Cathedral grounds. Leave the Cathedral by the south door, passing Edith Cavell's grave, and walk down Lower Close to Pulls Ferry. 6. Turn left into Riverside Walk to Bishop Bridge (14th Century), cross the road and continue along Riverside Walk to pass the Medieval Cow Tower. Continue until you reach the Magistrates Courts where you turn left to join Bishopsgate. 7. To visit the Great Hospital, turn left along Bishopsgate, otherwise go right along Bishopsgate, across Palace Place and into Palace Street. 8. At the mini roundabout, go right into Wensum Street and then left through Elm Hill. (St. Peter Hungate is at the top of Elm Hill.) 9. At the top of Elm Hill, go right into Princes Street as it leads down to St. Andrews Plain, where you can visit St. Andrews & Blackfriars Hall. Continue along St. Andrews Street. 10. At the junction on your right with Duke Street either return to your start or continue ahead into Charing Cross to visit Strangers Hall Museum, retracing your steps back to Duke Street.

Approx. Distance: 2.75 Miles
Approx. Time: 2 Hours

The Broads

With very few towns excepting those of Acle and Stalham in the Broadland district, the following Chapter seeks to examine the Broads within the context of the very many small villages and substantial nature reserves which make up the area. An artificial divide has been drawn between the northerly and southerly Broads, the former commencing for this purpose at Wroxham and the latter at Acle.

Wroxham

Given that Wroxham is the main Broads holiday resort we begin our tour of this part of the northern Broads here. Although the village is somewhat tarnished as a result of its vacational pre-eminence, from Easter onwards it is crowded with boats and boaters, it is nevertheless an ideal place either to stock up on provisions if you are on a boating holiday or to hire a boat if you are just visiting for the day. Roys of Wroxham probably rightly claims to be the 'biggest village store in the world' and is still expanding; during the May 1995 VE Day celebrations, however, a substantial part of the store caught fire but no doubt all will be

155

up and re-running before too long. Additionally, there are more than 15 boat-yards in the village offering a variety of water craft for hire.

Yet before the coming of the railway in about 1880, Wroxham was little more than a tiny settlement centred around the Church and Manor House. Thereafter, it became home to the visionary, broads-cruiser builder J. Loynes & Sons Ltd (established circa 1880). It was they who recognised early on the need for day-hire boats and mini-cruisers. Other firms quickly followed Loynes successful beginnings, notably Blakes Norfolk Broads Holidays Ltd (established 1908) and which initially acted solely as a booking agent for other companies. Now something in the order of 13, 000 boats are registered for Broads use alone.

For those wanting to hire a boat, try any of the following: ***Royall & Son*** *(01603 782743);* ***G. Smith & Sons*** *(01603 782527);* ***Moore & Co*** *(01603 378311),* ***Faircraft Loynes*** *(01603 782280),* and ***Fineway Cruisers*** *(01603 782309).* For guided boat tours, try ***Broads Tours*** *(01603 782207)* who run a regular and varied programme (one and a quarter hour and three and a half hour tours) from their base close to the Station; two boats have wheelchair hoists.

Additionally, ***Wherry*** Cruises on board traditional Norfolk craft can be chartered for variable length holidays, anything from a day to a week. *Contact: P. Bower,* ***Wherry Yacht Charter***, *Barton House, Hartwell Road (01603 782470).* Another wherry, *White Moth,* can also be chartered from the ***Norfolk Broads Yachting Company***, *(01493 488479).*

Food & Accommodation

Garden Cottage *(01603 784376), The Limes, 96 Norwich Road, Wroxham.* The very high standard B & B accommodation here makes use of a converted 18th Century barn and stables (the owners live in the nearby farmhouse). Packed lunches available. No evening meals.

Regency Guesthouse *(01692 630233), The Street, Neatishead.* A 17th Century house in the heart of this pretty village. Comfortable B & B accommodation amidst beamed ceilings. Packed lunches by arrangement. No evening meals.

On the other side of the River Bure is ***Hoveton***, a much more attractive spot - quaint shops and houses - than nearby Wroxham. It is a typical Broads village, although at one time seemingly more prosperous than many of the others as evidenced by the number of large houses here.

Chief amongst these is ***Hoveton Hall***, its 10 acre ***garden***, in a woodland setting, open to the public *(01603 782798).* Large walled gardens predominate here, one with an iron gated entrance in the shape of a spider and suitably named the 'spider garden'. The formal walled garden was planted in 1936, and there is also an interesting Victorian kitchen garden. The whole area is laced with streams and bridges and best visited during May or June particularly if you want to catch the

Horning village

many rare varieties of azalea and rhododendron. ***Open Wed, Fri, Sun & Bank Hols, 11-5.30, Easter to mid-September. Admission charge. Wheelchair access.***

Hoveton House, one mile south-east of the village, although not open to the public was built towards the end of the 17th Century, and as Pevsner says, is "... one of the most attractive, if not most perfect, houses of its time in Norfolk." Say no more, except that the gardens were laid out by Humphrey Repton in the early 19th Century. To the northwest is Hoveton Old Hall, again privately owned and not open to the public, and built in the earliest part of the 18th Century with its unusual adjoining barn enhanced with oval windows.

Part of Bure Marshes, ***Hoveton Great Broad*** is only accessible by boat from Wroxham; *weekdays only from May to mid-September*. The trail around it, only half a mile, takes you through a range of fen and wet woodland and is designed to illustrate the origins and wildlife of the area.

Nearby ***Neatishead*** is a charming Georgian village in an unspoilt and little explored area of the northern Broads. The Church of St. Peter on Threehammer Common is late 18th Century but retains elements of a Medieval building.

Gothic Beeston Hall, built in 1786, stands on rising ground overlooking a serpentine lake. Until recently, the gardens to the south of the house were open to the public; whether or not its new owners (1994) intend to continue this practice remains to be seen, but we can at least hope so. The park originally laid out by Richmond, a contemporary of Capability Brown, has now largely been given over to farming though a decent pathway did wind its way down through cornfields to a woodland and lakeside walk.

Another interesting place to visit is Norfolk's **Dried Flower Centre** *(01603 783588), Willow Farm, Cangate, Neatishead*. This is a small, specialist farm growing and supplying quality dried flowers direct to the public. The shop stocks a large selection of flowers, baskets and related sundries. Additionally, the showfields are open during the summer, and workshops can be arranged for groups of six from October to March. The Centre is **open all year, excluding 23 December to mid January, Tue-Sat, 10-4, & Sun 11-4. Also open Bank Hol Mon and Mon during July and August, 10-4.**

On to **Horning** now, a few miles east of Wroxham, and an attractive village surrounded by woodland, and with countless private inlets from the River Bure leading to the homes which grace its banks. Hobbs Mill, an open-framed, trestle windpump, also stands by the River. Horning is once thought to have been a Roman staging post with a ferry operating to Woodbastwick for almost 1,000 years; it is now no longer. Additionally, what were once boat building sheds have now given way to new property developments but most have been attractively deployed. As was the case with most Broadland villages, peat digging here was once a major industry with the villagers themselves allowed to cut 3,000 turfs each year for every property in Horning.

Try to visit Horning either in early June when the Three Rivers Race is set or in August when there is a colourful Regatta on the River. Alternatively, why not take a **Mississippi River Boat** along the River Bure *(01692 630262)*. If you want to explore the waters for yourself, boats can be hired from **Ferry Boatyard Ltd** *(01692 630392)*, **Kingline Cruisers** *(01692 630297)*, and **Horning Pleasurecraft Ltd** *(01692 630128)*.

Coltishall

To the north-west is Coltishall, one of the prettier of the larger Broads villages, and once more important than Wroxham, with a long main street, a rich arrangement of 18th Century houses, and an attractive flint-built school. The

The **Norfolk wherry** was specifically designed for sailing the very shallow Broads and rivers and so facilitating trade in the area and particularly trade between Great Yarmouth and Norwich. To many isolated communities, these boats were their only lifeline with the outside world and their only access to all but the most basic of local commodities. The wherries had to be able to tack in very narrow waters, drop their masts quickly and deftly to shoot the countless bridges along these waterways, be man-powered when the winds failed, be capable of negotiating reed beds and of carrying a heavy cargo at great speed. Quite a tall order! Inevitably, there was much competition between the various building yards to produce the fastest and most efficient boats. Usually, however, they were about 58 feet in length, with a long, straight keel, and a 40 feet high adjustable mast. They also had to be capable of carrying something in the order of 40 tons of cargo.

Old Maltings on the banks of the River Bure have now been converted to residential use, and the old boat sheds on Anchor Street have also given way to a new housing complex. At one time, Anchor Street was renowned for its boat building. Coltishall, legend has it, was the birthplace of the wherry and from the 1850's onwards John Allan's yard in Anchor Street perfected its design, building some of the fastest wherries in Norfolk; *Ella*, the last wherry to be built in Norfolk was appropriately launched from Coltishall in 1912.

Today, Coltishall has gained a reputation for itself for antiques: try **Eric Bates** (01603 738716) on the High Street for furniture, and opposite is the **Coltishall Antiques Centre** (01603 738306) where amongst other sought-after collectibles, a good choice of pistols and other armoury can be found. For cycle hire contact **Just Pedalling** (01603 737201), 9 Church Street, Coltishall.

Food & Accommodation

The Chequers (01603 891657), Hainford. An attractive, thatched pub in a picturesque setting. Imaginative foods and good ales. **Wheelchair access.**

The Red Lion (01603 737402), Coltishall. Pleasantly situated close to the Staithe this is a sympathetically furnished pub, making use of several split levels. Good food and ales. **Wheelchair access.**

The Rising Sun (01603 737440), Coltishall. On the edge of the River Bure, this is a large family pub with a good range of food. Probably best appreciated on a bright, sunny day when you can sit outside and enjoy the soothing, lapping waters of the River. **Wheelchair access.**

Horstead pretty well adjoins Coltishall, just on the opposite banks of the River Bure; the weatherboarded Mill, with its ground floor on arches and topped with six little gables, marks the head of the navigation stream. What was the miller's house, built in the early 19th Century, using yellow brick, stands across the road. All Saints Church retains some of its 13th Century features though much is of a later 19th Century date; if you do go there, look for some notable stained glass by both Burne-Jones and Kempe.

Stalham

Moving to the northerly fringes of the Broads we come to Stalham Staithe, separated by the main A 149 from its busy Georgian market town, but nonetheless a popular holiday destination. On the Staithe side, note the former Granary of 1808 which still retains its riverside wharf running underneath the building to the wherry bays. Close by, are the remains of a Cornmill dating from the early 1800's but closed and truncated since the 1930's.

The town itself is worth looking over. St. Mary's Church with its large but squat, unfinished tower faces the main street with its modest, but nevertheless charming, brick-built Georgian houses. Best of all is Stalham Hall, built circa

1670 for a Robert Puckle, with its stepped gables. Back to the Church for a moment though for it originally came under the control of the Abbot of St. Benet's Abbey and as its tower was only in the build stage in around 1530 during the Dissolution movement, when the Abbey itself was closed, it, therefore, remains unfinished. Stalham's former wealth is testimony to the success of the hand-weaving industry in these parts, and also to its previous position as a basket-making centre - the prime product being the 'skeps' or 'peds' used by the Great Yarmouth fishermen.

Boat hire from Stalham is via *Stalham Yacht Services* *(01692 580288)*, *John Williams Boats* *(01692 580953)*,or *Richardsons (Stalham) Ltd* *(01692 581081)*.

Food & Accommodation

The Butchers Arms *(01692 650237)*, East Ruston. A well restored village pub with an attractive and colourful garden and known for good food and ale. ***Wheelchair access.***

The Swan Inn *(01692 581099)*, Ingham. A 14th Century, thatched freehouse, originally forming part of the Priory and which has lost none of its charm in the renovation process. An excellent range of ales and generous, wholesome food is offered. Quality accommodation is in the nearby stable block.

Sutton Staithe Hotel *(01692 580244)*, Sutton. An attractive, 17th Century former farmhouse where the waters of Sutton Staithe lap close to its doors. The bar is regularly used by locals, and no wonder with its small alcoves, built-in-seating and antique settles. The accommodation is also of a good standard. ***Wheelchair access.***

At nearby *Ingham*, the Church of the Holy Trinity, founded in 1360 by Sir Miles Stapleton, was once closely interlocked, at least on the north side, with the former Trinitarian Priory. Very little now remains of the Priory - traces of the cloister arches, for example, can be found to the north of the nave - but it is thought the Church was partly used by the Priory. Unusually, and considered a rarity by the architectural scholar Nikolaus Pevsner, the south porch is three-storeys high, the upper floors probably forming the parish priest's living quarters. A very interesting tomb-chest and effigy commemorating Sir Oliver de Ingham (d. 1344) can be found in the chancel.

Not far from Stalham is *Sutton Windmill* *(01692 581195)*, an impressive 18th Century, nine-storey Tower Mill. In working order until 1940, its internal mechanisms and sails have recently been rescued from dereliction by its owners. If possible, do climb the stairs to the top for some really splendid views of the surrounding Broadland countryside. Also here is the *Broads Museum of Social Life*. Exhibits in the Museum building and Engine House include considerable displays of cooper's, blacksmith's, plumber's and carpenter's tools. There is also an authentic 1880's pharmacy as well as extensive domestic and kitchen paraphernalia. *Open daily, 10-6, April to end September. Admission charge.*

Walk 22: Dilham Canal

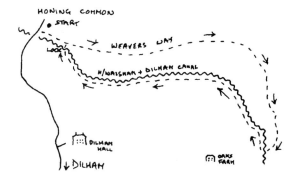

Directions:

1. From Honing Common, walk towards the railway bridge but do not cross it. Instead, follow a track which runs to the right hand side of it and turn left onto the Weavers Way along a dismantled railway line.
2. Cross a small bridge over a dyke and go through a gate. Just before the second gate turn right and off the Weavers Way. Follow the farm track which passes by the former crossing-keeper's cottage; the keeper had the enviable task of ensuring that cattle did not stray from the meadow onto the line. Continue along the farm track as it runs along the left hand side of the field. Go through a gate and continue along the path. 3. After a second gate, bear diagonally right across the field to reach the Tonnage Bridge. Cross the bridge and turn immediately right onto the other bank of the Canal. Follow this beautiful stretch of the canal's bank for about one and a half miles and then cross the footbridge at the end of this stretch. 4. Cross the bridge over the lock and follow the path round to where it rejoins the Weavers Way. Turn left to return to Honing Common along the opening stretch of this walk

Start: Honing Common
Approx. Distance: 4 Miles
Approx. Time: 2 Hours
Map: Landranger 133

Dilham, between Stalham and North Walsham, has always been very much a Broads backwater and despite the opening, in 1826, of the North Walsham & Dilham Canal. Sadly, the Canal never became the success that was intended; the last wherry bringing its cargo upstream from Bacton Wood Staithe in 1934, and even in its heyday only three wherries per day could use the Canal due to shortages in the water table. The walk described above is one of the most beautiful in Broadland and must, therefore, be strongly recommended. The wooded glade along the canal's banks on the second leg is quite idyllic; if you are lucky, you may also see the occasional kingfisher. The half-way mark is an unusual brick-built structure, the Tonnage Bridge, restored in 1982 at a cost of around £30,000. The walk also makes use of the *Weavers Way*, a 56 mile long pathway between Cromer and Great Yarmouth and no doubt used by the weavers of years gone by for distributing their wares.

Perhaps appropriately, it was here, in Dilham, that Sir William Cubbitt, a miller's son was born. Throughout his distinguished career, he was responsible for cutting canals, improving rivers, initiating vast drainage schemes and building many a railway tunnel; in 1851, he was knighted for his efforts towards the Great Exhibition of that year.

Irstead, north-east of Wroxham and south-west of Stalham, is a small settlement, dominated by the thatched Church of St. Michael, along the banks of the River Ant. The octagonal font is a fine 14th Century example depicting the Head of Christ and the hand of God together with other motifs, and standing on a stem of eight statuettes.

Nearby, between Horning and Irstead, is *Alderfen Broad*, sufficiently isolated to protect itself from pollution in the River Ant. Here is one of very few Broads still supporting a wide variety of water plants, especially the rigid hornwort and yellow and white waterlilies. The area also supports a good range of birdlife - including grebe and heron - and large colonies of frogs and common toads. The Reserve is managed by the Norfolk Naturalists Trust; a public footpath runs across the Reserve and a track from Threehammer Common leads directly to the Broad.

For those wishing to enjoy a day's fishing, Alderfen Broad is reputedly good for a catch of bream, pike and trench. The fishing here is from boats only and permits can be had from *Wroxham Angling Centre (01603 782453), Station Road.* Note the Broad is currently closed for the 1995 fishing season but may possibly re-open in 1996.

Close by is *Barton Turf*, a small Broadland village, the origin of which probably lies in the seasonal efforts of workers in digging peat (i.e. turf). Visit St. Michael's Church with its fine rood screen, considered to be one of the best in England, dating from the 15th Century and depicting three saints and an order of angels; this is what is known as a Heavenly Hierarchy. Also depicted is Henry IV; this is a rare portrait of the man and consequently is of great historical interest. Following a spate of burglaries, the Church is now sadly only accessible by prior arrangement; details are posted on the door. Nearby is Barton Broad Nature Reserve administered by the Norfolk Naturalists Trust. The Reserve provides a mixture of wet alder woodland, bulrush, reed and sedge beds. The bearded tit, great crested grebe and swallowtail butterfly all breed in the area. There is also a small heronry but access to this is strictly prohibited. The Broad itself is almost unapproachable by land though a short boarded walkway runs along Paddy's Dyke. The best access is inevitably afforded by boat from the River Ant.

Walk 23: Alderfen Broad

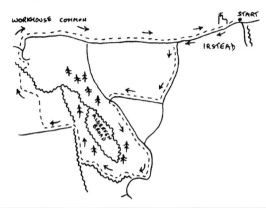

Directions:

1. From the Staithe at Irstead Shoals, follow the road to a junction and on to another junction where you turn left (the second left on your map after the Church). When you reach a thatched farm, go right and follow this lane to its end where you go left. 2. At the end of this, near a group of bungalows, turn right into Irstead Street. Follow this road round a right bend but as the road later bends to the left cross the rails near a sluice into the woodland carr. 3. Follow the yellow path marks around this southern corner of Alderfen Broad to a bridge over the ditch. Once over this, go left (but keeping the ditch on your left) until you meet another path. 4. Go right here until you reach the Staithe. At the Staithe, bear left for about 100 yards and then right into a farm track. Following the left hand side of two fields, aim for the field corner and then go left through a gap following the right edge of a field. Just before a cottage go right through a hedge, over the ditch and into another field. The path leads straight ahead and follow this until it joins a road. 5. Go left and follow this road round for about one and a half miles (ignoring the left hand junctions) as it skirts Workhouse Common and leads back to Irstead Staithe.

Start: Irstead Staithe
Approx. Distance: 4 Miles
Approx. Time: 1.75 Hours
Map: Landranger 134

Potter Heigham

None of the main Broads holiday centres are especially attractive and Potter Heigham is no exception. Its only appealing feature; the Medieval bridge with its particularly low and narrow arch. Larger hire craft using the River Thurne here *must* have an official bridge pilot to take them through this structure, and some hirecraft operators even have their own pilot service to assist holiday-makers along this stretch. Potter Heigham's saving grace is probably the easy access it affords to the Broads, either on foot or via local boat hire, and its shopping facilities which enable holiday makers to stock up on supplies. For boat hire, try: **Maycraft** *(01692 670241)* or **Herbert Woods** *(01692 670711)*. Alternatively, **Broads Tours/Herbert Woods** *(01692 670711)* operate one and a half hour and two and a half hour guided trips along the River Thurne from their base here.

The village originally gets its name from its once famous pottery industry which flourished from as early as pre-Roman times through to the Middle Ages. Sometime ago, a huge mound of ash, as tall as a cottage, was found in the near-by field of pot-hills. This mound, apparently, represented the remains of the former Roman furnaces.

Having given Potter Heigham a quick once-over, head for **Ludham** with its attractive houses and a large 14th Century Church. Inside St. Catherine's is a fine screen with paintings of 11 saints and a king on the dado. Other unusual features include a large 15th Century poor box, a mysterious stone hand which reaches out from the south aisle, and a 15th Century painting of the Crucifixion. Ludham Hall, with its plain Georgian front, was remodelled from a Jacobean house and, together with the brick and towered 17th Century Chapel at right angles to it, formed part of an old palace of the Bishops of Norwich (Pevsner says Bishops of Lincoln but this would seem highly unlikely) and later belonged to the poet Cowper's mother. It is now a farmhouse. The other particularly attractive house is the 17th Century Hull Common with its wooden cross windows, gables, and chequered brickwork. Two derelict windmills add to this picturesque environment - one stands below Ludham Bridge and the other, still with its sails intact, is about a mile north-west of the Church.

One of the few surviving wherries, *The Albion*, can be found at Womack, Ludham. Indeed, for many years it was the only surviving wherry and is that much more unusual for being carvel rather than clinker built (it was originally a Bungay built boat). It is maintained by the **Norfolk Wherry Trust** *(01603 505815)* and can be visited by prior arrangement. Better still, it is *available for*

St. Benet's Abbey

private charter from April to September. Day hire boats can be obtained from **Ludham Marine** *(01692 678322).* If you are an experienced yachtie then why not try a gaff-rigged sloop from the Norfolk **County Sailing Base** *(01692 678263).* The collection here was used for the BBC's serialisation of Arthur Ransome's *Coot Club.* (Note, negotiations are currently underway for the sale of this collection but hopefully the County Council will ensure the fleet is kept together and the service continued.) The nearby Ludham Marsh, now under the care of the Nature Conservancy Council, abounds with wild flora and fauna, and in particular the rare Norfolk aestina dragonfly. There is also free coarse-fishing - bream and roach - along a two mile stretch of the river, upstream and downstream, from Ludham Bridge.

About two miles south-west of Ludham, on the banks of the River Bure, is **St. Benet's Abbey**, founded on land granted by King Canute in 1020. The Abbey grew to be one of the wealthiest Benedictine houses in the country, reaching its height of prosperity in the Middle Ages but declining before the Reformation. St. Benet's was the only English monastery to escape Dissolution; Henry VIII and the last Abbot Bishop agreed a deal, in 1536, whereby the Bishop handed over the Estates belonging to Norwich Cathedral but was able to hold onto those of the Abbey. None of the ruins date from an early period and the best preserved is the gatehouse, owing to the fact that an 18th Century brick Windmill was built inside its ruins; sadly the cap and sails were lost in a gale in 1863.

The Bishop of Norwich still holds the title of the Bishop of St. Benet's - the only mitred Abbot in the House of Lords - and still attends a service, travelling there by water, usually on the first Sunday in August. The Abbey and its grounds, however, are today, owned by Norwich Union and leased to a local farmer. Legend also has it that the ghost of the monk who treacherously granted access to William the Conqueror - until then the Normans had unsuccessfully besieged the Abbey for several months - can be seen hanging from the former bell tower on each night of 25th May. The Abbey ruins *can be visited all year, free of charge* but do be mindful that this is private property, and liberty should not be taken with the access which is granted

To the north-west of Ludham is *How Hill* best known for its Nature Reserve representing as it does a microcosm of Broadland habitat - from carr woodland to reed and sedge beds, and supported by clear dykes. The whole area is managed by How Hill Trust and includes Reedham Water and Cromes Broad. Two Windpumps can be visited: B*oardman's Drainage Mill* with its open-framed, timber-trestle windpump and working turbine is *open daily,* and *Clayrack Drainage Mill* is especially interesting for its double scoop wheel and has a full set of patent sails. Furthermore, Toad Hole, a tiny thatched cottage once the home of a local marshman and eel-catcher, is now an environmental centre for the Broads. *The nature trail around How Hill is open all year, free of charge.* The *house and gardens at How Hill* *(01692 678555)* are only open on special azalea days during May. A formal, Edwardian terraced garden overlooks the valley, and the less formal water and woodland garden is thickly planted with a superb display of azaleas. Phone for opening times. ***Admission charge. Wheelchair access.*** Alternatively, take a trip aboard *The Electric Eel*, an Edwardian-style boat, accompanied by an experienced Broads guide. Trips run every hour from How Hill Staithe, June to September, and a reduced service is operated Easter to May and October. Booking is advisable; phone *01692 678763*.

Walk 24: Womack Water and Ludham Marsh

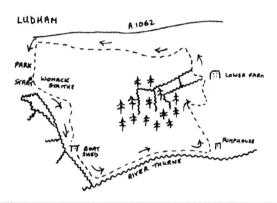

Directions:

1. From the car park at Womack Staithe (Ludham), go right in a south-easterly direction along the track (houses to your left and right). Ignore a left junction and continue towards a boatshed on Womack Water. Follow the path along Womack Water until you reach the River Thurne. 2. Go left along the banks of the River Thurne for about three-quarters of a mile until you come to a single storey pumphouse. 3. Turn left here and cross a footbridge, following the path which runs alongside the dyke (on your left). 4. At a meeting of paths, bear right onto a grassy lane for a short distance, and then left onto a track which leads alongside Lower Farm and then to a group of cottages. 5. Look for a path on your left in between these cottages and continue along here into Ludham. Finally turn left to return to your start.

Start: Womack Staithe
Approx. Distance: 3.5. Miles
Approx. Time: 1.5 Hours
Map: Landranger 134

Martham, a few miles south-east of Potter Heigham, derives its name, 'the home of the marts', from the vast numbers of pine martens or 'marts' which nested in the once extensive oak woodlands around here. A group of fine Georgian houses skirt the spacious village green. St. Mary's Church with its enormous lead-spiked west tower, however, dominates the skyline; story has it that the flints for the tower were hauled from the seashore by women parishioners. Look out for the curious gravestone in the churchyard commemorating

Alice Burraway with its inscription:

> *"... in this life (she was) my sister*
> *my mistress, my mother and my wife."*

Placed by her husband, it summarises a rather sad and bizarre personal history; he was born following an incestuous relationship between his sister and father. Unknowingly, he later marries the woman, having previously worked for her (i.e. his mistress).

Martham Broad is made up of two small Broads, north and south, with the River Thurne running between them. The extensive reed and sedge beds here support a variety of plantlife including the rare holly leaved naiad, and white and yellow waterlilies. Dragonflies, damselflies and butterflies are also in abundance. Managed by the Norfolk Naturalists Trust, the Reserve has two public footpaths which facilitate good access. For the more adventurous, yachts and cruisers can be hired from **Martham Ferry Boatyard** *(01493 740303)*. Alternatively, free coarse fishing on a three and a half mile stretch along the left hand bank of the River, between Martham and Repps, is available. Fishing from the private bungalow frontages, however, is definitely not permitted.

Hickling

One of my favourite places on the Broads, especially out of season, is Hickling where the village can be found to the north of Hickling Broad, midway between Potter Heigham and Stalham. The Broad here is the largest stretch of open water in Broadland and is probably best approached by the Pleasure Boat Staithe. Some of the original buildings of an Augustinian Priory, established in 1185, can still be found at Priory Farm. The other buildings of note are Hickling Hall, built circa 1700, and the now sail-less but seven-storey high tower Cornmill, built 1817, and retaining its traditional Norfolk, boat shaped cap.

Hickling Cornmill

The 1, 361 acre site at **Hickling Broad** was bought by the Norfolk Naturalists Trust in 1945, and is a haven for birds migrating between Africa and the Arctic - waders, sandpipers, osprey and spoonbill among others. Prior to the Norfolk Naturalists Trust ownership, much of the **Reserve** was a world-famous wild-fowl shoot used by kings and cabinet ministers alike. Thankfully, however, rarities such as as the Norfolk hawker dragonfly and swallowtail butterfly still breed here. The Broad is also renowned for its fishing - especially pike and bream - and its excellent reeds, used locally and further afield, for thatching. There are a number of nature trails of varying length around the Broad starting from the Warden's House in Stubb Road *(01692 598276); **admission charge for adults but children go free.** A **Water Trail,** in a replica lighter (the traditional craft for carrying reeds and sedge), can be taken from the Pleasure Boat Staithe and requires two and a half hours. Booking for this is essential *(01692 598276); admission charge..* The Reserve is **open daily from April to October.** Boats -cruisers, lug sails and rowing boats - can be hired from **Whispering Reeds Boats** *(01692 598314).*

Walk 25: Hickling Broad

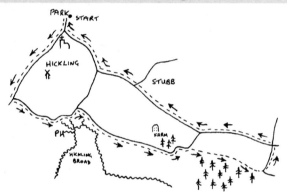

Directions:
1. From Hickling Green car park, go left past the Church, using the path behind the back and continue along here until you reach a junction, signed Hickling Broad. 2. Go left here and continue along Staithe Road round the edge of the Broad until you reach a junction. Ignore Ouse Lane straight ahead of you, and instead turn right along the edge of the Broad leading past Hill Common. Continue along this lane until it reaches Willow Farm where you bear left and then right. 3. Ignore the next left and continue straight ahead along the path which leads to the Warden's House. (If you want to use the Reserve you must get a permit from the Warden.) 4. At the Warden's House turn left until it reaches a road and then left again into Stubb Road. Stubb Road continues for about one mile. Ignore the next right junction known as the Causeway, and go on to the next junction, this one with Ouse Lane. 5. Go right here which will take you back to a junction on the corner of which is your start.

Start: Hickling Green Approx. Distance: 4 Miles
Approx. Time: 1.75 Hours Map: Landranger 134

Horsey Mill

Horsey

Further east and situated just a short distance from the coast, most of Horsey is now under National Trust care and is typically unspoilt. Its best known feature is the Mill, a four-storey red-brick Waterpump, complete with cap and sails and used for draining the surrounding land. Rebuilt in 1912, it was working until 1943 when it was struck by lightening, rendering it inoperative. The area is prone to flooding, although new sea defenses, completed in 1988, should go some way to alleviate the worst effects. In 1938, for example, thousands of acres of land were flooded here, only 100 acres of Horsey remaining above water level. It took four months just to drain the land and a further five years before farming could once again commence.

Food & Accommodation

The Nelsons Head *(01493 393378), Horsey.* Basically furnished and where appropriate a nautical theme pervades. Decent food and ales, and a warm welcome.

The National Trust *(01225 791199)* has three properties available for self-catering just a ten minute walk from Horsey beach and Mere. The accommodation has been converted from traditional thatched farm buildings. (Sleeps 4; 4-6; 4-6.)

Horsey Mere, an attractive and rich expanse of water, over 1,700 acres in extent, is easily explored whether by foot or boat. Legend has it that on every 13th June, the wails of small children who drowned in the Mere years ago on that day can still be heard. The Mere is today known worldwide for its winter wild-fowl; in particular it is a stronghold for the marsh harrier, so do keep your eyes peeled. Horsey is one of the few places where the Broads and the coast can be explored within a few hundred yards of each other; to do so follow the walk described below.

Walk 26: Horsey Mere

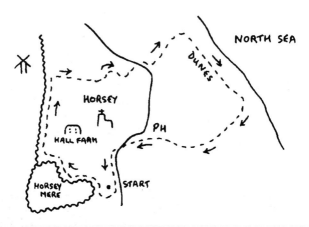

Directions:

1. From the National Trust car park at Horsey Mere Windpump, go up the bank and with the Windpump in front of you, go right following the path along the boat dyke and the edge of the Mere. Follow this path round to the boathouse and go left until you come to a bridge down on the bank. 2. Once over this, keep to the left across the marsh to a series of small bridges - five to be exact - until you reach a long straight dyke. 3. Once on the dyke, go right for approximately one mile until you reach Brograve Mill, now derelict. 4. From the Mill, go right to a series of wooden rails and cross into the field following the right hand edge of that field to a fence. Continue through this to a field corner where you bear left to a plank bridge. Once over this, continue beyond the plantation to Horsey Corner following the lane eastwards until you see a path to your left. 5. Follow this left hand path until it joins the Sea Palling road and go right. Shortly after, look for a track on your left which leads down to the beach. Beyond the sand dunes, follow the coastline to your right. (Note: if it is very windy, follow the path behind the dunes which will afford you some protection although sight of the sea will be lost.) 6. At the first major break in the sea defenses, go right over the dunes along an obvious path which leads into a track. At a junction, bear right on a road which takes you past the pub and an old barn dated 1742. 7. At the junction with the main road, go left and follow that road until you reach the car park: some care is needed along this stretch of road as it is narrow and in places there is little in the way of a path.

Start: Horsey Mere car park   Approx. Distance: 6 Miles
Approx. Time: 2.5 Hours Map: Landranger 134

Acle

Acle, a pleasant market town - the market dates back to the 13th Century - is our first port of call in the more southerly Broads region. The Thursday auctions (market day is also on Thursday) here are known for their bicycle bargains. Acle Bridge, one mile north-east of the town, was once the site of many executions, the hapless criminals hung from its parapets. Sadly, this former stone structure has been replaced by a concrete one but is is nonetheless not a bad spot. Boats can be hired at Acle Bridge from either *Horizon Craft (01493 750283)* or *Anchor Craft (01493 750500)*.

Stokesby is an unspoilt village by the River Bure with its thatched Church and Windmill even though the latter is minus its cap and sails; several drainage mills are dotted around the immediate area here but best of all is the *Stacey Arms Windpump* which also houses an exhibition on the Broads drainage mills. *Open daily, 9-8, April to September.* Free moorings are available for those on boating holidays. The brasses in St. Andrew's Church, mainly to the Clere family, are worth spending a few minutes over.

Food & Accommodation

The Ferry Inn (01493 751096), Stokesby. A pleasant, characterful pub on the banks of the River Bure. Free moorings are available for boating customers. Good generous food is only available during the summer months, and occasional guest beers add to the decent ales otherwise available.

Ormesby, Rollesby and *Filby Broads*, also known as *Trinity Broads,* lie approximately three miles north-east of Acle Bridge and are worth exploring for their beauty and isolation; they were originally Saxon peat excavations filled by the rising sea water. Just outside Filby is *Mautby Post Mill* - a rare example in Norfolk where the sails are made to face the wind by completely rotating the mill on a central post. Most mills in Norfolk have just a rotating cap. The area is fun when explored on horseback and the following BHS approved establishment is helpful in this respect: *Hillcrest Riding School (01493 730394), Hillcrest Farm, Filby Heath,* which can be found on the A 1064 between Acle and Caister.

Brundall, almost midway between Norwich and Acle, and just off the A 47, is a select riverside village with an Edwardian air, enjoying marshes and reed beds to its south. Although tradition, perhaps legend, has it that the Romans had a shipyard here, today a large marina makes a sound base for many boating companies. The tiny 13th Century Church of St. Lawrence stands in the middle of fields; it is reported to have the only lead font, decorated with fleur-de-lis, in Norfolk, together with some good stained glass dating from the 16th Century. Boats can be hired from *Buccaneer Boats (01603 712057), Fencraft (01603 715011), Harvey Eastwood (01603 713345),* and *Bees Boats (01603 713446).*

On various days throughout *April and May, Lake House Water Gardens* are *open to the public*, and were once part of a 76 acre estate and arboretum plant-ed around 1880; its history has been written up by the owners, Mr & Mrs G. Muter. Here you can enjoy an acre of water gardens set in a deep cleft in the river escarpment. Wild flowers are plentiful as are many rare and unusual species in the more formal planting arrangement. A small *admission charge* is made and a variety of plants are offered for sale. There is, however, only limit-ed parking.

At *Strumpshaw Fen*, five miles of footpaths are provided through a full range of Broadland habitats and is well worth the visit just to explore these. Strumpshaw is a tidal Broad, overgrown with reed sweet-grass. As for its birdlife, all three native woodpeckers can be seen, and warblers, harriers, and bearded tits all breed on the Fen. A visitors' centre and hide is by the entrance to the Broad, over the railway crossing at the head of Strumpshaw Road. The village itself, is small, built around the minuscule slopes of Strumpshaw Hall; there is a fine colourful 15th Century screen in St. Peter's Church.

Cantley

Salubrious, Cantley is not, but if nothing else it does at least remind us of how the Broads were once used as a commercial transport system. For on the edge of the River Yare, south of Acle, is an imposing sugar beet factory where the sugar is extracted from the crop and the remaining pulp waste packaged and returned to the farmers as cattle feed. Sugar beet forms a significant element of the local farming economy as seen by the volume of smoke which bellows from the factory's chimneys during the autumn and winter months, and by the con-stant stream of trucks which hurtle their way through the village.

The factory is the only industrial site to be seen on the Broads, and was first con-ceived by Dutchman, Jerald van Rossum. Cantley was chosen as the site for two obvious reasons - it afforded boat access to and from Great Yarmouth via the Yare, and was further supported by the Norwich - Great Yarmouth railway line. Building of the factory was begun in 1912 at a phenomenal cost, at least then, of £170, 000. Early days, however, were unsuccessful, further compounded by a shortage of growers during the years of World War I, and four years later, in 1916, the factory closed. All was not lost though for in 1921, the English Beet Sugar Corporation moved in, and within the first 12 months profits were begin-ning to show; doubtless, such profits have continued to grow and especially with the processes here handling over one million tonnes per year of the crop. Interestingly, the factory continues to make use of the Yare for transporting its products - the tanker *Blackheath* being a regular caller.

A short distance north of Cantley and marooned on the banks of the River Yare is St. Nicholas' Church, Buckenham, considered exceptional for its octagonal tower - octagonal from base to top. Until the mid 1970's it also housed one of Norfolk's oldest bells; this is thought to have been stolen around that time.

Halvergate

A few miles south-east of Acle will take you to Halvergate Marshes which remain the most substantial area of grazing marsh in the east of England. In earlier times, cattle would have been herded all the way from Scotland to be fattened on these marshes before their journey to London, and their eventual slaughter. It is an ideal habitat for wildlife - wildfowl and waders - and the fact that this remains so is due to the fact that Halvergate Marshes was the first experimental scheme whereby farmers were paid for retaining the traditional management of the land.

Rising over 70 feet high, with seven-storeys, the ***Berney Arms Windpump*** *(01493 700605)* is one of the finest windmills in the country, and hopefully will always remain a prominent feature of these marshes. It was originally built in 1870 to grind cement clinker, but was later converted for marsh drainage and in use until the early 1950's. In the care of English Heritage, the Mill is in perfect working order and houses a permanent exhibition. It can be approached by boat or train (Berney Arms Station) or via a three mile walk from Wickhampton ***Open Mon & Tue, 10-6, and Wed-Sun, 9-5. Closed 1-2. April to September. Admission charge.*** If you are using the rail service, remember when you are wanting to pick the train up from Berney Arms to give a hand signal to the driver, otherwise the train will go straight through the station - it is after all the smallest station in England, built circa 1843, and one of the most desolate. Note the pub near the Mill, is only open during the summer. Managed by the RSPB, the ***Berney Marsh Reserve*** (part of Halvergate Marshes), consisting of over 1, 300 acres of grazing marsh, hosts a large population of Bewick swans, snipe and yellow wagtails. In winter, it also supports lapwing and lapland bunting among other species. Additionally, just before the Berney Arms Windmill, the Rivers Waveney and Yare merge to form Breydon Water, a 925 acre estuary also managed by the RSPB. Look out for cormorants and seals.

Berney Arms Windpump from across Breydon Water

Walk 27: Halvergate Marsh and the Berney Arms Windpump

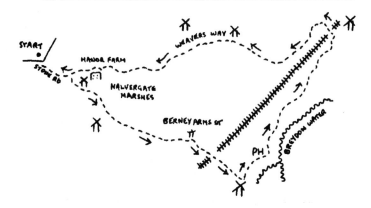

Directions:

1. From the car park at the end of Stone Road, go right over the stiles and avoiding the left hand return route along the Weavers Way. This is a winding, grassy track permitting views of the Berney Arms Mill in the distance. Before this, however, you will come across two other windpumps, both sail-less. 2. Just before one of these derelict mills, turn right over a bridge into a field. Follow the ditch on your left round this field and so to another bridge. Once over this, go a short distance towards a gate and into a meadow, and on over another meadow until a track from Wickhampton Marsh, on your right, is reached.

3. Go along this for a short distance, approximately 200 yards, and then cross the ditch via a footbridge on your right. The path now seems to head directly towards Berney Arms Mill. 4. After a gate, make for the bridge in the distance, and turn left onto the right hand bank of the dyke as far as Berney Arms Station. The path leads across the railway track to the Mill. 5. From the Mill, go left along the riverbank, passing the pub. Follow the bank as far as the Berney Sluices, early on you will pass the point where the Rivers Yare and Waveney meet and so run into Breydon Water. 6. At Breydon Sluices (i.e. Breydon pump) cross the railway track once again and into a concrete road; this twists left and right but just before a deep ditch go left into a faint track, a Weavers Way signpost gives you the added encouragement you may need. 7. Continue along this for about three-quarters of a mile to a gate. Once through the gate, the path goes between two farms and past another disused windpump.

8. Opposite a second disused windpump, the track veers to the left and stays reasonably close to the edge of The Fleet for about one and a half miles. 9. At Manor Farm, go left behind the cottages until after the last half mile you rejoin Stone Road and your start.

Start: At the end of Stone Road, south-east of Halvergate
Approx. Distance: 9 Miles
Approx. Time: 5 Hours (slow conditions when muddy)
Map: Landranger 134

Reedham

Make a special journey within the southern Broads region if you possibly can to Reedham, if only to use one of very few private ferries (this the only one in East Anglia) still in operation, and even the future of this is now threatened. The chain ferry provides the only vehicle crossing over the River Yare and the marshes between Norwich and Great Yarmouth, and it is a service which has been in use, in various guises, since the 16th Century. Only three cars can be carried at any one time, so a wait in the summer months is to be expected. Large sea-going vessels are often to be seen along this stretch of the Yare, especially in winter, the *Blackheath* which carries oil to the sugar beet factory at Cantley. Please note that caution should be exercised by anyone using the River Yare here as it has an unusually fast-running tide involving a rise and drop of about three feet. Reedham was also once an important wherry building centre with the reputable Hall's Yard only closing in 1906, but the boatyards are still to be seen here.

The Church of St. John the Baptist is worth visiting - gutted by fire in 1981 but rebuilt by the villagers in just 15 months. Ironically, the fire revealed some interesting structural features - blocks of freestone interlaid with bricks, and flax tiles of Roman origin (thought to have once been part of a Roman lighthouse or Pharos), and herringbone brickwork both inside and out.

Food & Accommodation

The Ferry Inn *(01493 700429), Reedham.* Good food and ales in very pleasant surroundings on the edge of the River Yare; if you have arrived by boat the mooring fee is refundable against what you consume. The secluded back bar is probably the most interesting with its antique rifles and open log fire. Much care is taken to ensure you enjoy your stay, including the provision of showers in the toilets for those who use the moorings. *Wheelchair access.*

Mornington House *(01508 528572), 33 Church Plain, Loddon.* A former inn, this 16th Century house stands close by the Church; Charles Wesley is once said to have stayed here, presumably following a service he attended. The B & B accommodation is of a high standard and the welcome warm. No evening meals

South-west of Reedham, **Loddon** was once a Broads Port. A predominance of Georgian houses continue to line Loddon's main street and a watermill on the River Chet reminds us of how this water connects with the main River Yare. The Church of the Holy Trinity, built by the Hobart's of Hales Hall, stands amidst a vast graveyard and is thought to have succeeded an earlier one founded by St. Felix in 630 AD. Inside, there is an unusual screen decorated with scenes from the Martyrdom of St. William of Norwich and from the Life of Christ. Additionally, there are some excellent brasses and monuments, and an oak almsbox thought to be the last relic of the first church. Chedgrave is the northerly continuation of Loddon. It is thought that the Church of All Saints houses some 16th and 17th Century stained glass from Rouen Cathedral no less. Boats can be hired from *Aston Boats (01508 520353)*, *Loddon*, *Gale Cruisers (01508 520300)*, *Maffett Cruisers (01508 520344)*, and *Pacific Cruisers (01508 520321)*; the latter three to be found at *The Pits, Chedgrave*.

Hardley Flood, near Loddon, is an important site for winter wildfowl (teal, gadwill and shoveler amongst others) and for bearded tits. Spring migrants include osprey and a variety of waders. The Flood is a spillway for the River Chet, and the river wall is permanently breached in two places ensuring that tidal waters move freely and constantly between marsh and river. A public footpath follows the north bank of the River Chet either from Chedgrave Common or Hardley Hall. Two bird hides are also available; the keys are with the Norfolk Naturalists Trust Warden.

Hales Hall, just south of Loddon, was built by Sir James Hobart, Attorney General to Henry VII. A moat surrounds the last remaining wing of what was a large, early 15th Century Manor. The gardens here have undergone extensive restoration after centuries of neglect - rare and unusual perennials are a feature, as is the National Collection of citrus fruit, figs and greenhouse grapes. The adjoining nurseries offer an extensive range of conservatory plants, vines, figs and even mulberries, and can provide planting advice should you need it. The Great Barn, built in 1478, is also open and especially noteworthy for its roof timbers. *The gardens and nursery are open Tue-Sat, 10-1 & 2-5, (01508 548395),* and other times by appointment. There is an honesty box by the entrance.

Walk 28: Hardley Flood

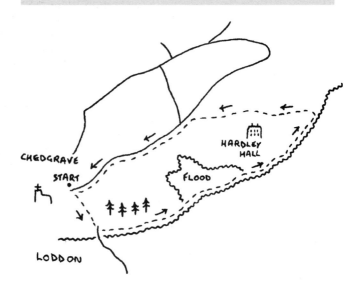

Directions:

1. From All Saints Church at Chedgrave, cross the playground to the road. Bear right along this road until it becomes a right hand bend where you cross the stile in front of you and head towards the River Chet. 2. Turn left onto the riverbank to another stile. Once over this continue along the banks of the Chet to Hardley Flood (a series of footbridges will be crossed). Continue along the bank to the head of the Flood to a stile. 3. Once over this, go left along a path which joins the one you are now leaving and which leads to a group of cottages and a little further on a crossroads (look out for Hardley Hall on your left). 4. Go straight over the crossroads and continue along the track until it joins a road. 5. At the road, bear left and within a little more than a mile you will arrive back at the Church.

Start: All Saints Church, Chedgrave
Approx. Distance: 5 Miles (good footwear needed)
Approx. Time: 2 Hours
Map: Landranger 134

Continuing in a north-westerly direction from Reedham sees us first to Langley, where the ruins of a Premonstratensian Abbey are visible on the western banks of the Yare; these are privately owned, but what is left of the west cloister range and the former early 13th Century chapter house are clearly visible from the road side. Nearby Langley School, formerly Langley Hall, was built in the mid 1700's by Matthew Brettingham who was also responsible, using Kent's designs, for Holkam Hall. The likeness between the two buildings is immediately apparent.

Again heading north we find another typical Broad at Rockland St. Mary, connected to the Yare by a long, narrow channel. The River here provides a good supply of thatching reeds - occasionally, if you are lucky, you can see a traditional reed punt at work. The reeds being cut in water, tied in bundles and laid out on the banks or road sides for drying. And at *Surlingham*, the main attraction is the *Nature Reserve* under the Norfolk Naturalists Trust control. Here Broadland life can be enjoyed to full advantage and its preservation owes much to the efforts and lifes-work of naturalist writer and broadcaster, Ted Ellis. A wide variety of wildfowl and waders use the site and it was the first place in Norfolk to be colonised by Celt's warblers just a few years ago. Please note, *land access to the Reserve is extremely dangerous* but boat access is possible to Bargate Water from the River Yare. One other place to visit nearby is *Daphne Ffisk Herbs (01508 538187), Bramerton*, a well-know specialist nursery offering a wide range of culinary, medicinal and fragrant herb plants. A small display garden can also be visited. *Open Thur-Sun, 10-4, March to September.*

P.H. Emerson was one of the early pioneers of documentary photography in England and spent much of his time recording life on the Broads. His *Life and Landscape on the Norfolk Broads* (1886) is just one of seven such collections depicting the marshdwellers' life here. Furthermore his *Birds, Beasts and Fishes of the Norfolk Broadland* is considered to be one of the finest natural history books to be illustrated entirely by photographs.

South Walsham

During the 12th Century, South Walsham, approximately five miles north-west of Acle, was actually two separate parishes each with its own church, but sharing the same churchyard. St. Lawrence's was all but destroyed by fire in 1827, leaving St. Mary's to stand proud against its ruins. St. Mary's is mainly a 14th Century structure and look for the 1907 stained glass in the south aisle window by Pearson and depicting astronomy.

Near the Church, the road crosses a narrow stream and it is hard to imagine that in the last century, wherries carried cargoes of barley along this - albeit at the time a wider waterway - to Ranworth. The whole area around here is most picturesque and both walkers and boaters can enjoy it to its full extent. For example, you can easily reach Malthouse and Ranworth Broads on foot or use the Bier Way, leading to Kingfisher Lane with its pretty thatched cottages, to get to South Walsham Broad. Until recently, the Bier Way was used for carrying the dead from the low end of the village to their churchyard resting place. If time permits, follow the seven-mile circular walk described below, created by Anglian Water and the Broads Authority, and which will take you along the River Bure via South Walsham, Upton and passing on the other side first St. Benet's Abbey and then the village of Thurne with its windmills dominating the flat expanse of marshland around them.

For those wanting to fish, there is free coarse-fishing along a one mile stretch of the right hand bank of the River from South Walsham Broad to its confluence with the River Bure. It is considered good for a catch of roach, bream or pike.

Fairhaven Garden Trust (01603 270449), *South Walsham,* is an important woodland and water garden with many rare shrubs and plants, particularly lysichitons, astilbes and gunneras of extraordinary size. The majestic oaks, one the 'King Oak' is over 900 years old, add a touch of grand natural beauty and try not to miss the azaleas and rhododendrons in late spring. A vintage-style river boat *The Lady Beatrice* runs regular, half-hourly, trips around the inner Broad on days when the gardens are open. *The gardens are open Tue-Sun & Bank Hols,11-5.30, & Sat 2-5.30, mid April to mid September. Plant sales, refreshments and toilet facilities. Admission charge. Wheelchair access.*

Food & Accommodation

South Walsham Hall (01603 270378), *South Walsham.* The Hall is thought to have been built in the 16th Century and is now a hotel and country club. Until his death in 1973, it was owned by Lord Fairhaven and his gardens have been retained, as above, as a separate entity. Nonetheless, the grounds in which the Hall is set are at once both majestic and soothing. Good standard accommodation and restaurant ensure a restful stay in one of the most picturesque parts of Broadland. *Wheelchair access.*

Ranworth is something of a quiet Broads backwater but well worth the visit. Start at St. Helen's Church, with its superb 15th Century screen spanning the nave; the paintings depict saints, apostles and martyrs. Occasionally, during the summer you can also see the *Sarum Antiphones*, a leather bound, illuminated manuscript created by the monks of Langley Abbey and bought by the Church for 50 guineas some years ago. Much of the Church's prosperity, incidentally, was gained during the Middle Ages when the parish was heavily involved in the wool industry. Take the trouble to climb to the top of St. Helen's tower - it involves 89 steps and two ladders. From here you can see right over to Ranworth Broad and beyond to the River Bure as it weaves its way through the marshes. Closer to the Church is the Broadland Conservation Centre with its floating gallery for birdwatching.

Like most of the Broads, Ranworth is a flooded peat-digging, flooded in the 14th Century as the sea level rose. It has been a private water since the 19th Century, now managed by the Norfolk Naturalists Trust, and is renowned for its winter waterfowl - teal, wigeon, shoveller and Bewick swans. Also, in winter, something like 400 cormorants roost on the Broad. Ranworth is also intriguing for the number of wherries which have been sunk here - during World War II this was done to prevent enemy hydroplanes from landing, though more recently it is a practice aimed to help prevent erosion of the Broad's delicate banks .

A half mile trail leads through mature oak woodland to carr woodland dominated by alder and sallow. Further along you will find yourself in open fen which supports a variety of plant life, including hemp agrimony, meadowsweet, milk parsley and yellow loose-strife. Finally you arrive at a thatched floating building on pontoons - the **Broadland Conservation Centre** *(01603 270453)*. ***Open daily, excluding Mon and Sat mornings, 10-5, April to October. Admission charge.*** There is also an Information Centre at Ranworth Staithe *(01603 270453)* which is open between April and September. Please note there is no car park at the Reserve entrance (use the Norfolk Naturalists Trust park near Malthouse Staithe and then follow the signposts).

Upton Fen together with its Broad, a little to the east of South Walsham, are isolated from the polluted river systems and are fed by clean spring water. They, therefore, form one of the most important open water sites in the area. A great diversity of plants and an extensive dyke system can be found here. The more unusual plants to be noted include black bog rush, marsh fern and the lesser tussock sedge. The site also boasts an exceptional number of dragonfly species and a good colony of swallow butterflies.

At Upton village, are two interesting items. The first is Palmers Post Mill, the only hollow windpump of its type remaining. The second can be found in Eastwood Whelptons boatyard and is none other than the wherry *Maud*. Built in 1900, and one of only two surviving craft of its type.

Walk 29: South Walsham Broad and Upton Fen

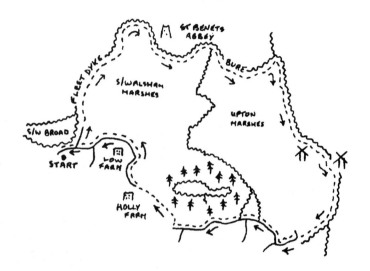

Directions:

1. From South Walsham Broad follow the road which runs down to the Staithe (about 400 yards). From the Staithe, follow the footpath (marked with Broads Authority green arrows), alongside the Broad, and so along Fleet Dyke. Occasionally the pathway is separated from the river but at the top of Fleet Dyke are the remains of St. Benet's Abbey. 2. Continue to follow the bank alongside the River Bure until the pathway bends south-east at Thurne Mouth with its two windmills on the opposite banks of the river. 3. Continue along the bank past Thurne Mouth for approximately another two and a half miles until you reach the mouth of Upton Dyke, passing Upton Mill, now a private home, and later passing derelict Oby Mill on the opposite bank. At Upton Dyke, turn right with the bank for about half a mile until you come first to Palmers Post Mill and then the boatyard belonging to Eastwood Whelptons. 4. Bear right out of Dyke Lane, and go along Marsh Lane as it leads to the modern housing of Cargate Green. Go right along a footpath (signed) by the edge of a field. The path leads through the edge of woodland to Holly Farm; the path here can be wet but wooden planks have been laid over the worst stretches. 5. At Holly Farm, go right through the farmyard until you reach a crossroads and then go right again. 6. After about 200 yards you reach the entrance and car park to Upton Fen Nature Reserve. The path continues along the edge of Low Farm along Marsh Road and beside a thatched barn. Go left to Tiled Cottage and then right, over a stile, along a footpath which runs beside a field. Follow the path round to the right to return to your start.

Start: South Walsham Broad car park
Approx. Distance: 7 Miles
Approx Time: 3.5. Hours
Map: Landranger 133.

Oby Mill

Just north of the confluence of the Rivers Bure and Thurne, the unspoilt village of *Thurne* is accessed north of Acle i.e. not via South Walsham. Walk down to *Thurne* Dyke *Drainage Mill*, with its distinctive white-painted brick tower, housing a small local exhibition. *Open Sun afternoon, 3-6, May to September. Nominal admission charge.* On the opposite bank is another drainage mill but this one is privately owned.

If you are near the Church, look for the circular hole driven through the west side of the tower - if you have reasonably decent eyesight you should be able to see as far as St. Benet's Abbey (one and a half miles away). Story has it that a light would be placed in the hole if any of the villagers were sick. This would bring the Abbey monks, skilled in medicine, to the villagers' aid. This practice continued until Henry VIII's reign when the Abbey's powers were severely curtailed.

Three miles to the west of South Walsham is *Woodbastwick*, bordered by the River Bure and rightly considered one of Norfolk's most beautiful villages and at the heart of conservation Broadland. Since the early 1800's, all but a handful of properties have been estate owned, by the Cator family, and their holdings include the 1, 000 acre Bure Marshes Reserve.

The thatched Church of St. Fabian & St. Sebastian stands at the heart of the village and is the only church in England to be so dedicated. Note the unusual tie-beam roof here. Adjacent to the Church is the village green with its charming, round, thatched pumphouse, thatched cottages and almshouses, one of the latter with the following delightful inscription: 'At Eventide It Shall Be Light.' The village is also home to **Woodforde's Brewery** *(01603 720353)*, specialist producers of local ales.

To get to the River, go down Ferry Road (about one mile) and from here you can make use of the nature trail (about half a mile in length), a wooded walkway which follows Cookshoot Dyke to a hide overlooking the Broad. Only in 1982 was the Broad dammed off and pumped to restore it to its former condition. The result today is clear water and an abundance of wildlife. Visitors by boat can moor at the end of Cookshoot Dyke, which has recently been extended to cope with the extra demand. Coarse-fishing, opposite the Horning Ferry pub, along this stretch of the River Bure is free and the catch variously bream, roach or pike.

Finally to **Salhouse,** north west of South Walsham and a relatively short distance from Wroxham. This is one of few places on the Broads which affords direct access for walkers to the open Broads. During the summer months, the Broads Authority, via Beccles Tourist Information *(01502 713196)* run occasional boat trips from here to Hoveton Great Broad; the only way to gain access to the nature trail there and well worth the effort. One of the most beautiful of the Broads, Salhouse gets its name from the abundance of sallows or pussy willows which grow along the damp ground here.

Upton Mill

South-Norfolk
and the
Waveney Valley

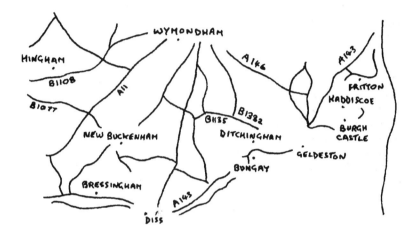

Oour tour of southern Norfolk and the Waveney Valley begins in and around Wymondham (pronounced Windham). From here, bit by bit, we head further south into the Valley proper to take in Diss, Bungay, Geldeston and the most southerly reaches of the Broads as they join the River Waveney near Haddiscoe and Fritton.

Wymondham

Founded in 1107, by William d'Albini for the Benedictine order, Wymondham Priory was to become the Abbey in 1448 and what remains of it can be found in the Churchyard. The twin towers are a legacy of the many, often ferocious, quarrels between the towns people and the monastery. These reached such a climax in the 13th Century that the Pope awarded the nave, north-west tower and the north aisle to the towns folk leaving the remainder for the Benedictines use. The latter walled off their part whilst the town built its great west tower in 1445. Not to be outdone, the monks retaliated with their octagonal tower, and only this was to survive the destruction of the rest of the east end during the Dissolution of the Monasteries. But it is those aspects which belonged to the people which are classed together as one of Norfolk's greatest buildings. More recent additions include Comper's altar screen which is exceptionally lavish,

Wymondham Abbey

heavily gilded, and obviously 'High Church'.

Wymondham though is perhaps best known for having been the place where Kett's Rebellion began in 1549. The rebels, mainly peasants revolting against 16th century land enclosures, were led by Robert Kett, a local farmer, who secured the capture of Norwich before he himself was caught and hung at Norwich; his brother was similarly executed at Wymondham. On Norwich Castle walls hangs a plaque commemorating Kett's fight for England's common people. It reads: *"In 1549 AD Robert Kett Yeoman Farmer of Wymondham was executed by hanging in this Castle after the defeat of the Norfolk Rebellion of which he was the leader."*

In the centre of the Market Place is an attractive octagonal Market Cross raised on arcades and erected in 1617. The timbered upper-floor was once used for meetings of the town's market court and later as a library. From the Cross, narrow streets run in all directions and many of the buildings along these are timber-framed with over-hangs and date from 1615 onwards; a fire of that year destroyed most of the 16th Century buildings, though there are occasional 15th Century buildings which survived the ravages of that fire. One of these is the Guild Chapel, dedicated to Thomas a Becket, although it was rebuilt during the 14th Century; it is now the County Library.

A few miles north-west of Wymondham is *Wicklewood Cornmill* which can be visited *on the 3rd Sun in the month, 2-5, May to September.*

A few miles south-east of Wymondham are *Rainthorpe Hall Gardens (01508*

470618). Here, the five acres of garden adjoin an Elizabethan manor house, the lawns to which run down to the River Tas. Of the original 16th Century garden, there still remains elements of the knot garden, the nuttery and a serene, ancient yew tree. Other trees of botanical interest include a collection of bamboos. Altogether, a most peaceful environment. *Open occasional days during May as part of the National Gardens Scheme; other times by appointment.*

Food & Accommodation

The Bird in the Hand *(01508 489438)*, *Wreningham*. A well- kept establishment, where the bar was once the stable and the restaurant part of a former farmhouse. An extensive menu ensures busy week-ends with locals and visitors alike. There is usually a pianist to entertain you on Wednesdays and occasional jazz evenings are another feature. On a summer's day, you can also take advantage of the landscaped gardens. **Wheelchair access.**

Just a short distance south-east of Wymondham is *Forncett Industrial Steam Museum (01508 488277), Forncett St. Mary,* which houses a collection of 18 stationary steam engines, including one which once opened Tower Bridge, London. On steam days, many of the engines can be seen running, most in pristine condition. *Open and in Steam on the 1st Sun in the month, 10-5.30, May to December; otherwise by appointment.*

Hingham

Travelling west from Wymondham will lead to Hingham, recorded as belonging to King Athelstan (Alfred the Great's grandson) as early as 925AD. Its royal privileges, confirmed by several Charters, in 1414, 1610 and again in 1703, continued until the beginning of the 18th Century.

Evidence of Hingham's former wealth is clear from the grandeur of its 14th Century Church. St. Andrew's dominates the Market Place and its tower stands as a landmark for miles around.

Detail of Hingham Village Sign depicting emigrants to the USA

One of the finest groups of Georgian buildings in Norfolk can be found around the eastern side of the Market Place. Now minus its sails and fantail, Hingham's Windmill was built in 1928, and the Watermill in Deopham Road is unusual as it is not sited on a river but is rather fed by several nearby springs.

A few miles south of Boston, USA, is a settlement founded by Puritan emigrants from Norfolk in 1635, and also named Hingham. Between 1633 and 1643, as commemorated by the village sign here, approximately 200 people from Hingham left for America, and among these were the Lincoln family; from which Abraham Lincoln, himself, was able to trace his ancestry. Today, the Village Hall is called Lincoln Hall and a bust of President Lincoln can be found in the Church.

Walk 30: Hingham

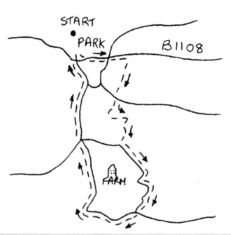

HINGHAM

Directions:
1. From your park near the Market Place, head east along the B 1108 to a group of council houses. Opposite these look for a path across the field on your right. 2. At Seamere Road, turn left for a few yards until you see a footpath sign on your right. Follow this across the field, turning left along its southern perimeter to a plank bridge. Once over this, go right following the path along the edge of the field until it becomes a track. 3. Turn left along the next road, up a hill and then go right at Money Hill Lane, down the hill (i.e. avoid the track to Money Hill Farm.) 4. Turn right at the bottom into Hall Moor Road. You will pass on your left an unusual group of cottages known as Pitts Square, and a little distance on the former Windmill. 5. Continue along Hall Lane back to the Market Place.

Start: Hingham Market Place
Approx. Distance: 4 Miles
Approx. Time: 1.75 Hours
Map: Landranger 144

Diss

Now into the Waveney Valley proper and so to Diss. The older part of town can be found around Diss' Market Place and Mere, the latter a six-acre lake and a haven for wildfowl; the fishing here is also reputedly good. The name Diss is thought to derive from the Anglo-Saxon *dice*, meaning standing water. Many period buildings, part-timbered and with jettied upper-storeys, can be found in or near the Market Place. Perhaps the most interesting is the half-timbered Dolphin Inn with its over-hangs. A number of fine Georgian buildings are also evident as is the Corn Exchange of 1854 and the Maltings built for Lacon's Brewery in 1788. The early 14th Century tower of St. Mary's Church is surmounted by a lantern and arches on either side. John Skelton, Poet Laureate during Henry VIII's reign, was the rector here; during one difficult period during his career, he was forced to take refuge from his enemies in Westminster Abbey.

Market Day at Diss is on Friday, and early closing on Tuesday. *Auctions,* managed by *Thos. Gaze & Son (01379 650306)* are also held on Fridays. On Park Road, on the A 1066, near Diss town centre, you can find the Water Garden and Aquarium Centre of *Waveney Fish Farm (01379 642697)*. Hardy water lilies, floating and aquatic plants together with moisture loving shrubs and alpines are their speciality. *Open daily 9.30-5.*

A few miles south-east of Diss is *Billingford* tower *Cornmill. Open daily, 11-3, and from May to September also between 6-9.* Keys are available from the Horseshoes Pub. If you do visit the Mill, also take a look at the interesting, early 14th Century wall paintings high on the south wall of St. Leonard's Church. Good views of the Waveney Valley can in any case be had from the churchyard. Also nearby is *Thelnetham Windmill*, a 19th Century four-storey Towermill complete with sails and in working order. The flours milled here are for sale.

For those looking for horse-riding facilities, the following are BHS approved: *Rosebrook Farm Equestrian Centre (01379 687278), South Lopham,* and *Willow End Equestrian Centre (01379 608296), Pulham Market.* Something of a different flavour can be found at *Pulham Market Vineyard (01379 676672), Mill Lane, Pulham Market.* Close on 25, 000 bottles of wine are produced each year here and the vineyard has won a number of awards especially for its Magdalen Rivaner and Magdalen Auxerrois wines. Guided tours are available by prior arrangement. *Open for wine sales May to September, 9-7, and October to April 10-3. Tours of the vineyard itself by appointment only.*

Pulham Market village itself is especially charming, its thatched cottages sited around the green and much sleepier than in earlier years when a busy market was once held here. The village sign here commemorates "The Pulham Pigs", and recalls the airships once stationed at the old airfield south of the village. In the neighbouring village of Pulham St. Mary, the Church, also called St. Mary's, is worth a visit for its 15th Century stone-fronted, two-storey south porch.

Food & Accommodation

Salisbury House *(01379 644738), Victoria Road, Diss,* is a privately owned restaurant with limited but homely bedroom accommodation. It was originally built as a store for the nearby windmill, and only its facade is Victorian. The menu at this popular venue changes regularly to take advantage of seasonal produce, and additionally a choice of over 200 wines, mainly French, is offered.

The Old Rectory *(01379 677575), Gissing, nr. Diss,* is a private home offering B & B styled accommodation. The Old Rectory is a spacious and well-furnished Victorian building standing in three-acres of garden and woodland. Personal touches in the bedrooms and bathrooms are very welcoming. Dinner is usually only available on Friday and Saturday, and only by prior arrangement.

Strenneth Farmhouse *(01379 688182), Fersfield, nr. Diss.* An old brick built farmhouse offering B & B accommodation in a remote but peaceful setting (do not be put off by the motley collection of farm buildings around it). Un-even floors, beams and low ceilings abound. The bedrooms are well furnished, and the good no-choice dinners are optional.

Scole Inn *(01379 740481), Scole.* Although Scole itself is not a very attractive place, the Inn itself is well worth a visit. Originally built for a wealthy wool merchant in 1655, its Dutch gabled front is most dignified. A Grade 1 listed building, it still boasts weathered timbers, leaded windows and beamed fireplaces amongst other features. In his hurry to escape the law, highwayman John Belcher would regularly ride his horse up the huge oak staircase here. In some of the bedrooms in the main building, antique furniture - tester and half-tester beds - is very much in evidence. If you are staying, try to avoid those bedrooms in the converted Georgian stables as they are small and lacking in character as compared to the rest. Choose from a good range of bar food or the separate restaurant. *Wheelchair access to restaurant and toilets only.*

The Old Ram *(01379 676794 or 608228), Tivetshall St. Mary.* A former 17th Century coaching inn retaining its exposed timbers and has old craftsmens tools hanging from the ceiling. A large, wholesome menu means it can get very busy at weekends; there is a separate dining room. There is also a good range of traditional ales and a decent selection of house wines. Accommodation, all en-suite, is available. *Wheelchair access.*

Manor Farm, *Pulham Market,* managed by *The Landmark Trust (01628 825925)* is self-catering. This is a vernacular, Elizabethan building once the home of a yeoman farmer, and now well preserved (oak panelling and moulded beams) by The Landmark Trust. (Sleeps 8.)

The Buckenhams

A few miles north of Diss sees us in New Buckenham. In its planning, a grid-iron Medieval town, the layout of which is still evident. Although called New Buckenham, it was originally founded in the 12th Century by William d'Albini II. He built the Castle as a replacement for the one he had inherited at Old Buckenham. Parts of the old stone circular keep, with its huge walls, can still be seen, as can fragments of the former gatehouse behind the keep. The Castle was demolished in the mid 1600's by Sir Philip Knyet, its then owner. (The key to the Castle can be had from the garage in the village for a nominal charge.) The town consists of three elements: the Castle ruins at one end, the large common with pasture rights for 80 cattle at the other, and the town and former marketplace, little more than a village green now, in the centre. The parish Church of St. Martin's, dating from the 13th Century, is sited to the west and it is a particularly fine Church due to many handsome endowments from benefactors.

A number of interesting buildings can be seen, including the Old Guildhall on the edge of town, and close to this is a red-brick barn which apparently was once the Castle Chapel; it occupies the outer bailey of the former Castle. There are some fine 17th Century buildings, especially one; Market House, which is timber-framed and stands on wooden pillars with cast iron supports. A whipping post equipped with a variety of fetters, forms the central part of this structure. The old ditch still runs behind the gardens; it was originally diverted to edge the pattern of the square in the 12th Century.

A traditional English willow basketry workshop at New Buckenham

At Old Buckenham, the village itself is attractive, the houses and cottages arranged around a huge green. The former Castle ruins were given by William d'Albini II to the Augustinian Canons such that they could use what materials were left to build a Priory. Little now remains of this Priory except fragments of wall in Abbey Farm gardens. But look for Priory House, a handsome timber-framed building, erected by the Canons between 1520 and 1540, and probably intended for the use of guests. Scheduled to re-open in the summer of 1995, the Cornmill here has the largest diameter tower in England.

Walk 31: Buckenham Castles

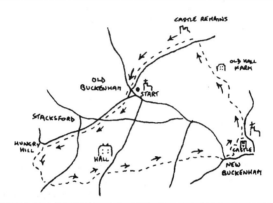

1. From your park near the Church at Old Buckenham (i.e. just off the village green), walk away from the Church towards the green, which you cross diagonally to its left hand corner to reach Mill Lane. Walk past the substantial remains of this Towermill until you reach a junction. 2. Go straight across here (signed Wilby) and continue to another junction, where again you go straight across into Stacksford. 3. Where the lane bends sharply to the right at the farm, turn left instead towards Hungry Hill. When you reach a wood, just before another farm, go left over a rickety wooden footbridge across the stream and through the edge of the wood. At the end of the wood, go through a gate and continue over a meadow (this can be quite wet) and so into a field. Head towards the farm buildings, over a metal gate and along the right hand side of a meadow in front of the farm buildings. 4. Once on the lane, go left to a junction of sorts and straight over this along a track which leads to the remains of a large tumulus and then to a lane. 5. Turn left here, ignoring a track immediately on your left, so following the lane as it heads back to Old Buckenham. Look for a pair of gates on your right which take you through to a track on your right. Continue along this path (along the edge of cultivated fields and meadows) until you reach another lane. 6. Cross over the road, through the gate in front of you to a paddock. A series of paddocks and meadows are crossed to reach a row of houses and so the road. Turn left for a few yards to reach a junction, and go straight across here along the B 113 into New Buckenham. If time permits, explore the village and the Castle. 7. Assuming you have explored the village, aim for the Church and with this on your

right and the Castle on your left, continue along Cutter Lane in the direction of Old Buckenham. Once passed Hunts Farm, and just before the point where the road goes round to the right, look for a path on your left through a field, near a telegraph pole. 8. Walk diagonally over this field aiming for the left hand corner. This will pick up another track and on through a field to a lane just right of a house. Turn left into Harlingwood Lane and continue to Old Hall Farm. 9. Go right here, along a farm track passing a farm building on your left and so to another road. Turn left into Abbey Road, where you can see what remains of Old Buckenham Castle. Continue along Abbey Road until you return to the village, turning left at the junction to return to your vehicle.

Start: Old Buckenham Church
Approx. Distance: 7 Miles
Approx. Time: 3.5 hours
Map: Landranger 144

Bressingham

Travelling west from Diss we arrive at Bressingham, known principally for its large garden and nursery, *Blooms of Bressingham (01379 688133)*. Begun by horticulturalist Alan Bloom, he and his family have created an informal, bedded collection of over 5, 000 species of hardy perennials, alpines, heathers and conifers. *The nursery, open daily, 10-5,* adjoins the garden, and Blooms have achieved high regard as growers and suppliers to the retail trade. In addition, Blooms also own and operate the *Bressingham Steam Museum (01379 687386)* within their grounds. More than 50 engines and roundabouts are on display in the Exhibition Hall, including a model of the famous *Pacific Type 4-6-2*. A narrow-gauge, steam hauled train runs through the grounds enabling visitors easy access to these enviable gardens. *Open daily, 10-4.30 (last admission), April to 2nd September. Reduced opening times during October. Admission charge.*

Food & Accommodation

Garden House *(01379 687405), Thetford Road, Bressingham.* Dating from the 16th Century, this rambling old pub oozes with charm, not least because of its thatched roof and multitude of timbers. Good food and traditional ales complete the picture.

A little further west sees us in *Garboldisham,* where many of the houses have been built from clay lump. This material was once common in south Norfolk, just as it was in north Suffolk, and consists of large blocks of unfired clay, laid on top of each other. It is reputed to last for centuries, provided it is kept very dry, (pretty difficult, I would say, with this country's climate). Additionally, there are several unopened tumuli near the village, and an earthwork, known as the Devil's Dyke, which runs for approximately two miles on the west side of the parish; it is thought to have been built for defensive purposes by one or other of our distant ancestors.

Bungay

Although a Suffolk town, Bungay is literally just over the county border on the southern banks of the River Waveney, and is sufficiently important within the context of the Waveney Valley as to warrant its inclusion in this guide to Norfolk. Bungay must have provided an important river crossing for the Romans, for when the Normans arrived there was already a castle and settlement which they quickly turned into a strong place. Now only a few ruins of a later Castle remain. Running diagonally from the west to the south side of these ruins is a small gallery in the middle of which are two small cross cuts through the masonry. Theory has it that this is a sappers tunnel, which would have been reinforced with timber and set alight as a means of seizing the Castle. It is thought that Henry II's troops drove this sap into the keep in an effort to repel Hugh Bigod for his part in the uprising against the King; their efforts were halted when Bigod chose instead to pay a fine as punishment for his misdemeanours. Another Bigod, Roger, rebuilt the Castle at the end of the 13th Century and its primarily the ruins of this structure which can be seen today. The *Castle* is managed by English Heritage and is *open all year, free of charge.*

A network of paths, collectively known as the ***Bigod Way***, begin at the Castle. Additionally, the section along the marshes here was well characterised in George Baldry's classic work of Norfolk country lore, *The Rabbit Skin Cap*.

As many people will know, Bungay is a famous printing town. The industry was originally begun in 1795 by John Brightly, a local school master who set up an early wooden press. He was later joined by grocer J.R. Childs, who was to marry Brightly's daughter. For years known as John & R. Childs, the company was later taken over by Richard Clay and the business continues to thrive today.

Nor should we forget that Bungay was also once an important wherry building centre and William Brighton, considered the foremost builder of these boats, worked from the town. Here he built the unconventional *Albion* which still sails the Broads; unusual in the sense that it was made as a carvel (smooth) rather than as a clinker (overlapping) built hull, probably so that she could navigate the shallow waters between Bungay and Beccles more easily.

Another Bungay industry is the working of leather sheep skins into clothing. *Nursey & Son Ltd* first began in 1790 and the same family continues this tradition in the town. Their shop can be found at *12 Upper Olland Street (01986 892821)*. Furthermore, Bungay was once a well known weaving centre; until 1855, hemp was grown in the locality and many homes had their own hand looms. Indeed, 'Bungay Canvas' was a highly rated sailcloth.

The Butter Cross marks the town centre and a market is still held here on Thursdays. Its octagonal structure is surmounted by a leaden figure of Justice (1754) and was built to replace an earlier market-cross after the fire of 1688 destroyed much of the town. The stocks were also here as was a large cage which held prisoners in the centre of the Cross; this was only removed as late as 1836.

> Near the Butter Cross is an electric light standard with a black lead-en panel at its top depicting **Old Shuck.** It commemorates one Sunday in August 1577, when Old Shuck, the terrifying black dog of East Anglia, appeared in the Church and wrought his havoc:
>
> *All down the Church in midst of fire*
> *The Hellish monster flew;*
> *And passing onwards to the Quire*
> *He many people slew.*
>
> Stories of Old Shuck abound in East Anglia and sightings of him are still reputedly common!

Other worthwhile places to visit include St. Edmund's R.C. Church, built in 1892, and known for its very lavish statuary both inside and outside. To the east of St. Mary's Church, the ruins of a former 12th Century Benedictine Nunnery, founded by Gundrede, wife of Roger Glanville, can be found. *Bungay Museum, (01986 892176)* housed in the Waveney District Council Offices on Broad Street, depicts the history of the town mainly by means of old photographs and prints. *Open Mon-Thur, 9-4.30 & Fri 9-4. Closed 1-2.*

Of a different bent is *The Otter Trust (01986 893470),* one mile west of the town, at *Earsham.* Here, otters live in conditions as close as possible to their natural habitat. The Centre is *open daily, April to October,* and riverside walks are a further plus. Earsham itself is an ancient village with Saxon, Viking and Roman beginnings. In a field opposite All Saints Church, evidence of a Saxon burial ground has been found, and although the oldest parts of the Church are Norman, it is nonetheless thought to have been built upon an earlier Roman encampment. During World War II, Earsham was an important centre for Allied Air Operations - much of the estate lands around here being used for storing bombs and armaments. It is now home to the *Norfolk & Suffolk Aviation Museum,* with its collection of warplanes and associated memorabilia.

Bungay Butter Cross

Before we leave Bungay and its immediate environs, however, we should add that just north-west of the town is Bath Hills, the slopes of which in Roman times were a mass of vines. A cold-spring, considered as health improving as early as 1730, ensured Bungay achieved a reputation as a spa town long before the likes of Bath.

Walk 32: Bungay & The Bigod Way

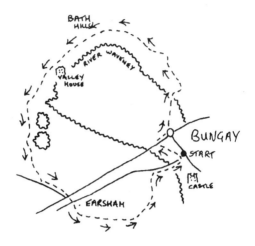

Directions:

1. From Priory Lane Car Park in the centre of Bungay, continue along Priory Lane as it goes round Castle Orchard. Shortly, you will come across a bridleway on the left and follow this as it runs in front of the Castle. From the bridleway, a footpath leads into a pub yard and on into Earsham Street. From here, go left so as to pass the Post Office, and look out for Outney Road on your right. Follow Outney Road as far as the footbridge. Cross this bridge over the by-pass, and then take the track on your right. This track soon joins a footpath running along the side of a pond. 2. Before long, the path takes you away from the common and onto the marshland (via a kissing gate) and so along part of the Bigod Way across the marsh. Once at the banks of the River Waveney, bear right and so over the River and into Norfolk. 3. Once out of the trees, bear left, eventually going through another kissing gate and so into a meadow and on up a relatively steep hill. From the summit, continue westward, over the valley's top, and on underneath a wooden footbridge. 4. The path joins a farm drive at Bath Hills and now your descent is begun. After Bath House, the track continues through pleasant woodland and on through a gate (note the old ice house on your right). 5. The track continues just above Valley House from where it becomes a metalled road. To begin with the lane winds through some lovely woodland but later on a number of gravel workings somewhat mar the scene (a number of earlier workings though are now ponds which, thankfully, attract a wide variety of wildlife). 6. Eventually you will reach a road junction. Go left here into

Earsham, crossing the main road on to a footpath, and leading onto a blocked-off road. Walk past the Post Office and pub, and once again cross the road to a footpath. Turn left at the lane end passing the Church and over the hump-back bridge. Continue over the next footbridge but turn left to walk along the riverbank back to Bungay. 7. Once at the road, turn right at Roaring Arch Bridge, cross another bridge, and take the right turn into Castle Lane. From here, take the left turn into Castle Orchard, then Priory Lane and so back to your starting point.

Start: Priory Lane car park, Bungay
Approx. Distance: 5 Miles
Approx. Time: 2.5 Hours
Map: Landranger 156

Ditchingham

Sir Henry Rider Haggard, author of *King Soloman's Mines* among other literary favourites, was born and grew up at Ditchingham (he lived at Ditchingham House), just north of Bungay, and although he later turned his attentions to agriculture and farming his writings are what he is especially remembered for. The glass in one of St. Mary's Church windows commemorates the Rider Haggard family. Another memorial, this time to those who were unfortunate enough not to return from World War I, can be found in the village. This bronze was commissioned from Derwent Wood and depicts a soldier lying in his trenchcoat, his head on a lumpy haversack, and his helmet close by.

The village has clearly enjoyed substantial wealth during its history, evidenced not only by the somewhat opulent and Perpendicular Church but also by the early 18th Century Ditchingham Hall (some elements of the Hall though are 20th Century), its gardens designed by Capability Brown. The Old Farmhouse and Alma House are both of a similar period, around 1700, but the Community of All Hallows, just east of the village, dates from the mid 1800's. This originally began life as a 'House of Mercy' for young women, though later additions to the complex include a house for the sisters and a Chapel. Close by, on Broome Heath, is a substantial Neolithic longbarrow measuring 160 feet by 83 feet; to date excavation work has not been carried out on the site although a number of shards have been found in the vicinity.

One other item to look out for is the old inn sign, called a 'Triple Plea', which depicts three men - a divine, a lawyer and a doctor - arguing over a woman whilst the Devil looks eagerly on. The origin of the story lies in a piece of verse which concludes:

> *"Now if those three cannot agree*
> *The Devil shall ride them three times three."*

Further south-west, following the course of the River Waveney, is **Harleston.** A small, quietish market town with a handful of interesting buildings. In partic-ular, in the Old Market Place are a number of good houses dominated by the three-storey Post Office, and in the New Market Place note the former Corn Exchange built 1849. Close to the Georgian-fronted Swan Hotel, is a charming but small 16th Century timber-framed house, and just east of the Railway Station is perhaps the most notable building of all, Candler's House, an early Georgian two-storey structure.

Places to visit nearby include *Cranes Watering Farm Shop* *(01379 852387), Starston, nr. Harleston.* Using milk from their own Jersey and Guernsey cows, the farm specialises in making fresh dairy ice cream, yogurt, cheese, butter and lemon curd. Other local produce - pork and poultry - is also available. *Open all year, except Mon, 9-5, & Sun 9.30-12.30.* Between Bungay and Harleston, on the banks of the River Waveney, you can find potter *Clive Davies (01986 788144) at Valley Barn, Homersfield.* He specialises in highly decorative but functional stoneware - anything from jugs to cups and saucers, all with a bit of a difference. Visitors are welcome, but you should phone first to see whether or not it is con-venient.

Geldeston

Food & Accommodation

Locks Inn(*01508 518414*), *Geldeston.* An unspoilt inn which retains its wooden settles, benches, tables and log fires. Closed weekdays during the winter. Live music on most evenings is a bonus.

The Wherry *(01508 518371), Geldeston.* A 16th Century, character pub serving traditional food and ales. **Wheelchair access.**

This time heading just north-east of Bungay, we arrive at the village of Geldeston which marks the limits of navigation on the River Waveney; a useful and attractive public footpath runs from Geldeston Dyke here to Beccles (approx. 3 miles). The lock here was in use until the mid 1930's and was amongst three such structures enabling wherry traffic to sail the few miles to Bungay. Although its original dating is unsure, it is certainly known to have been restored as early as 1670 by an Act of Parliament.

Walk 33: Geldeston Lock
Directions:
1. From the Information Centre on Beccles Quay, head back into town passing the Loaves & Fishes pub. At the top of Fen Lane, bear right to cross the bridge over the River Waveney. Look for a footpath marker pointing immediate left and go down steps onto the riverside, and on through the boat and timber yard. Shortly after you will come across the old railway bridge pier and from here the track now nar-rows to a footpath along the riverbank. 2. Continue along this foot-path, through the small stretch of woodland at Dunburgh Hill, and

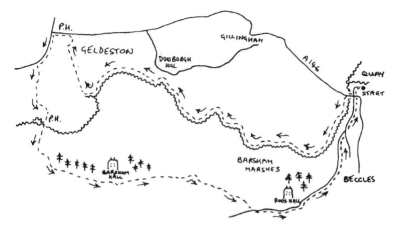

eventually onto the Dyke at Geldeston. 3. To get to the village, pass under the old railway bridge and through the boatyard. Reaching the street, via left until you reach a point where the road goes round to the right. At this point, turn left following the road into Dockeney. 4. Look for a track, Locks Lane, on your left which will take you over the marshes and to what was once the most isolated of all Broads pubs, Lock Inn. 5. Before reaching the pub, bear right crossing the bridge over the dyke and then over the bridges at the Lock (three of them). Continue straight across the marsh until you reach a junction of pathways. 6. Go left, following the path around the edge of a copse of trees until it joins another pathway. Again, go left here along what is the Angles Way. Continue along this as it skirts another stretch of woodland, crosses the driveway leading to the remains of Barsham Hall, and as it crosses Barsham Dyke. 7. Just before Roos Hall, the track then joins the B 1062. Use the footpath, which keeps you off the worst of the road. Look for a road to your left, after the Hall, which provides a pleasant entry into Beccles. 8. Once at the Market Place, go left into Northgate and on into Bridge Street which will get you back to the Quay.

Start: Information Centre on Beccles Quay
Approx. Distance: 7 Miles
Approx. Time: 3 Hours
Map: Landranger 134

Haddiscoe

Also north-east of Bungay is Haddiscoe. The village stands just over a mile south of Haddiscoe Bridge, which gave its name to a new cut, an artificial canal, between St. Olaves and Reedham. It was built, in 1832, by Lowestoft men as part of an ill-fated scheme to allow coastal boats access to Norwich without having to pass, and so pay at Great Yarmouth. The Church of St. Mary has an 11th Century Saxon/Norman round tower, complete with battlements, and built in

197

four telescopic stages. Two interesting features are the rare Norman sculptured figure above the south doors, and a stone on the nave floor commemorating Jan Piers, the Dutchman responsible for draining the marshes in this area.

> **Raveningham Hall Gardens** *(01508 548222), nr. Loddon.* The plantings around this elegant Georgian Hall include a variety of rare and variegated shrubs, hardy plants and trees. Specialities include hardy euphorbias and agapanthus. The walled kitchen garden and greenhouses are still in use and an arboretum is being developed. **Open Sun & Bank Hols, 2-5, & Wed 1-4, mid March to mid September. Admission charge. Wheelchair access.** The nursery is open weekdays throughout the year and Sat-Sun, 2-5, mid March to mid September.

Fritton Lake

Still following the eastern course of the River Waveney, *Fritton Lake & Country Park*, owned by Lord and Lady Somerleyton, can be found five miles south-west of Great Yarmouth, off the A 143. Although the entrance is a rather unattractive collection of commercial paraphernalia, do not be misled by this as the large lake beyond is still unspoilt. The half-acre, Victorian garden is also an unusual feature with its irregular beds and clipped box hedges, all planted with a wide variety of herbaceous perennials and shrubs. Amongst the more commercial attractions are the craft workshops, putting green and boat-hire facilities. *Open daily, 10-5, Easter to October, (01493 488208). Admission charge. Wheelchair access.* Coarse fishing on the lake is also available.

Burgh Castle

Finally, and leaving the River Waveney, by heading north towards Breydon Water we come to *Burgh Castle*. Here the visitor can find the substantial remains of the Roman fort of *Garianonum*. Spread across an area of six acres, the site affords excellent views of the Berney Arms Windmill, the marshes and Breydon Water. *Garianonum* formed one of the main naval bases for the 'Count of the Saxon Shore', a position once held by Roman Emperor, and is a complimentary fort to that which can be found at Caister to the north-east. The ruins are managed by English Heritage and are *open all year, free of charge.* For those wanting to explore the area by boat, *Goodchild Marine Services (01493 782301), Butt Lane*, provide boat hire facilities from near the Castle.

Breckland

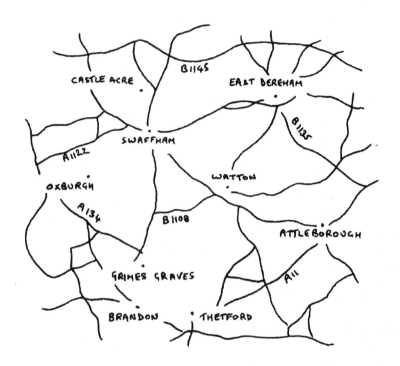

We begin out tour of Breckland in the charming market town of Swaffham, an ideal base from which to explore the benefits of the immediate surrounding area and which takes in Castle Acre and Oxborough amongst other nearby villages. From here we will then move on to the other typically Breckland towns of East Dereham, Watton, Attleborough and Thetford.

Swaffham

Swaffham is predominantly a Georgian market town, once the winter retreat of prosperous farmers and landowners who took the opportunity during those cold weeks to host extravagant soirees and parties. As a result, the town became an important venue on the flourishing theatre circuit during the early 1800's; the Nelsons and Lady Hamilton, amongst other dignatories, are recorded as occasional visitors. Another well-heeled activity in Swaffham at this time was hare-coursing. In 1776, Lord Orford, formed his coursing association, the Swaffham Club, and in the heaths around the town Orford coursed his dog, Czarina, considered the ancestor of all thoroughbred greyhounds. Greyhound Racing, a diluted form of the original sport is still very much on the agenda and regular events are held at *Swaffham Raceway (01760 724761)*, just outside the town. Stock car, hot-rod and banger racing are also part of the Raceway's programme.

The Market Place at Swaffham is of an attractive, somewhat irregular, shape and has at its centre an elegant rotunda topped by a figure of Ceres. It was given to the town by the 4th Earl of Orford, Horace Walpole, in 1783. The many fine Georgian buildings which skirt the Market Place give an air of expansive tranquillity and former prosperity. An open-market of ancient origin is held here every Saturday, much of the local produce - for example, samphire, eggs, and flowers - is of an exceptionally high standard and very modestly priced. A livestock, produce and bric-a-brac auction is also a feature of this Saturday market; here you can replenish your stocks of rabbits, chickens, cockerels and much more!

Close to the Market Place is the imposing but majestic Church of St. Peter & St. Paul, built from Barnack stone and rightly considered one of East Anglia's finest Medieval churches. Its grand exterior was completed during the 15th and 16th Centuries and inside is a fine hammberbeam roof complete with angels. One of the bench end carvings celebrates John Chapman, reputedly a 15th Century street pedlar, who donated his find of treasure to the Church such that the north aisle could be repaired. Legend has it that Chapman dreamt that if he went to London and stood on London Bridge something would happen to his advantage. This he did, meeting a shopkeeper who questioned his loitering and said if he paid attention to dreams then he would, coincidentally, have gone to Swaffham and dug in the garden of a pedlar. On hearing this, Chapman quickly returned to Swaffham where he discovered a crock of gold under a tree at his

The Swaffham Pedlar, as commemorated by the Town's Sign

own home. The real Chapman, incidentally, was not a pedlar but rather a local merchant and Church Warden. Nonetheless, his elaborate story is further encouraged by what is one of the most attractive town signs in Norfolk.

Food & Accommodation

Stratton House *(01760 723845), Swaffham.* Hidden behind the Market Place and enclosed within its own peaceful and attractive grounds is this large 17th Century and part 18th Century country house hotel. Good furnishings and antique furniture are lavishly deployed. For example, the Venetian Room has a walnut Renaissance bed and red Chesterfield. A good, freshly cooked English menu can be enjoyed in the building's basement.

Castle Acre

A few miles to the north of Swaffham is Castle Acre. It is well worth allowing a full free day to explore its fascinating features and to enjoy a leisurely walk around the surrounding countryside.

Earl William de Warenne, son-in-law of William the Conqueror and 1st Earl of Surrey, was granted the Manor of Castle Acre (together with 139 others!) shortly after the Norman Conquest. Although archaeological investigations have revealed pre-Norman, possibly Iron Age, ramparts, it was de Warenne who constructed the great **Castle.** Today, only the 11th Century bailey gateway and earthworks remain, the former representing the heart of the current village. *Both are open all year, free of charge,* and are under the care of English Heritage.

Sitting on high chalk uplands, Castle Acre's enclosed village green is one of the most charming in Norfolk. Formerly the outer Castle bailey, it is now surrounded by a delightful mix of houses, village shops and pubs with the gateway standing in the middle. The large parish Church of St. James is also worth a

Castle Acre Priory

look for its fragments of Medieval glass in the south aisle windows, the carved shields of de Warenne and Fitzalen over the door, and the painted rood screens.

To the west of the village, astride the ancient Peddars Way, is the Priory, thought to have been begun by de Warenne's son, the 2nd Earl, for the Cluniac Order. 25 monks lived here in great style, the Prior commissioning his own lavish residence in 1500. Shortly afterwards, in 1527, as part of the Dissolution movement, Thomas Malling, the last Prior, surrendered the Order's holdings at Castle Acre to Henry VIII. Thereafter, it passed through Thomas Gresham and Thomas Cecil (Earl of Exeter) to Sir Edward Coke whose descendent, the Earl of Leicester, appointed HM Works as guardians. The remains, including the magnificent, elaborately decorated 12th Century west front of the Priory Church, are now in the care of English Heritage. Other aspects of this monument not to be missed include the walled herb garden and the rather opulent Prior's Lodgings. The site is *open daily, 10-6, April to October, and Wed-Sun, 10-4, November to March (01760 755394). Admission charge. Wheelchair access to ground floor and grounds only.*

Food & Accommodation

The Ostrich Inn (01760 755398), Stocks Green, Castle Acre. A large, former 16th Century coaching inn which has retained much of its character including a stunning, vaulted, timbered roof in the back bar. In winter you can warm yourself by the inglenook fireplace here. A good range of food and traditional ales are a bonus. *Wheelchair access.*

Willow Cottage (01760 755551), Stocks Green, Castle Acre. Situated next to the Church, this is an attractive listed 18th Century cottage offering B & B styled accommodation - all of it comfortable and cosy. Downstairs are the hugely popular Tea Rooms open to all. No evening meals. *Wheelchair access to Tea Rooms.*

Down the valley of the River Nar, at *West Acre,* are the ruins of an Augustinian Priory constructed in the 12th Century to match the efforts of their Cluniac rivals; it was once significantly larger than that at Castle Acre. Beside the Church is the Priory's flint built gatehouse, dating from the 14th Century. Other elements still standing include bits of the former 13th Century chapter house.

Immediately south-west, on the opposite bank of the River Nar, is Narford Hall. Although it is not open to the public, it can be seen standing grand against the lake and park. The most appealing part of the building dates from the 1690's when the left hand side of the southern facade was built. Later additions followed, many of them Georgian but some Victorian. Nothing, however, remains of Narford village and even St. Mary's Church, originally built in the mid 1800's, is now disused; nonetheless it stands serene, close to the shores of the lake.

At nearby *South Acre* do take the trouble to get the key to St. George's Church (details of how to obtain this are posted on the door), the earliest part being the

Detail of the monument to Sir Edward Markhem in St. Geroge's Chuch, South Acre

north chancel of the Chapel which can be dated to the late 13th Century. In particular, look for the effigy of a Knights Templar, thought to commemorate Sir Endo Harsyke, the beautiful five-feet long brass to Sir John Harsick (d. 1384) and his wife, and a particularly fine alabaster monument to Sir Edward Markhem (d. 1623), once Lord Mayor of London, and his wife, somewhat gruesomely decorated, some might think, with a collection of skulls and a skeleton in a shroud.

Walk 34: Castle Acre and the Nar Valley

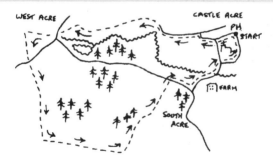

Directions:

1. From Castle Acre's village green head towards the Church and beyond this to the Priory ruins. At the end of this lane, bear right (the Priory entrance is to the left), and then left along a track as it winds its way down towards the wood and a pond. 2. After the pond, a path leads off to the left (through a gate) away from the main track. Follow this but note that it can be very boggy if the weather has been wet: if this is the case, instead of going through the gate, follow the edge of the field to your right which runs parallel to the path you need - after a while you will be able to pass through the thinning hedgerow on to your route. The path winds its way along the edge of the Common, wild marsh marigolds a particular feature in spring, and heading

towards another woodland. 3. Cross the stile and continue along the firm path through the woods. A gate at the end of this stretch leads into a meadow, over another stile, and over two footbridges (Mill House will be on your left). 4. Turn left at the lane and then right onto a sandy track. Before you reach the next ford (just before West Acre), look for a path along the edge of a field (not signed) which heads south. At the road, cross over onto a track which runs along the right hand side of a field, towards a pylon, and up a gradual incline. 5. At the top, go left following the hedge on your right towards Three-Cocked-Hat Plantation. You will then need to follow the field on your right (the hedge now on your left). 6. Go straight across Washpit Drove to Petticoat Drove where you bear left along it. From here the track descends into South Acre, passing the Hall on your right. 7. Turn right at the road taking you past the Church. Shortly beyond the Church, bear left following this lane down to the ford and over the footbridge. 8. Cross into the field to your right and walk along this idyllic stretch of the River Nar (keeping the River on your right). This joins a lane, where you turn left, heading back up towards the centre of Castle Acre village and through the ancient gateway. Once here turn left onto the village green to return to your start.

Start: Castle Acre village green
Approx. Distance: 6 Miles
Approx. Time: 3 Hours
Map: Landranger 132

Oxborough

A few miles south-west of Swaffham, approximately six miles, is *Oxburgh Hall* built by Sir Edward Bedingfield in 1482 and much renovated in Victorian times; Bedingfield's descendents continue to live here although the Hall is now under

Oxburgh Hall

National Trust management. It is without doubt one of the most charming of England's great country houses.

The impressive seven-storey fortified gatehouse stands to the front of the moat but the bridge over the moat is 18th Century and replaced the former drawbridge. Inside the main building, head for the King's Chamber which holds the famous Oxburgh Hangings, made circa 1570, which contain over 100 panels of needlework crafted by Mary Queen of Scots during her imprisonment here, and by Elizabeth Countess of Shrewsbury. Outside, the pretty parterre gardens were laid out in 1845 and are well worth walking around. Also look out for the 1835 Chapel in the grounds, built by Pugin; it contains a magnificent Flemish altarpiece. If time permits, try the woodland walk (marked), you will not be disappointed. The Hall *(01366 328258) is open weekends only April and October, and daily, 1.30-5.30, excluding Thur and Fri, May to end September. Admission charge. Wheelchair access to ground floor rooms and gardens.*

The original settlement of Oxborough (note the different spelling) centred around Oxborough Hythe on the River Wissey, linking the village to the Fenland rivers and, thereby, to King's Lynn and Cambridge. Sadly, nothing remains of this township and even the parish Church is in ruins. The tower of St. John the Evangelist, over 150 feet high, fell in 1878, and even though it was rebuilt it nevertheless collapsed again in 1948 causing much damage to the north aisle and nave. Its ruinous state is all that remains but it is very picturesque.

> **Gooderstone Water Gardens** *(01366 328645), Crow Hall Farm.* Close to Oxborough, Gooderstone Water Gardens are rather awkward to find - along a path between industrial buildings. The rewards are well worth the effort, especially in summer, for the owners have produced an excellent, landscaped garden with a mix of flowers, shrubs, and aquatic plants bordering pools and a lake. A series of broad streams, with bridges across them, add further interest and variety. *Open daily, 10.30-5.30 (Sun 1.30-6), April to October. Admission charge. Wheelchair access.*

Close by is *Cockley Cley*, Cley pronounced 'Cly', and the village itself is thought to occupy an original Iceni site dating from the times of Queen Boadicea. The reconstructed *Iceni settlement* here will provide further insight into the lives of these early, first Century AD Britons. The site is also home to a collection of carriage and farm implements dating from the early 1800's, and to the *East Anglian Museum* with its collection of archaeological and historical exhibits and housed in a small Elizabethan cottage. The Centre which comprises all these elements is *open daily, 2-5.30, Easter to October, and 11.30-5.30, July to September, (01760 721339). Admission charge.* The Centre also includes a Saxon Church dating from 630 AD and hence one of the earliest in Britain; during the 16th Century, it was converted to the village priest's house and only restored in the late 1960's.

Walk 35: Cockley Cley and Oxborough

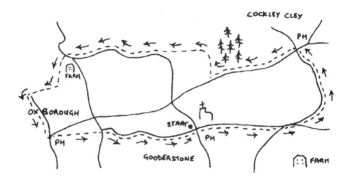

Directions:

1. From your park near Gooderstone's St. George's Church, continue along the village's main street in the direction of Cockley Cley (i.e. with the Church on your left) and passing the entrance to the Water Gardens also on your left. Go straight on at a junction and at the next junction the road bends round to the left. At the next junction, go left into Cockley Cley. (Note: the whole of this section makes use of country lanes but they are usually very quiet.) If time permits, explore the many attractions the village has to offer and on your way out take the road leading past the Church (with that on you right) and signed Oxborough. 2. Walk for about three-quarters of a mile along this stretch and at the point where the forest ends turn right along a track which leads up the western fringe of Deadman's Plantation. 3. Where the plantation cuts in sightly to the right, look for a track on your left which leads to some farm buildings. 4. Go left for a few yards and then right along a track. At the junction, go right which takes you past an isolated cottage and at the next junction turn left and continue along this until it reaches a lane. 5. Go straight on here to Caldecote Farm but look for a track a few yards ahead on your left (i.e. leave the lane just after the farm). Take the left hand route, ignoring a path which forks right and follow the track to a junction of tracks. Go right here until you join the lane leading to Oxborough and turn left. 6. Follow this road into Oxborough village, and if possible do visit the Hall. To do this, turn right at the junction. Otherwise aim for the Bedingfield Arms and just beyond this go through some wooden gates into a field. Follow the left hand edge of the field and continue right and left along another field until you reach the road. 7. Turn right here to follow the road back to Gooderstone.

Start: St. George's Church, Gooderstone
Approx. Distance: 10 miles (half on easy country lanes)
Approx. Time: 4 Hours
Maps: Landrangers 143 & 144

East Dereham

Another typically Breckland town is East Dereham; equally typical is the area surrounding it. East Dereham is usually known simply as Dereham and should not be confused with West Dereham. Having said this the town is an odd mixture of some unsightly shop fronts but with some fine Georgian buildings amidst them in the Market Place.

George Borrow, the author of *Lavengro,* published 1851, was born just outside the town at Dumpling Green. Another famous literary character, the poet William Cowper, is buried in the Churchyard, as is the French prisoner-of-war, Denarde. Although the latter was initially successful in escaping his guard whilst on his way to Peterborough jail, he was nevertheless shot down from the tree in which he had sought refuge.

> **George Borrow** was born at Dumpling Green near Dereham in 1803.
> Much of his work depicts the everyday life of the gypsies (he even
> collated a dictionary of gypsy language). He is most well known
> though for his autobiographical novel *Lavengro* (1851), and its sequel
> *The Romany Rye*. In 1840, following years of wanderlust travelling,
> he married a wealthy widow and settled down on a small estate
> belonging to her at Oulton, near Lowestoft. He died in 1881.

St. Withburga - daughter of the Anglo-Saxon King Anna - and founder of the 7th Century convent here was also once buried in the churchyard. The Abbot of Ely surreptitiously removed her remains, and the spring which gushed from her desecrated grave, is known as St. Withburga's Well. The unusual town sign, stretching across the road, just before entry into the Market Place, celebrates the Saint's powers at a time of famine. It depicts two does which in answer to Withburga's prayers, found their way to the nunnery such that they could be, milked. St. Nicholas' Church, partly of Norman origin and with a 16th Century bell tower, stands on the site of this former nunnery; it is usually now locked and access details were not posted at the time of visiting.

*Bishop
Bonner's
Cottage*

Bishop Bonner, who was to send many Protestants to the stake during the reign of Queen Mary is also remembered at Dereham, for he was the Church Rector here, from 1534 -1538, before his appointment as Bishop of London. The small houses, knocked into one, are collectively known as ***Bishop Bonner's Cottage*** and have the date 1502 set into the colourful and attractive pargetry which adorns their frontage. It is now home to a Museum of local history but the building itself, with its three staircases and extremely narrow passageway (you will need to walk sideways) is undoubtedly the main attraction *Open Tue-Sat, 2.30-5.30, May to September. Note: the Museum is currently undergoing restoration and is scheduled to re-open in 1996. Admission charge.*

Food & Accommodation

Clinton House *(01362 692079), Well Hill, Clint Green, Yaxham.* A few miles south-east of Dereham and set in an acre of mature gardens is this handsome 18th Century house. High standard B & B styled accommodation is assured as is use of the tennis court. No evening meals.

Bartles Lodge *(01362 637177), Elsing.* A few miles north-east of Dereham is the quiet and unspoilt village of Elsing. At Bartles Lodge, renovated and refurbished in 1992, the B & B accommodation is also of a high standard. Guests additionally have use of a spacious conservatory. Evening meals by arrangement.

Three miles north-east of Dereham is the ***Gressenhall Museum of Norfolk Rural Life*** *(01362 860563)*, which holds a wide range of photographs and artefacts depicting rural life in East Anglia over the past 200 years or so. The many reconstructions of tradesmen's premises, for example a blacksmith's, saddler's, dairy and a general store provide added atmosphere. *Open Tue-Sat & Bank Hols, 10-5, April to September, and Sun, 2-5.30. Admission charge.*

Close by is ***Sparham Pools***, an attractive site with a mix of deep and shallow pools with islands and under the care of the Norfolk Naturalists Trust. A wide variety of plants have colonised the banks and gravel here, including hound's tongue and evening primrose. Furthermore, kingfishers and sandmartins are known to nest in these banks. A public right of way providing good views of the pools passes along the edge of the Reserve. There is also a small path around the edge of the pools themselves.

Another Reserve, this to the south of Dereham, is ***Lolly Moor***. A short trail can be followed over the Reserve but do keep to the paths as the site contains a large variety of delicate plant, animal and bird life. Amongst the tree and shrub species can be counted guelder rose, wild cherry, wild plum and alder blackthorn. Additionally, the streamsides are especially attractive when primroses and lesser celandines are in flower; wild orchids are another feature. The Reserve is home to a wide range of birds - from tawny owls to greater spotted woodpeckers, warblers and tits, and in winter to redpolls and goldcrests - and is also important for its butterflies, especially brimstones, ringlets and gatekeepers. The shallow ditches which run across the open area of the Reserve are thought to be the remains of a Medieval ridge and furrow ploughing, and the hedgerows along the lane near the Reserve are considered to be Tudor in origin

A few miles south-east of Dereham at **Runhall** is a 25 acre centre for those determined to try their hand at off-road driving around a three-mile course. Either take your own vehicle or phone first *(01362 850233)* for availability of the **Mid Norfolk Off-Road Centre's** own.

North Elmham, can be found approximately six miles north of Dereham. Much controversy surrounds the ruins of the **Bishops Chapel** here, managed by English Heritage. Many are of the opinion that these ruins were once part of a Saxon Cathedral. The surviving features are indeed remarkable and unusual; for example, the transept is something of a Greek 'Tan' Cross and is a very early symbol of Christianity, and the shallow apse is certainly pre-Norman.

It is thought a church, at least, was on the Elmham site in 920 AD. Following Archbishop Lanfranc's decision that the Bishops' seats should be in towns, Elmham was demoted in favour of Thetford, in 1071. About 1100, Bishop de Losinga replaced the small Saxon place of worship with a stone Chapel, and later work was done in the 14th Century when Bishop Despenser converted the Chapel into a hunting lodge. The ruins here lay forgotten until an amateur digger came across them in 1871. A series of excavations have been carried out, some dating the masonry to 1090 and 1120 and identifying the Saxon structure as a wooden one. A Saxon village and cemetery have also been unearthed. Whatever the true story, the ruins are worth exploring and are *open all year, free of charge.*

Close to the Chapel ruins is St. Mary's Church part of which was constructed from stone belonging to the Chapel. Much is 13th Century with 15th Century modifications. Unusually, and further suggesting the Church's importance, the two interior chapels here are dedicated to St. James in the south and to St. John in the north. Other notable features include the figurative painting on the chancel screen and the Jacobean pulpit.

Nearby Elmham Park was landscaped in the 18th Century and later remodelled by Lord Sondes, as was the Hall. His efforts include the brick dovecote and larder of 1840. The Sondes family crest can still be seen on several Victorian Estate houses in the village. The old stable block at Elmham houses **Elmham Park Vineyard** *(01362 668167)*, producers of dry white wines and apple wines from the estate crops. The vineyard is *open daily for wine sales. Tastings and guided tours by appointment only. Occasional open days.*

Take the trouble to seek out the County School Station built in 1886 on the GER Wymondham to Wells line and serving the former school here. Little of the latter survives but it began life as a public school and later as a Naval College for Dr. Barnardo's boys. It closed in 1953, and was subsequently demolished. The Station was in use as a passenger line until 1964 and for goods traffic until 1985.

It is now a *Visitors Centre* with displays on the Wensum Valley, the railway and County School. The Dereham & Fakenham Railway Society occasionally operate a Ruston diesel train and van along a short stretch of the remaining track.

At nearby *Swanton Morley*, All Saints Church stands large and proud and is one of the earliest, complete examples of the Perpendicular style in East Anglia; work was begun in 1378 following a bequest from Lord Morley. The tall bell openings are especially memorable. Other interesting buildings include the red brick Georgian Mill House and the early 19th Century White House with its grand pilasters.

Food & Accommodation

Darby's *(01362 637647), Swanton Morley.* Once a row of derelict cottages and now a cosy, attractive, beamed pub. Farm tools adorn the walls, and an open fire ensures a warm welcome in winter. Good food, real ales and lively locals. **Wheelchair access.**

For those with a head for heights and adventure, trial microlight flights through to full flight training can be arranged with *David Clarke Microlight Aircraft, (01362 637405), Unit 1, The Black Hanger, Worthing.* Aircraft and equipment sales are another feature of David Clarke's enterprise; he can be found only a five minute drive from North Elmham.

Built in 1460 on an earlier site, *Elsing Hall,* near East Dereham, was once the seat of the Hastings family. Although much restored and embellished in both the 19th and 20th Centuries, the front shows considerable knapped and squared flint. Set in deep parkland and surrounded by an ancient moat, it is perhaps one of Norfolk's most alluring of halls. Handsome 16th Century chimneys, timbered gables and mullioned windows all adding to its mysterious charm. The *gardens* here are *occasionally open as part of the National Gardens Scheme* - odd days between the end of June and the beginning of July, and by appointment. Nominal admission charge. Of particular note are the 200 plus varieties of old-fashioned roses, the kitchen garden and the recently planted knot garden with its combination of clipped box, thyme, lavender and iris.

Whilst you are here, take a look in St. Mary's Church at the incredible brass, on the floor, to Sir Hugh Hastings (d. 1347). Although incomplete, it is nonetheless five and a half feet long and is one of the oldest and most important church brasses in the country. Embellishments to the same include two angels holding Sir Hugh's pillow, Sir Hugh on horseback, and a collection of mourning relatives among them Edward III, Henry Plantagenet Earl of Lancaster, and Thomas Beauchamp, Earl of Warwick. Sir Hugh, himself, was responsible for the building of the Church around 1330 and no doubt ensured his own place therein. Note also the stained glass with a figure of the Virgin which is thought to date from the Church's beginnings, and those depicting the Apostles which are also 14th Century.

Watton

Moving on now to Watton, one of Breckland's five regional towns, we find that it is little more than a long high street. Whilst it is not especially attractive it is interesting because of its central Breckland location. It was a market town long before the 13th Century, with Wat meaning 'hare,' and presumably an abundance of them being sold at the weekly market. The 17th century Clock Tower in the centre of town has an attractive weathervane on its cupola which depicts a hare jumping over a barrel. Unfortunately that is about all there is to see in the town itself but nearby, approximately one mile south-west, is **Wayland** or **Wailing Wood**, an ancient woodland of oak, hazel and bird cherry recorded in Domesday and still managed in the traditional way.

This is the only site in Norfolk where the yellow Star-of-Bethlehem flowers (in March), and in spring the ground is a mass of bluebells. Both lesser and greater woodpeckers breed here as does the golden pheasant. Tradition has it that this is the setting for the *Babes in the Wood* story; according to legend, the Grey children were dumped here by their wicked uncle from nearby Griston Hall. Their wails can reputedly still be heard at midnight and their grave can still be seen in the wood. *Wanelund*, from the Viking, means sacred grove, so the site could in earlier times have been a pre-Christian place of worship. Today, it is managed by the Norfolk Naturalists Trust. A little further south-west than Wayland Wood is **Little Cressingham Watermill**, unique because it is a combined wind and watermill. *Open on the 2nd Sun of the month, 2-5, May to October.*

Food & Accommodation

The Windmill Inn *(01760 756232), Great Cressingham.* Despite its deep, rural location, this is a very popular pub with a warm, friendly atmosphere. The building dates from the 14th Century, and rural artefacts, open fires and the like provide added charm. Traditional pub games can still be played here and music evenings are another feature. Good food and ale. **Wheelchair access.**

A short distance south of Watton is **Thompson Common and Water**, an attractive area of open water, pools, streams, wet meadows and woodland. It is especially rich in flora - marsh marigolds, marsh orchids, water-violets and bog-beam - and the meadows provide rich grazing for the roe deer here. From the Car Park at the former Stow Bedon Railway Station on the A 1075, begins the **Great Eastern Pingo Trail,** a superb circular walk of approximately eight miles taking in Stow Bedon Covert, Thompson Common, Thompson Water, part of the Peddars Way and part of the typical Breckland heath around here. See the information boards at the Car Park for full details, and although the trail is usually well-marked is its advisable to carry a copy of *Landranger 144* for additional reference.

The Great Eastern Pingo Trail derives its name, Pingo, from the relics of glaciation which are to be found in this area. During the Ice Age, the frozen water beneath the surface of the ground pushed up the surrounding soil. Once these melted, crater-like depressions, pingos, were the result.

Thompson Water itself is an artificial lake occupying about 40 acres; it is a popular site with local fishermen after a good catch of carp. The walk referred to above misses the village of Thompson but it is typically and attractively Norfolk in style. Well spread out, the Church can be found at one end, whilst the school, pub and greater residential element can be found at the other end.

Food & Accommodation

The Chequers *(01953 483360), Thompson.* A pretty 16th Century thatched pub set back from the lane. The original timbers are covered with interesting oddments from old corkscrews to boot scrapers. Each of the bars is characterful and one of the ceilings is only five feet high, so do mind your head. Good food and real ale. **Wheelchair access.**

Thatched House *(01953 483577), Pockthorpe Corner.* Characterful and comfortable , you can be sure of a relaxing B & B in this charming 16th Century cottage. Beams, sloping ceilings and a narrow staircase all add to the charm. No evening meals.

Attleborough

Since the days of Daniel Defoe during the first part of the 18th Century, Norfolk has been renowned for its turkeys. Defoe was amongst the first to describe the droves of turkeys, (each comprising about 500 birds), being driven on a three-month trot to London for the Christmas market, their feet covered with tar to afford a modicum of protection. Attleborough was once the centre of Norfolk turkey-rearing and an annual fair where the birds were sold, was ,until recently, held here. Today, the main production-line centre for turkeys in Western Europe is Bernard Matthews operation at Great Witchingham

Attleborough is also noted for its cider, made at Gayners Works, though sadly considerable contraction of the same took place during the mid 1980's. Otherwise, and excepting St. Mary's Church, Attleborough too has very little to offer the visitor. But do visit the Church which was largely rebuilt in 1436 by Sir Robert Mortimer. Particularly outstanding are the mural of the Annunciation painted circa 1500, and the 52 feet long rood screen dated 1475. The altar is the only screen in Norfolk to stretch continuously across the nave and both sides of the aisles and is complete with painted panels and a finely carved rood loft.

For those wanting to go horse riding, try *Eden Meadows Riding Centre (01953 483545), Sandy Lane, Attleborough* which is BHS approved, as is *Hockwold Lodge Riding School (01842 828376), Davey Lodge, Hockwold.* Alternatively, motor racing can be enjoyed at nearby *Snetterton Motor Racing Circuit (01953 887303). Thetford Golf Club (01842 752258), Brandon Road, Thetford,* is a sandy course with tree belts, heather and gorse acting as strategic features. *Visitors are welcome but do take your handicap certificate.*

Other interesting outlets include *Thorncroft Clematis (01953 850407), Attleborough.* This is a small family-run operation growing around 200 varieties of clematis. The display garden is *open daily, excluding Wed, 10-4.30, 1 March to 31 October.* Also in Attleborough is *Peter Beales Roses* (01953 454707). Here over two acres of display gardens reveal hundreds of different varieties of roses with old fashioned roses being a particular speciality. *Open all year, Mon-Fri, 9-5, Sat 9-4.30, & Sun 10-4 excluding Sun in January when the nursery is closed.*

Thetford

The 'capital' of Breckland, Thetford, was a thriving community even before the Norman Conquest and is reputed to have been the foremost settlement of the Iceni tribe of ancient Britons. Thetford's prosperity and importance as East Anglia's principal city continued until the 11th Century when the Bishop's throne was removed from here to Norwich. It is now relatively quiet and modest but like Swaffham is one of the more appealing of Breckland's market towns.

In 1979, **Arthur Brooks,** an amateur archaeologist, discovered, using his metal detector, one of the greatest Roman treasures to be found in England this Century - mainly jewellery (brooches, bracelets, rings, many of them gold and inlaid with jewels) and ornate silver spoons. All in all over 80 objects dating from the latter part of the 4th Century were uncovered. *The Thetford Treasure* is now to be found in the British Museum, London. Sometime later, archaeologists working on the same site unearthed the remains of three large, Iron Age, round houses; an equally remarkable find.

Of the Norman Castle, little more than the moat has survived. The remains of the *Priory* are somewhat more extensive especially the 14th Century gatehouse and the cloisters. It was originally founded in the 12th Century by Roger Bigod, 1st Earl of Norfolk, for the Cluniac monks and continued as an important religious centre until Dissolution in 1539. The ruins are *open all year, free of charge,* and are managed by English Heritage. The ruins of the *Priory Church of the Holy Sepulchre* are also managed by English Heritage and are again *open all year, free of charge.* These are unique in being the only surviving remains in England of the Order of the Canons of the Holy Sepulchre.

Food & Accommodation

The Bell Hotel (01842 754455), Thetford. A 16th Century, half-timbered coaching-inn, now part of the Forte Heritage group, and overlooking the River Ouse. The bedrooms in the main building are beamed whilst those in the wing are of a more contemporary style. The bar gives off an old-world atmosphere and is well-used by both locals and residents alike.

Colveston Manor (01842 878218) Mundford, nr. Thetford. An excellent location for exploring Breckland and itself a Georgian farmhouse surrounded by substantial acres of farm land. Very high standard B & B accommodation and food; choose from either a full evening meal or light supper.

The 15th Century, early Tudor, timber-framed *Ancient House Museum (01842 752599), White Hart Street* contains displays on the history of the town and surrounding area. Especially interesting is the story of Breckland man, as is the beautiful ceiling with its moulded and decorated beams. *Open daily June to September, 10-5 (closed Mon, 1-2), & Sun, 2-5. Admission charge.*

Thetford was also once home to Thomas Paine, 'Father of the American Revolution,' and author of *The Rights of Man.* A gilt statue by Charles Wheeler was presented to the town by the American Thomas Paine Society. Also here and well worth the visit is the *Burrell Museum (01842 751166),* with its impressive collection of world famous Burrell steam traction and showmen's engines. *Open Tue, Fri, Sat & Sun, 10-5, April to October. Admission charge. Wheelchair access.*

> **Thomas Paine** was born in 1737, son of a Quaker stays-maker. He left school aged 13 to work in his father's shop and, thereafter, variously held jobs as a preacher, teacher, tax collector and tobacconist. Somewhat disillusioned by life in England and after two failed marriages, he emigrated to America in 1774. Soon after, in 1776, an anonymous pamphlet was published in Philadelphia entitled *Common Sense*; this was Paine's plea for independence and basic civil rights. That same year he went on to help formulate the American Bill of Rights. After his success in America, Paine ventured to work with French Revolutionaries during their Civil War. *The Rights of Man* was published in England, in 1791, and this argued that only the people and their chosen representatives were legitimate rulers; Paine was subsequently accused of treason for his efforts. He fled to Paris where he was made a Member of the National Assembly, and although he rejoiced at the fall of the French monarchy, he opposed their execution. Consequently, Robespierre, in turn, had Paine arrested for treason. Inevitably, he returned to America where he died in 1809, alone and friendless, in a New York boarding house.

Close to the town is *Thetford Forest* with over 70sq. miles of woodland, being the second largest forest in England. Deer and red squirrel shelter here and nightjars and nightingales can also be heard in the evening. The Forest is also home to the rare stone curlew.

Thetford Heath, three miles south-east of the town, is a good example of a typical Breckland heath. Bank after bank of acid-loving heathers can be enjoyed in season and other plants of interest include field wormwood and small medick. The area is also rich in birdlife. *Visitors must obtain a permit* from the *Nature Conservancy Council's Regional Office (01284 762218), North Tower House, 1-2 Crown Street, Bury St. Edmunds IP331QX.* Alternatively, and easier to enjoy, just north of the town is *East Wrentham Heath.* This is a unique area of Breckland combining deciduous and coniferous woodland with open heath. There are two attractive meres - Langmere and Ringmere - and an area of ancient pines planted during the Napoleonic War and called the Waterloo Plantation. Another plantation is mainly hornbeam. Over 250 plant species - the sandy soil supports continental plants unusual in England - and 130 species of bird have been recorded at the site. Butterflies, grass snakes, lizards and newts are equally abundant, and the resident roe deer can occasionally be seen. The *nature trail is open daily, excluding Tue, and permits for the same can be had from the Warden's house near the entrance.* A leaflet on the trail is available, otherwise just follow the arrows.

The ancient *Peddars Way* passes close to Thetford and although accepted theory has it as being of Roman origin, built immediately after 61 AD, there are those who believe it to be a much earlier structure, possibly Iceni. Those that accept the Roman argument see the Way as a military and policing road following suppression of the Boadican (Iceni) Revolt, and that it may have linked a series of Roman fortifications. The width of the Way, in places as substantial as 45 feet, would further seem to support this contention. The Way, itself, stretches over a distance of 46 miles, from Knettishall Heath, just east of Thetford, to Holme-next-the-Sea on Norfolk's north facing coastline. It is also quite plausible that at one time the Way linked directly with Colchester further south, and furthermore that it could be crossed by northbound ferry at the Wash.

Over time, its original military purpose would have been superseded by general supply needs i.e. the movement of livestock, for general agricultural purposes and for the supply of local goods and produce. It was also well used by pilgrims en route to Walsingham. The name itself is certainly not of Roman origin and whilst there can be no precise attribution, Peddars Way may well simply be a generic word for footpath. It is nonetheless an important historic route which passes through a significant part of Breckland, through some of Norfolk's finest farmland, open countryside and the important site of Castle Acre. For details of accommodation and camping facilities along the Way contact T*he Peddars Way Association* (01603 623070), *150 Armes Street, Norwich.*

Walk 36: West Harling Heath

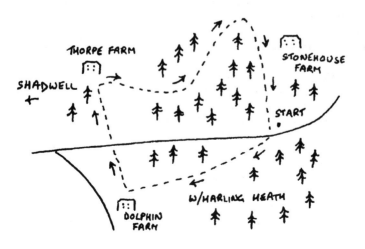

Directions:

1. From the main forest Car Park cross the road and bear left. Look for a footpath immediately on your left. 2. Follow this for approximately one and a quarter miles as far as Dolphin Farm; along the way you will pass tumuli, typical of what remains of the Breckland landscape. 3. At Dolphin Farm, go right along another path, crossing the road and continuing along the eastern aspect of Boundary Plantation as far as Thorpe Farm. 4. Once at Thorpe Farm, bear right through Thorpe Woodlands following a way-marked Forest Walk as it goes along a well-defined track. At another footpath sign, go right thus avoiding the driveway to the campsites. When the path again forks, bear left to follow the course of the river and go straight on at the next path intersection. After a while the path will gently bend to the right, eventually meeting a broad sandy track. 5. Go right into Bridghar Lane which is a straight south-easterly track through the Forest which after about one and a half miles will take you back to the Car Park.

Start: the main Forest Car Park at West Harling Heath, found between Shadwell and East Harling
Approx. Distance: 4.5 Hours
Approx. Time: 2 Hours
Map: Landranger 144

Brandon

Finally to Brandon on the Norfolk-Suffolk borders, and for centuries the home of Britain's oldest industry - flint knapping; inevitably much of the town is also built from flint. Although it is not the most attractive of places, Brandon's history and surrounding countryside more than compensates. In the early days arrowheads and prehistoric tools would have been hammered out of mined flint slabs. Later, flints from Ling Heath were brought to a yard behind the Flint Knappers Arms and here chips would be struck off for gun-flints or knapped for building materials. Local records reveal a wealth of specialist flint knapping families, notably the Snares, Fields, Edwards and Carters, who supplied amongst others the British Army with gun flints during the Napoleonic Wars. In fact, flints are still in demand today, especially by American collectors of muzzle-loading, flintlock guns.

The Little Ouse flows through Brandon to Thetford and although the lighters which once plied their way along the River ceased commercial carrying after 1914, canal boats can still occasionally be seen negotiating holiday makers along its banks.

Brandon Country Park can be found just outside the town and is a small element of what was once a large estate owned by Edward Bliss during the early 1800's and now owned by Suffolk County Council. It is an ideal place to see some of Breckland's wildlife; jays, long-tailed tits, feral golden pheasants, red squirrel, deer and adders. There is a ***Visitors Centre*** here equipped with a small shop and toilet facilities, as well as providing details of the history and natural history of the area. Enjoy your picnics here, take a waymarked forest walk or just explore the grounds - the former Brandon Park House is now a nursing home but provides a beautiful backdrop to the lawn and lake. There is also a recently restored mausoleum and walled garden in the grounds.

Weeting Heath can be found a couple of miles north-west of Brandon; this is one of the best remaining heathlands in Breckland with its chalk grassland peculiar to the area. These dry stony soils support a host of rare plants including spiked speedwell. Others include hound's tongue and early forget-me-not. Additionally, the Heath is a well known haunt for green woodpeckers, stone curlews, butterflies and rare spiders. A warden is on the site *from the beginning of April to the end of August* and the *hides can be used* during this time.

Grimes Graves, three and a half miles north of Brandon and now managed by English Heritage, are unique Neolithic flint mines comprising over 340 pits or shallows, almost circular depressions, on a 43 acre site. Visitors can go down one of the excavated shafts and see for themselves the mining gallery. Although the shifts were first discovered in 1869 by the Rev. Canon Greenwell of Durham, the main period of their exploitation was during the late Neolithic and early Bronze Ages, from around 3100-2200 BC. In the earliest pits, the chief mining tools would appear to have been the bones of red deer and flint wedges. *Open daily, 10-6, April to October, & Wed-Sun, 10-4, November to March. Admission charge.*

Nearby *Weeting Castle,* built by Ralph de Plais in the late 12th Century, was probably more of a domestic residence than a defensive structure. The ruins of the moated aisled hall and three-storey residential keep-like tower are now under the protection of English Heritage. *Open all year, free of charge.*

Walk 37: Weeting Castle and Grimes Graves

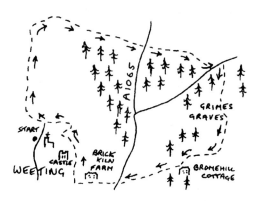

Directions:

1. From your park at the entrance to Weeting Castle, worth a few minutes exploration, take the narrow road leading north past St. Mary's Church. Go through the yard of Home Farm and at the next cottage, on your right, take the track left leading to a farm shed. 2. Just beyond the shed, go right along a wide track which is now the Pilgrims Way, follow this for approximately one and a quarter miles, ignoring all left and right diversions, and shortly after where the ground rises on your left (a tumuli) you will reach a wide forest track. Go right along here. 3. Continue straight ahead for approximately one and a half miles - the hoggin being replaced by another grassy track - until you reach the A 1065. Cross the road to the right of Forest Cottage and continue along the forest track which runs straight ahead of you and leading through Snake Wood. 4. At the junction with a minor road, go left for a couple of hundred yards and then turn right into a tarmac lane signed Grimes Graves. If time permits, take the opportunity to go down the flint mine excavated here. Otherwise, head towards the Information Centre and just before that go diagonally right across the open area, there is a path if you look closely, to a metal gate. 5. Once over the gate, go straight ahead to where you reach a junction of paths. Go right here until you reach another such intersection and take the second left path - this is a wide track leading in a very straight south-westerly direction. Continue along here for about one and a half miles passing the very scanty remains - little more than builders rubble and an old metal bedstead - of Bromehill Cottage on your left. 6. At the junction with the A 1065 again, cross straight over following the track to Brickiln Farm. A short distance past the Farm, take the path to the right which skirts the edge of a copse. Follow this to its natural end, then bear left towards some semi-detached cottages. Just before these follow the track round to your right, then left until you come to a meeting of farm tracks (cottages on your left). Turn left here to return via Home Farm, Weeting Church and so back to your start.

Start: Weeting Castle.
Approx. Distance: 8.5 Miles.
Approx. Time: 3.5 Hours.
Map: Landranger 144

Tourist Information Centres

Aylsham (01263 733903), *Aylsham Station, Norwich Road.*

Beccles (01502 713196), *The Quay, Fen Lane, NR34 9BH.*

Cromer (01263 512497), *Bus Station, Prince of Wales Road, NR27 9HS.*

Dereham (01362 698992), *Bell Tower, Church Street, NR19.*

Diss (01379 650523), *Meres Mouth, Mere Street, IP22 3AG.*

Downham Market (01366 387440), *The Town Hall, Bridge Street.*

Fakenham (01328 851981), *Red Lion House, 37 Market Place, NR21 8DJ.*

Great Yarmouth (01493 842195), *Marine Parade, NR30 2EJ,* and at *Town Hall, Hall Quay, NR30 2PX* (01493 846345)

Hunstanton (01485 532610), *Town Hall, The Green, PE36 5BQ.*

King's Lynn (01553 763044), *The Old Gaol House, Saturday Market Place, PE30 1BY.*

Mundesley (01263 721070), *2a Station Road, NR11 8JH.*

Norwich (01603 666071), *The Guilldhall, Gaol Hill, NR2 1NF.*

Ranworth (01603 270453), *The Staithe, NR13 6HY.*

Sheringham (01263 824329), *Station Approach, NR26 8RA.*

Swaffham (01760 722255), *Market Place, PE37 7AB.*

Thetford (01842 752599), *Ancient House Museum, 21 White Hart Street, IP24 1AA.*

Walsingham (01328 820510), *Shirehall Museum, Little Walsingham NR22 6BP.*

Wells-next-the-Sea (01328 710885), *Staithe Street, NR23 1AN.*

Wroxham (01603 782281), *Station Road, Hoveton, NR12 8UR.*

Chronology of Monarchs

Anglo-Saxon & Danish Kings
Egbert 802   Ethelwulf 839   Ethelbald 855
Ethelbert 860   Ethelred I 865   Alfred the Great 871
Edward the Elder 899   Athelstan 924   Edmund 939
Edred 946   Edwy 955   Edgar 959
Edward the Martyr 975   Ethelred II the Unready 979   Edmund II Ironside 1016
Canute 1016   Harold 1035   Hardicanute 1040
Edward the Confessor 1042   Harold II 1066

Norman Kings
William I 1066   William II 1087   Henry I 1100
Stephen 1135

House of Plantagenet
Henry II 1154   Richard I 1189   John 1199
Henry III 1216   Edward I 1272   Edward II 1307
Edward III 1327   Richard II 1377

House of Lancaster
Henry IV 1399   Henry V 1413   Henry VI 1422

House of York
Edward IV 1461   Edward V 1483   Richard III 1483

House of Tudor
Henry VII 1485   Henry VIII 1509   Edward VI 1547
Mary I 1553   Elizabeth I 1558

House of Stuart
James I 1603   Charles I 1625

The Commonwealth   1649-60

House of Stuart (restored)
Charles II 1660   James II 1685   William III & Mary II 1689
Anne 1702

House of Hanover
George I 1714   George II 1727   George III 1760
George IV 1820   William IV 1830   Victoria 1837

House of Saxe-Coburg
Edward VII 1901

House of Windsor
George V 1910   Edward VIII 1936   George VI 1936
Elizabeth II 1952

Index

*Principal references are in **bold** type*